The more I read of your book, the more aware I became of just how comprehensive it is! It seems you left no stone unturned, no aspect of this family dynamic untouched. Quite an undertaking! **With a scientist's mind, you analyzed. With a counselor's heart, you empathized.** The feelings of pain and yet joy are hard for a lot of GRANDS to understand and reconcile for *themselves,* let alone explain to others - you recognized both, legitimizing them.

The personal stories of grandfamilies are so numerous and yet the common threads in them are...well, common. The fact is, it's usually a heartbreaking story that leads up to a grandparent raising a grandchild. The fact is, this is indeed a 'silent epidemic hiding in plain sight' to quote ABC's Cynthia McFadden. For years, study after study cites statistics marking its growth and attempting to explain the causes. The frustration is that *realistically*...very little is done to help these families. Most grandparents will step up, sacrifice whatever needs to be sacrificed, do whatever needs to be done, to give these children a chance. **Drama aside, they're saving lives.**

—Gayle Byrne, a grandmother raising her granddaughter
Author of *Sometimes its Grandmas and Grandpas:
Not Mommies and Daddies*

Courageous Love begins with honoring the value of a grandparent, and it is from this place of honoring that Laura Montané Bailey takes the reader on a journey toward understanding from a wounded child's lens, while completely respecting and validating the experience of the grandparent. She respectfully delineates the stages of "normative" development while explaining how that may have been interrupted for this child for various reasons, in an easy-to-read format. She gives solid "how to" instructions that a grandparent can use to assist their grandchild with mastering a stage of development.

Additionally, *Courageous Love* offers realistic solutions to many challenges that emerge when grandparents raise grandchildren, such as: understanding a new genre; seeking resources; claiming authority in the new role of grandparent/parent; all while instilling family and values.

This book is a must read for any grandparent, raising a child who is with them due to a trauma. It is a highly recommended tool for mental health professionals for their libraries for working with this at-risk population.

—Sherry A Blair, PhD, MSSW
CEO of ISIS, LLC
Serving New Jersey Wraparound System of
Care for children and families
Author of *Positivity Pulse* and *Tribal Warriors series*

COURAGEOUS
LOVE

INSTRUCTIONS FOR CREATING HEALING CIRCLES FOR CHILDREN OF TRAUMA

For Grandparents Raising Grandchildren

Laura Montané Bailey, LMFT

iUniverse LLC
Bloomington

COURAGEOUS LOVE
INSTRUCTIONS FOR CREATING HEALING CIRCLES FOR CHILDREN OF TRAUMA
For Grandparents Raising Grandchildren

Cover Art: Larissa Michelle Hamel
Interior Book Design: iUniverse

iUniverse books may be ordered through booksellers or by contacting:

iUniverse LLC
1663 Liberty Drive
Bloomington, IN 47403
www.iuniverse.com
1-800-Authors (1-800-288-4677)

ISBN: 978-1-4917-0376-2 (sc)
ISBN: 978-1-4917-0377-9 (hc)
ISBN: 978-1-4917-0378-6 (e)

Library of Congress Control Number: 2013914672

Printed in the United States of America.

iUniverse rev. date: 08/21/2013

TABLE OF CONTENTS

ACKNOWLEDGEMENTS

This book began in my heart on July 4th, 2010 at the Cheesecake Factory in Marina Del Ray where I met with three of my closest work comrades from the Loma Linda University Marriage and Family Therapy Clinic, Dr. Lana Kim, Sharita Bates, and Autumn Jimmerson, also family therapists. That night, overlooking the bay, with fireworks crackling overhead, they challenged me to write a book and I promised to start it before the three of us met up again. That challenge has been in the back of my mind throughout the writing of this book. Each of them have contributed to the book whether by sending encouraging notes in the mail or by sharing their own accomplishments and writings with me. Just knowing they were behind me and believed in me gave me the courage I needed to complete it.

In December of 2010 I wrote two chapters to a book and then quit writing because I couldn't figure out what the book was about. During the next year I met David Sparks and Maryanna Young from Boise, Idaho. It was because of their encouragement, inspiration, and influence that this book started to come into focus. Finally, the team at iUniverse helped me pull it all together and actually complete and print Courageous Love. They have been wonderful to work with from start to finish.

My daughter Larissa Hamel has been involved in everything to do with the artwork of the cover, the web site, social media and marketing. As a voracious book reader herself, she knows the difference between a mediocre book and a great book. To her a big thank you for helping me rise above mediocre and for making my online presence first class. Also, a great big heart-felt thank you to Larissa for making me a grandmother so I could personally understand the great love that flows between grandparent and grandchild.

For my deep connection to the topic of grandparents raising grandchildren I have much gratitude:

- To the wonderful memory of my grandmother who was a powerful role model for me. She went to college in her 70s to learn to write and published several stories and a song. She made me believe I was someone special and unselfishly helped to raise many children who were not her own. I wish she were alive to celebrate this book with me.
- To my parents who provided a safe and loving home for me to grow up in. They have loved me and my children unconditionally. Their love and support during the years that I was a single parent carried us through many difficulties. Their home was always a welcoming safe harbor.
- To my two children, Michael and Larissa, who taught me much more about love than I ever taught them, who have made me very proud by being and marrying wonderful people, and who are providing me with delightful grandchildren.
- To my first granddaughter, Hazel, who completely stole my heart before I even met her. Without her I would have written

the book without fully understanding what it feels like to love a grandchild.

- To my dear friend Myla, Hazel's other grandmother, who has freely shared with me her journey in parenting her granddaughter, Payton, over the past decade. She made the book real for me and contributed a great deal to my insight and perspective.

- To Marisol, my sister's amazing daughter-in-law, who was raised from forty-three days of age by her grandmother, proving that grandmothers make really good moms! Pieces of her story are scattered about in this book.

- To the many children and teens that I have known and worked with through the years. Your courage in the face of such trauma and loss has shown me the great strength of the human spirit and how eagerly children seek and respond to healing relationships.

- To many other grandparents and their adult children and grandchildren who have trusted me enough to share their stories and who have honored me by allowing me to be part of their journey. I will never forget you.

- And to the more than 2.5 million grandparents all over the United States of America who get up every morning, put their "marathon-running" shoes on, and set themselves to the task of raising their grandchildren. You are making a huge positive contribution to a special life and to the very fiber of our country. Our world is a better place because of you.

Countless clients, friends, co-workers, professors, supervisors, therapists, and colleagues have been part of my journey. Hundreds and hundreds of authors have touched and changed my life and have helped me to understand the incredible power of the written word. I would especially like to thank two authors for their contributions: Eugene Peterson for his book *The Message*, which helped me to deepen and broaden my understanding of love; and Howard Glasser for his first book on the Nurtured Heart Approach®, *Transforming the Difficult Child*, which gave wings to that understanding and gave me the tools and the courage to teach it to others in powerful life-changing ways.

I am also grateful to the wonderful members of the West Michigan Word Weavers group for their part in turning this reluctant writer into a confident and driven author. Without them I would still be hunched over my desk struggling with piles of reference books, my stomach in a knot, and a kaleidoscope of words and ideas spinning around in my head.

I so appreciate those who helped to edit and review the manuscript: Bonnie Petry, Reference Librarian CSU San Bernardino; Sherry Blair, PhD, MSSW, Author; Donna G. Sage, PhD, CHt; Gayle Byrne, author and grandmother; Jan Voth, grandmother; Corinne Kluzit, grandmother; Dorothy Montané, grandmother, author's mother, proofreader/editor; Denise Combs, MFT; Whitney Bright, educator; Sharita Bates, MFT; and Sylvia Bowen, MSW.

Last, but not least, I am incredibly grateful to my husband Craig for his unconditional support, for his gentle strength that grounds me, and for the 573 amazing cups of coffee he has brewed to keep me going while writing this book. I have spent many days, evenings and weekends at the computer or with my head in a pile of books as I worked to create the 82,654 word original manuscript that I sent to my first editor and countless hours rewriting it in the year since then. Also, I am thankful to his daughter, Erica, who has graced my life and made room in her heart for me. She also contributed some ideas to the book as her grandmother helped to raise her, an experience she will always treasure.

Laura

INTRODUCTION

It was sometime late in the long, wet winter of 2012 and the phone on my desk rang for the umpteenth time that day. I answered as usual. "Hello. This is Laura." I was unprepared for the despair in the lady's voice as she begged for help in dealing with her teenaged granddaughter. "I am 73 years old. My body is old, and I get tired," she said. "I had her first when she was a newborn, but I just could not see me doing this again, raising a child from square one. So I let her go back with her mom who was married to an abusive alcoholic." As it turned out, Benita got her granddaughter back when she was nine years old and kept her for two years. There were signs of trouble then, but her mom took her back again. Now mom has gone to prison for five years and there is no one else to care for Rebecca, who now has been diagnosed with bi-polar disorder and ADHD. Benita is frantic to keep her out of the foster care system, but does not know what to do. "Please help me!" was her plea. I talked to her for over an hour, gave her some resources and then hung up the phone.

I thought of all the other calls I had received from grandparents in the last few months and then went through my records. Realizing that roughly one-third of my calls in had come in from grandparents raising grandchildren startled me. I had not considered this topic with any particular interest before that time. But now I realized that I had to. I needed to do something to help. Most of these grandparents did not have the means to access the type of care that I was used to recommending. They could not pack up the family, fly across the country and participate in a "family therapy camp" or pay the thousands of dollars per month needed for treating some of these kids. I decided to start by holding a workshop right there in the city where I was living and offer a few tools. I didn't know it then, but that was the start of this book.

In my efforts to be part of the solution for grandparents in crisis because of raising their grandchildren, and for grandparents who are still in a position to prevent a crisis, I read just about everything I could get my hands on. I already had hundreds of books in my personal library, but now I have at least a hundred more. In addition, I have read research articles and websites and talked to anyone that would answer my phone calls or emails that seemed to be an "expert" in this field. Eventually this quest turned into this book. Even so, I do not feel like an "expert" in this field because there are so many who know so much more than I do on this topic of grandparents raising grandchildren. But I was not able to find a book, or a resource that put in one place what grandparents need to know to do what they really long to do for their grandchildren: offer a healing love that will lead to Post Traumatic Growth rather than Post Traumatic Stress Disorder. They want to know that their time and efforts are not wasted and that what they are doing can really make a difference for these children.

I have read hundreds of books on relationships and family dynamics; I have a master's degree in Marital and Family Therapy; I have worked with many troubled children, teens, and families; and I am an effective child and family therapist. But while I can help you navigate the challenge of raising your grandchild, every story is different and only you can be the expert on your own situation. What I know and what I love, is working with traumatized children, and I believe that everyone should have access to the information that I paid dearly for as measured by time, effort, and money. I often take for granted this knowledge base because I can't remember what it's like to not know. *Knowing* this information and putting it into the form of a book are two wildly different things.

In this book, my goal is simply to take the gems out of each book, article, web site, workshop and any other resource I have had access to, put the best ideas that apply all together in one place, and present them in a way that is usable to you, the grandparent. I tried most of all to give you effective solutions that are easy to understand and that are doable. I did my best to give you the kind of information that would inspire change without extreme and discouraging effort. Once you have read this book, I think many changes will be easy to make because you will have the understanding that inspires change. I tried as much as possible to look at root causes because I don't believe in pulling the same weeds over and over again. I like to go for the root and be done with the whole problem.

I believe you picked up this book and began reading it because YOU want to make a difference for your grandchildren. You want to make sure that they do not fall through the cracks or get caught up in "the system" like others you've seen. You want to help them create the story of their lives and make sure it has a good ending somehow. To me, you are a hero, and I hope that the information this book offers can help you make the best of whatever bad things have happened in your family. Chances are pretty good that both you and the children in your care are suffering from broken hearts and/or trauma, some more than others.

Science and experience are teaching us so much about the heart and the brain and now there are powerful ways to go about finding healing for yourself, your family, and your relationships. I want to share some of what I have learned with you, the most powerful healing tools that I know of. The greatest gift you can give to your children and your grandchildren is to tend to your own emotional health and healing. Whether you have a childhood history that was very hurtful to you, or you are brokenhearted by what has happened to your children, you can heal and move on. I want to give you powerful, life-changing steps toward recovering from what has gone wrong so that it does not drain the life and joy out of your present moments.

In my own mind, I am writing this book as a regular person, just like you, who has been tossed around more than a bit by the waves of life. I've been down a few long tunnels where the light at the end really was an oncoming train. I've been dragged down the tracks a couple of times. The beautiful bubble I grew up in burst toward the end of my second decade. My rose tinted glasses were cast to the ground and crushed in the middle of my third. At that time I started looking for answers to all the painful questions of my life. I left no stone unturned in my attempts to repair all the ruptures that had occurred; hence the reading of hundreds of books.

I have always had the gift of mercy, but I did not have the wisdom I needed to protect me during those years. For the last two decades I have focused my intentions on seeking wisdom and the last ten years on reaching an active understanding of love. It was my belief in God and His power to heal that gave me the tenacity to continue my search for answers rather than to give up and become lost in hopeless despair, although I had many occasions when I was tempted to do so. During those times it was my personal relationship with Jesus that gave me the strength to keep going. I absolutely knew He had a plan for my life, that I was created for a purpose. I just didn't know yet what it was. It has only been through my sensitivity to the Holy Spirit, and my early resolve to follow His promptings that I have been able to achieve any of my major accomplishments. Among other things, those include raising two children as a single mom, and the writing of this book, which has been an extremely difficult process.

Out of respect for the wide variety of religious and spiritual beliefs of readers, the remainder of the book will not include any explicit religious content. It is not necessary for one to believe in God to give or to receive healing through love. Love, I believe is governed by laws just as strong as the law of gravity, which is why we are all so drawn to it. It is only fear that keeps us from giving and receiving love. Perfect love is the light that shines on the intense darkness of fear and causes it to disappear.

I wrote this book specifically to help grandparents know how to use the love they already have in the most healing way possible. I wrote this book not only for the grandparents and the grandchildren, but also for the lost or marginalized generation between them. I care about them all. Whatever their stories, I include them in this book and hope that it may have a positive impact on them.

If I could, I would sit and listen to the personal story of each reader and continue listening until, in each case, I hear how tragedy turns into triumph. Thank you for choosing to read this book. I am honored to be part of your journey. May you be blessed. ~Laura

ps. Typos and other imperfections are scattered throughout this book to remind all of us that none of us are perfect, and that all of us are beautiful and capable of accomplishing many great things in spite of it.

"Understanding, forgiveness, gratitude, and love are what you need to turn the crap of the past into fertilizer for your present garden"

~Laura Montané Bailey

CHAPTER 1

The Great Gift Exchange

As she held the sleeping child in her arms, she was at once overwhelmed by feelings of deep love and by a fear that spoke in a loud voice, "Love will never be enough to fix all that's gone wrong here." Even after three and a half months of devoted care, her grandchild's night-terrors were not subsiding. Angelina was exhausted and filled with the knowing sense that it was going to take more to raise Samantha than she had ever imagined.

She had been disappointed when her middle daughter married Steven. Something about him just didn't seem right. From three states away she had known there were problems, but she had no inkling how bad those problems were until the morning three and a half months ago when she got the call.

"Hello, is this Angelina Rivera?" a strong male voice questioned.

"Yes, speaking."

"This is Dan Redding, with the Sherriff's Department in Tampa, Florida. There was a criminal incident last night involving your daughter, Caroline and her husband. We have them in custody and we are looking for family who can take their daughter. Caroline asked us to call you." His voice trailed off as Angelina's world crashed around her.

Everything that had happened since then was too complicated and heartbreaking to think about and there was nothing she could do about it anyway. Her heart ached for her daughter, but with her arms wrapped around three-year-old Samantha she knew in her heart that she had to do something for her. The child continued to whimper a bit as slumber settled in, and Angelina committed herself to finding answers for all the problems she was dealing with now. Samantha's night-terrors were just part of it.

Samantha screamed when she left her at daycare and that tore at Angelina's heart every day. She had taken two weeks off when she first got her but could not quit her job. She needed the money now more than ever. She was tempted to take second shifts to cover the extra expenses, but turned them down because she knew she had to be with Samantha as much as possible. The child clung to her and followed her all over the house. She wouldn't stay in her bed at night and woke up with night-terrors regularly. She was pulling chunks of hair out of her head, and already had a large bald spot around the crown on the back of her head. She sucked her thumb and reverted back to wetting her pants. When disciplined she would refuse to comply and other times she would sob without any apparent reason.

Angelina was exhausted, but her love for this lost little child got her up every morning to start the next day with just as much energy as she had the day before. She had to save her granddaughter, if it was the last thing she did. Samantha might just be all that was left of Caroline, who was going to be tried as an accomplice to a murder, apparently drug related. It seems that Steven was a meth dealer and Caroline had taken up with him and all the chaos and destruction that lifestyle brought. Poor little Samantha had been subjected to a life not at all suited to growing up and developing properly.

Raising her own three kids had been instinctual, nothing more than the regular challenges of weaning, potty training, making sure homework was done, and curfew kept. Getting them all off to college had brought both a sense of accomplishment and a serious case of the empty nest syndrome. But Angelina had focused on her work and recovered sufficiently from an unexpected divorce to enjoy life again. Sitting in the same old rocker she used when her kids were little, she couldn't help looking back over the years for a bit. What went wrong? Everything seemed good enough. Why would Caroline, having come from a good family, get involved in such a lifestyle? How could she neglect and abuse her own child? Now Angelina began to doubt her own parenting skills. If she couldn't raise Caroline right, even in good circumstances, how in the world was she going to raise Samantha who had been through so much. Would she be able to make a difference or was it already too late?

Many grandparents who are raising their grandchildren begin to have doubts as they experience difficulties with their grandchildren that they never encountered when they raised their own children. How will this all turn out? Will I cut my own life short from the stress of it for nothing? Is there any hope for my troubled grandchild? These are good questions and thanks to scientists, researchers and other people who devote themselves to finding real solutions for what ails the human condition, we now have answers to many questions, questions people did not even know to ask fifty years ago. And we have the reassuring truth that although it "takes a village," if a child has even one person in their life who truly loves them, it can make all the difference in the world. They just need that one ray of hope and the picture imprinted in their minds of what being loved feels like.

POWERFUL MEMORIES

> *"Now that I know about the trauma of being separated from my birth mother at 43 days old, the fights between my parents, abuse and abandonment from my dad, I realize that I would have had to be an incredibly distraught baby in the middle of a storm. I have always thought of my grandma as an angel that saved me from all that trauma and strengthened me, gave me resiliency to get through it all. I think that to a certain extent I was also what allowed her to finally be a mother—fully a mother, not just a mother that was DOING EVERYTHING,* (widow with 9 children) *but now being able to be the mother that was just nurturing for the first time—just being a mom. In some way I think it was healing to both of us."* ~ A grandchild

Erik Erikson was the first child psychoanalyst in the city of Boston, where he fled from Germany during the Holocaust years. He taught for many years at the Harvard Medical School and for the Institute of Child Welfare at the University of California at Berkeley. He worked with and studied children and youth in many cultures and areas of the United States, and through his research established what is still recognized as the most complete theory of life stage development. In 1969 Erikson received the Pulitzer Prize for his book *Ghandi's Truth*. His last book, published in 1986 just eight years before his death at age 92, was *Vital Involvement in Old Age*. This book discusses the final stages of life beyond childhood and adolescence to help people discover how, in looking back, they can accomplish the stages that remain incomplete and end their lives with integrity rather than despair. As a grandparent raising grandchildren, you now have the opportunity to examine your own life as you consider how best to help these children in your care, pulling you both into a healthier, happier, more fulfilling future.

I fondly remember my own grandmother, the way she rocked me and sang off key when I was a little girl. Yes, she was old (when you are four years old, fifty-seven seems really old), heavy set and a little wrinkled. But I thought she was beautiful and I loved hearing her sing. I always begged for one more song, and one more story about when she was a little girl. Spending time with her remains one of my best memories more than 50 years later.

I remember going to the beach alone with her and sitting in the sand, dipping Fritos into pimento cream cheese, and dipping our toes in the water. Later we went t. Universal Studios (before it became a theme park) to visit the studio where she worked for Lucille Ball and several other actors and actresses. I remember a myriad of craft projects, watching her sew, and eating hot tapioca pudding with strawberries from her garden. This is the magic of being a grandparent, there is nothing but love between you and this child for whom you are not responsible in an everyday sort of way. But all that changes when they come to live with you and you do have to tend to the daily stuff that real life is made of. Everything changes in that moment as both grandparent and grandchild experience the horror of a family tragedy such that parents are no longer able to be there for their kids.

My grandmother's husband abandoned her and then returned one day twelve years later with two sons she didn't know. She threw her door and her heart open and let them all in. She raised the boys as her own and through the years had a string of children both related and unrelated that stayed in touch with her until she died in her mid-70s. She also took in my troubled teen cousin whose parents were not able to care for her. Most of all, I remember that she loved me unconditionally. From start to finish, she loved every moment that she got to spend with me. She made me feel special and prized, and I have a feeling she did the same thing for each of the children whose lives she touched.

My own parents, now married for close to 60 years, were the best support system that I had after my divorce in 1984. My two very young children and I lived with them off and on for several years and my daughter, who was an infant at the time of the divorce bonded so closely with them that she spent most of her summers at their house through her mid-teens. I have no idea how we ever would have made it through those hard times without them. Without asking questions, they were just there for us. I won't sugar coat it, sometimes we were very angry with each other over different things. Sometimes we judged each other and sometimes we exchanged harsh words. But through all of it I knew they loved me and I knew they loved my kids. I couldn't have made it without them, and they wouldn't have wanted me to try to.

In the end, our relationships with each other have matured and grown because of our extra time together.

Of her grandparents' involvement in her life, my daughter, now 30, says this:

> *"What was most important to me during those years was having something and someone to count on. Unlike my family, they always lived in the same place and my friends knew where I lived from summer to summer. I loved helping Grandpa at his lab, and feeling like I was really helping out. I remember when he would put lotion on his hands and come over and put the extra on mine. Usually he went to work early and came home late and it was fun to wait up for him.*

> *I liked knowing what to expect. They had rules that never changed and that made me feel safe. And I loved running errands with Grandma. We would go to the bank and they always gave me a sucker. We went to the pond every week after church to feed the ducks and to the same park to hike. I liked knowing what to look forward to. Grandma and I had a special tradition. She would take me to eat at a nice restaurant and then to see a live theatre play every year. I loved it!*

> *Every summer they bought me a new dress. That new dress made me feel REMEMBERED. It was a tradition that made me feel like they remembered something*

they did with me. It was not so much about the dress,
really.

What was hardest was being homesick. I hated it.
That feeling at nighttime—of being really anxious. I
would get a terrible stomach ache from the anxiety and
Grandma would put me in her lap and rub my tummy in
circles. It felt like she really cared and wanted to help
me. It made me feel noticed, loved, cared about. When
you feel anxious and scared, it doesn't feel good, so
you feel sick PLUS worried. She helped with both, even
though she didn't say anything. She just tended me."
~Larissa

In all of the small groups and parent training classes that I have run or attended, when people are asked the question, "Who was your biggest cheerleader, your greatest source of love and support as you were growing up?" By far the most common answers to that question are "My grandma" or "My grandpa." Grandparents are known by many titles, Mamo, Papo, MiMi, Granny, Grandmother, Grandfather, Pop Pop, Nonnie, or Poppy . . . and I am sure there are hundreds more. I call mine "Gramma" and she was the only grandparent that I really grew up with. But whatever you call yours, chances are they were very important in your childhood and maybe even still today.

Although my grandmother has been dead for over thirty years, she is still a huge inspiration to me. In her 70s she went off to the local college to take classes in writing and politics and other topics that interested her. She had articles, stories, and even a song published. She had never written before that, so I have to say she is probably my biggest inspiration in writing my first book, which you are now reading. Somehow my grandmother knew that she could do anything she set her mind to and so she learned wig making, hat making, sewing, and pattern making. She became a costume designer in Hollywood back in the 40's. One time she needed some electrical work done on her house, during the years when she had no husband and couldn't afford to have it done. So she took an electrician course and wired it up herself. She was still doing electrical projects on her house when she died (not by electrocution). She moved doors and windows, and one time when I came to visit her she was up on the roof. "Gramma, what on earth are you doing up there?" I called out from below. "Oh, the house was too hot, so I am installing an attic fan." She announced it matter-of-factly as if she were baking a batch of chocolate chip cookies. She was like a pioneer of a new kind and even though she was gone by the time my first child was born, she was with me in spirit, showing me that I too could do whatever I needed to do, through my fourteen years of single parenting.

Here's some inspiration for you. Quite possibly the most difficult marathon on earth is the annual Leadville 100 held in Colorado. The course is one hundred miles of the most rugged, mountainous terrain. It begins at an elevation of 9,200 feet—one that would make most of us huff and puff just to get out of bed—then climbs to 12,600 feet. Half of the hundred miles is done at night and the athletes hope for a full moon. The participants have a motto, **"You are tougher than you think you are, and you can do more than you think you can."**

People who choose to pit themselves against the treacherous Leadville 100 course, and strive to finish it, are experienced super athletes. Grandparents raising grandchildren are experienced super parents.

You are running a "marathon" of your own over challenging territory that is often in the dark, one you have run before. Unlike the athletes, you may feel that you did not have a choice, but when you love someone this much and they need you, you don't just walk away because it's hard or because it's inconvenient. It will take a lot of COURAGE and a lot of LOVE to get to the end of your trail and this book was written for those of you who intend not only to finish, but to finish well!

Jeanne, who's had two of her grandchildren since their mother was arrested for crimes related to her crack cocaine addiction said,

> *"I admit, I have some resentment toward my daughter for putting me in this situation that I had no choice about. Really, I had no choice, or at least I never saw it as such. If I wasn't able there might have been another choice. I don't know. It started out just for the weekend and four years later here I am. I don't remember making a choice."*

Maybe she never felt she had a choice, but she did. Many people who could, do not choose to care for family members who need them. Although she feels she had no choice, this grandmother and many, many grandparents raising their grandchildren, have no regrets about taking them in. As hard as it might be at times, and some grandparents have been through some unbelievably horrible, nightmarish situations, nearly all grandparents that have raised or helped to raise their grandchildren share a similar sentiment:

> *"Yes, it was hard. There were periods of such stress and anxiety that I hardly slept for months. I have had*

*my heart ripped out of my chest in more ways than one,
and I have sacrificed many things. But this one thing I
know, if I had it to do over again, I would definitely do
it again. It was one of the best things I ever did in my
life." ~A grandmother*

A GIFT FOR YOU!

Why do grandparents feel this way in spite of all the challenges involved?
Grandparents report many benefits to raising their grandchildren
including:

- A very special bond with their grandchildren because they see
  them every day
- Gratitude for the extended years of parenting, getting a second
  chance to do it right
- Knowing they are making a positive difference for someone
  they love
- Enjoying the abandon that children and teens display knowing
  they are fully loved, noticed, and accepted, something
  grandparents may have been too busy to offer the first time
  around
- The peace of mind they have knowing their grandchildren are
  safe and fed and loved
- The kids bring youth and energy back into the home. They
  make you laugh 'til you cry and they keep life interesting
- Grandchildren introduce you to things you would never
  consider doing otherwise. They look at life in fresh new ways
  and they love that you love them.

These are just some of the hidden treasures that grandparents can stumble upon. Most of us begin our very first parenting journey full of high hopes and the very best of intentions. We may not have anticipated what it would be like to raise kids in the midst of the busyness of modern day life. Dealing with the stress of getting a career up and running; adjusting to married life; managing a household for the first time; and unexpected losses or challenges while raising kids is not something you can really prepare for. How could we have known it would be so hard or that we would go through a divorce or failed business or that one of our kids might not turn out okay, might turn to drugs and alcohol rather that to us? No matter how good our intentions were, everything didn't turn out perfectly and now it has come full circle and we get a second chance.

Whatever mistakes we made the first time around, whatever opportunities we missed out on, whatever went wrong that was totally out of our hands, this is our opportunity to use everything we learned in our practice run. Now we must use the wisdom and patience we learned along the way to set aside hurt feelings, to give up grudges and arrogance, and to embrace what is left that is good with a heart of understanding, acceptance, and forgiveness. We are now mature enough to say what we need to say, to ask for what we need, to say "I forgive you" and mean it, and to say "I am sorry" and mean that too. We also know that we can't please everybody all the time and that living on principle is the true road to fulfillment. In our youth, we usually do not have all of these important skills.

I titled this book *Courageous Love* because I know many grandparents raising grandchildren and that is what I see in them. One day, in an unrelated conversation, my husband used these two words to describe something we were talking about and I knew instantly that those two words capture the essence of grandparents who are called to do this labor of love—Courageous Love. I have not heard any stories as dramatic, valiant, and compelling as some of the stories I hear from grandparents. And yet these people that our youth-and-beauty-seeking society has come to look down on show their true grit when they come to the rescue of orphaned grandchildren. They show courage greater than the military requires, because grandparents usually must fight many battles with no strategizing team, no benefits, no vacation time, no MREs (Meal Ready to Eat), and no back up. In this very personal battle, your most powerful weapons are courage and love.

More often than not, the grandparents raising grandchildren are single women, but there are many grandfathers, step-grandparents, aunts, uncles, cousins, and siblings also involved in raising kids whose parents are not able to be there. Some of you have adopted your grandchildren or have sole custody by other means while many share some type of custody or visitation with the parents who are in and out of the home. Many others of you have the grandchildren and their adult parent or parents living in your home with you due to economic situations or divorce. Every situation is unique, but most of the time there are many challenges that come along with it. For those who have sole custody of the children from infancy, things may be a little easier because the kids have not had to live through so much trauma before coming to your home.

One mother raised nine kids, mostly as a single mom. Her husband died when the youngest was an infant, leaving her to raise the kids alone. She was not educated and worked every odd job she could possibly find to put food on the table and survive. Raising her kids was stressful and she was mostly gone to work. In some sense they raised themselves and each other. By the time her infant granddaughter came to live with her, a few of her kids were still living at home and supporting her so she was able to stay home and raise this one child the way she had dreamed of raising her own kids. She poured her love out daily and got more back than she ever gave. This is what her granddaughter had to say after grandmother's death:

> *"I remember just before she died and she was forgetting things and forgetting people. I feared so much that she would forget me too. But she never did . . . she forgot a lot of her own kids and mixed their names all up, but she never mixed me up with anyone. We had too much, too strong a connection, it never disappeared from her memory. I think that was sort of a confirmation for me once more that for whatever reason I was this very personal savior for her too—the one person she really connected with.*
>
> *She got to see me graduate from college and get married. Then 6 months later she died. It was good timing for her because she finally felt she could let go and someone was taking care of me." ~A grandchild*

WHY GRANDPARENTS ARE SUPER PARENTS

As grandparents, most people have mellowed and become wiser than when raising their children the first time around. Often, experience and age change us in ways that help us to be more tolerant of those around us, even those who have different ideas and habits. By now, many of us have learned to be more patient and realize what is important and what is not. It is easier now to adopt that attitude of "Don't Sweat the Small Stuff" because we realize that almost everything is small stuff. Four or more decades of life experience generally cause people to be more understanding and compassionate. For example, when I was a teenager, I would often say, "I will NEVER . . . . (fill in the blank)." There were so many things that I just knew I would never do! Like "get divorced" for one. Looking back, it seems that every time I said the word "never" life became laser-focused on making sure I knew that I, yes, even I, could stoop to these actions that I esteemed at the time so beneath me. Now, I never say "never" anymore. Oops, there I go again . . . I really try to avoid saying that word! I have become much more understanding of others who are doing things that I do not necessarily understand or consider wise.

Having made a series of our own mistakes causes most of us become less critical of others and a little slower to fly off the handle without all the information we need. In addition, we have seen enough of life by now that we are no longer easily shocked and perhaps more willing or able to sit back and see both sides of any situation. Even when we are "stuck in our own ways" we know we can still allow others to have different ways and be okay with that. A new kind of strength settles in to replace the idealistic vigor of youth, a strength that often comes with patience and tolerance for others. This may not be true for everyone, but you are reading this book which shows me that you are a person who is open to new ideas. So I am thinking that for you, it is likely true.

The experience of having already raised kids and now being in a position of reflection and introspection, allows us as grandparents to be more enthusiastic and less ambivalent with our grandchildren. For example, with my granddaughters, I am painfully aware that I will not know which time is the last time they will sit on my lap and snuggle in for a book reading or a song or just to be close. I don't know when the last time was for either of my kids. You just don't know. You simply wake up one day and notice that it has not happened for a very long time, and if by chance you are able to guilt them into sitting on your lap again, it is quickly clear that it is not the same experience that it was before and you know then, that childhood has slipped away in the night. Now, as grandparents, we fully know that each moment is precious and deserving of notice. We worry much less about the small stuff, and more stuff falls into the category of "small stuff."

One drug addicted mother told me that in some ways she feels like her mother owes her the raising of her daughter. She feels that her drug problems are a result of her parent's utter abandonment of her when she was a child. During their bitter and ugly divorce, the children became the true victims. Now, as she watches her mother care for her daughter she is, in a sense, nurtured vicariously.

Another young mom reports her father saying to her, "Well, you FINALLY did something right. You had a daughter that is everything you never were." Observers might think what a cruel thing that would be to hear, but instead of being hurt by it, this mother felt grateful that her daughter was getting from Grandpa what she herself had never received from him when she was a child. Her response was, "I am glad that you are doing something right and giving her everything you could never give me." Healing eventually occurred in their relationship and the child received good fathering from her grandfather in the meantime. That provided a great deal of comfort to the young mother who was unable to be there for her children in the way she wanted to.

These are generational stories. Generational habits of relationship and of doing life that get passed down or that cause other problems in the wake of their own power. We all have some of these habits that could use change and healing. If you are a grandparent who has regrets about what happened with your own children, then this might just be your opportunity for a redo. Like Bette Midler, grandmother in the movie *Parental Guidance*, said, "You know what grandparenting is, a second chance!" So if you need a second chance to do your very best job at parenting, now is your time! If you couldn't fit enough hugs and giggles in the first time around, you can do it now. If you need help to do your very best, take heart, help is in your hands.

GRANDPARENTING IN A STRANGE WORLD

Although grandparents have always been involved in helping to raise grandchildren in one way or another, it looks much different today than twenty, fifty, or a hundred years ago. In today's world, families are often scattered all over the country or all over the world. There is a much greater focus on individual accomplishment and a much higher incidence of divorce. There is much more information easily accessed, even by small children, through electronic devices. Older people are no longer looked to as the "sage's" or the great purveyors of wisdom. Now their vast experience and knowledge has been usurped by the power of the Internet. Things have turned upside down as any discussion or argument can be ended by the one who can find the answer most quickly on the iPhone or other such handheld device. That's usually the kids. "Sorry, Grandpa, we don't need you for that anymore! A whole big world of information is at our fingertips and YOU are out of date!"

The best antidote for this dilemma is active relational grandparenting. It offers the best in "vital involvement" that old age has to offer, benefiting both the grandparents and the grandchildren. It's the relationships with your children and grandchildren that make life most worth living during your old age. You may not be old yet, but someday, if you survive all this, you will be and your relationships can make all the difference between dying with a sense of a life well lived versus dying in lonely despair. In the beginning of life, in the end of life, and everywhere in the middle of life, relationships are everything. After all, we are humans and we are wired to connect. The good news is that whatever went wrong, we can begin wherever we are to make it better. An emotionally rich and vibrant relationship is something you cannot get from an electronic device but it is something your grandchildren desperately need. Can they get it from you?

Many grandparents rarely get to see their grandchildren due to divorce, strained relationships, or geographical distance. It's hard to say who loses more because of this. Grandparents lose out on the greatest joy of old age, watching their grand-children and great-grandchildren grow up. Grandparents give a sense of belonging to other family members by passing on stories of family history, and rich traditions that create strong bonds. And children lose out on the wonderfully healing role that grandparents play in helping fractured families to recover in an increasingly isolating world. According to Judith Wallenstein and Joan

Kelly in their book, *Surviving the Breakup*, children with supportive and involved grandparents adjust much better after a divorce than children without. The same goes for any other life tragedy. Grandparents matter. They make a difference—a very big difference.

If you are raising your grandchildren, you have been given the opportunity to permanently and positively impact future generations. And you belong to the clan of **super parents**, those who can parent with more patience, wisdom, calmness, purpose, and compassion. You might feel like you are struggling every step of the way, but you are doing it. If you are struggling while doing it and you are at the end of your rope, you are not alone. If you and your grandchildren are suffering from broken-heartedness because of what happened to their parents, you are not alone. If you feel resentment towards your adult child for leaving you and their children in this predicament, you are not alone. On the other hand, if you are enjoying every moment of your present journey, you are not alone either. I was a guest on a radio talk show and a grandfather called in and said, "We are raising our granddaughter and she is the sweetest girl you can imagine. We have not had any problems with her and she is a delight in our home." Whatever your experience, you belong to the special group of grandparents desperately needed by grandchildren in an unpredictable and chaotic world. You have been given a gift, the gift of a second chance—a second chance for you and a second chance for the children.

When I originally started this book, I was asked by a publishing company to write a book offering simple steps for grandparents raising grandchildren. I told them I couldn't do that because there is nothing simple about raising grandchildren in most cases. If it were simple, no one would buy a book for it. If you are caring for your grandchildren then likely a traumatic event of some kind has occurred. The events that lead to parents not being able to parent their own children generally include drug and alcohol addiction, incarceration (often a result of drugs and alcohol), neglect and abuse, and death or serious illness. Divorce, teen pregnancy, and economic hardship often lead to grandparents being involved in raising the kids, but usually in those cases, the parents are still the primary caregivers with grandparents taking a supportive role for the whole family.

Most of these situations have a huge impact on the children and always involve stress and loss. In many situations there may also be neglect, physical or sexual abuse, domestic violence issues, chemically induced disabilities such as Fetal Alcohol Syndrome, emotional and behavioral problems, Post Traumatic Stress Disorder (PTSD), shame, isolation, academic failure, and a host of other problems. When the parents are involved, or come and go from the home, there can also be very difficult issues of abandonment, authority, and guardianship. Dealing with too many of these issues at a time can be very overwhelming for both grandparents and grandchildren.

Children may resent the grandparents if they perceive that they were taken away from their parents and still want to be with them. Parents may blame grandparents for taking the kids, regardless of the fact they were in jail or the kids were removed by children's protective services. You may never get a single token of gratitude from either the parents or the children. The fact that you endure that and continue to do the right thing proves my point that you are courageous.

A quick search of Wikipedia tells us that "*Courage is the ability to confront fear, pain, danger, uncertainty, or intimidation. **Physical courage** is courage in the face of physical pain, hardship, death or threat of death, while **moral courage** is the ability to act rightly in the face of popular opposition, shame, scandal, or discouragement.*" Being courageous does not mean that you have no fear, no shame, no discouragement. It means that you do the right thing in spite of that, which is what you are doing. I think you deserve hero status!

What would inspire such courage? Well, let me ask you this question: How many other kids would you take into your home and raise as your own at this time in your life? My guess is that most of you could not come think of any other circumstances in which you would take some traumatized children into your home and devote the entire rest of your life to raising them as your own. The only explanation for this kind of courage is love, especially given the fact that grandparents in general do not get the kind of support, financial or otherwise that foster and adoptive families get. This is much more challenging than signing up to be a foster parent. So there you have it, COURAGEOUS LOVE. That describes you!

A GIFT FOR THEM!

While it is wonderful and commendable that you have been able to step more or less confidently "up to the plate" to care for these children that you love, there are many aspects of caring for them that may seem overwhelming. In addition to making room in your house; ensuring safety; taking care of legal and guardianship issues; figuring out how to feed the extra mouths; the impact on all of your other relationships, as well as your job and your marriage, the behaviors and emotions of these children are of utmost concern. The whole reason for taking them in is born out of love and out of a desire to help make a good life for them in spite of the family tragedy. If you don't take them, they will likely be farmed out to total strangers and possibly lost for good to a system that, in spite of its good intentions, all too often fails the children.

Foster care is important and it exists because many children have no better options. But is has been well known and well documented for many years that children do better when raised by family members than when raised by strangers in foster care. When children are taken away from their parents or lose their parents, they experience this as great trauma. One child I worked with was taken from her drug addicted mother who worked as a prostitute in order to support her drug habit. She describes an incident that occurred when she was 6 years old like this:

> "My mom used to work for a pimp who was really mean to her. He would cuss her out and hit her and push her around. It was awful. We were always moving and staying in different hotels, trying to hide from him, but he always found us. One day he was beating up on my mom really bad and I was so scared. I thought maybe he was going to kill her so I called 9-1-1. I thought that they would take him away and lock him up, but instead when they came they took me away. I was scared to death and I was screaming and crying and biting and kicking. I wanted to stay with my mom and I even pulled some of the lady's hair out, but I wasn't strong

enough to get away. Anyway, that was a few years ago. I was just a kid. I keep thinking my mom will get her life straightened out and come to get me but I guess she doesn't care that much. She keeps saying she is doing what they told her to do to get me back, but I don't think she is doing it. She keeps going back to the drugs and her pimp instead of coming to get me."

This is a child living in foster care. Her behavior had been so unmanageable that she could not live with a foster family and had to be in a more intensive program. She only had one grandmother living who was not able to care for her due to health concerns. This little girl lived from phone call to phone call from anyone in her family and she lived for the days her grandmother came to visit. She remembered who she was when she could be connected to her family. Her mother continued to fail and disappoint her time after time, but her large extended family was still there in the community where she grew up and she longed to be with them. Unfortunately, the last time I was able to get any information on her she had been moved two counties away from her family. Her contact with them is now minimal and she is not doing well. Her choices and aggressive behaviors continue to grow more negative with time and distance. I fear for her and countless others like her who have nothing stable to connect to. I watched her weep when her mother did not show up for visitation. I saw her cling to her grandmother on the one visit she made the year that I was in her life. She begged grandmother to let her live with her, but grandmother could not do it.

When grandparents (or other kin) are able to take their grandchildren in, it significantly reduces the trauma of the event and of the separation from parents because it provides continuity and familiarity, allowing kids to grow up and develop within a known community and culture. These children report being more satisfied with their home environment than foster kids because foster children must live with total strangers and deal with limited family connections, often in communities far from home. They must also live with the stigma of being a "foster kid," a fact that most of them want to hide. In contrast, children living with grandparents report feeling normal rather than stigmatized and they are less likely to change placements. This stability and sense of belonging contribute to fewer incidents of disruptive behavior at home and school and reduces the likelihood of the poor outcomes reported for foster care placement. If they do change in their placement from a grandparent's house, it is usually to another relative's home that the children know and love, keeping them connected to their birth and extended family.

Overall, grandparents provide a safer and more nurturing environment than foster homes, with significantly reduced reports of abuse. In foster homes, roughly half of such claims are due to sexual abuse. Also, grandparents have a greater sense of responsibility including a lifetime commitment to the raising of the child. Grandparents are more likely to have ongoing open dialogue with their grandchildren, giving advice and offering life direction, including the teaching of religious and moral values, as well as empathy and respect for others. These children have a sense of belonging and family. They feel cared about and loved, experiencing more hope for the future and better relationships with their caregivers. In fact, according to a research project reported in Solomon & Marx article, *To Grandmother's House We Go*, children who are raised by their grandparents (without parent involvement) do very well compared with children raised by single parents or in blended families, and almost as well as those raised in an intact family.

Apparently grandparents are excellent stand-ins for biological parents. Because of the pre-existing bonds between children and their grandparents, grandparents are more likely to view the kids through a more positive lens than foster parents are. In addition they are more likely to discipline when rules are broken and lines are crossed, as they would their own children.

Compared to foster care, the only identified weaknesses in grandfamilies are that grandparents get less support, less crisis intervention, and less formal training for raising children of trauma. Because of this, although experienced at parenting, grandparents are less prepared to handle raising traumatized children responding to the loss, neglect, and abuse they have experienced. Trauma brings with it a whole set of behaviors that are often misunderstood, misdiagnosed, and mistreated.

The purpose of this book is to give you the tools you need to understand and deal with the kaleidoscope of difficult and confusing behaviors that often come into grandparents' lives through their traumatized grandchildren. You will be happy to know that you are already doing many things covered in this book and some will just seem natural when you hear about them. Even if you are scared, and even if you feel overwhelmed sometimes, you belong to a group of courageous people who have a lot of love to give. So go ahead and slap that *Super Parent* button on your collar and wear it with pride!

IT'S ALL ABOUT THE CIRCLES

Probably the first thing you noticed about this book are the circles on the front cover. Throughout this book we will be talking about different circles so I thought I would start out with two circles that are referred to in Stephen R. Covey's book, *The 7 Habits of Highly Effective Families*. These two circles caught my attention back in 1997 when I first read this wonderful book and they have changed the way I live. Here is a brief description of Covey's two circles that highly effective people understand:

- **Circle of Concern**: This includes basically everything that we are concerned about, including flossing our teeth, health problems, bills to pay, terrorism, tornados, family vacation, world peace, world history and everything else that we might spend any of our thoughts, time and energy on.
- **Circle of Influence**: Things that concern us that we can actually do something about.

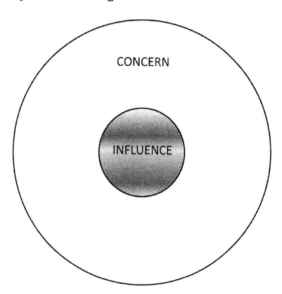

It is critical for success to carefully consider how we spend our time and energy. We have concerns that we have no control over, some that we have indirect control over, and those that we can directly control by our own behavior. Covey states that if we apply positive energy to what we do have control over, the Circle of Influence begins to grow. I have experienced this as truth in my own life. If we spend a lot of time and energy on things that concern us that we can't actually do anything about, it leads to blame, resentment, victimhood, and eventually frustration and bitterness. The purpose of this book is to bring things in your circle of influence into sharper focus and give you better tools so that you can do something about it. We will do that by giving you three powerful Healing Circles, but not until we first talk about the shattered circle.

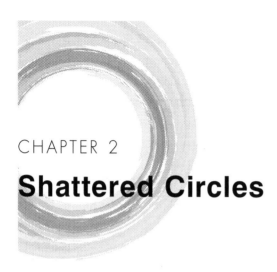

CHAPTER 2

Shattered Circles

"I was three when my dad died and yes, I remember it clearly. Not only did I lose him, but every adult in my life was very upset and badly affected by it. My mother was pregnant at the time that he was killed in an auto accident. He was just 25 and an only child, so my grandparents who helped a great deal in caring for me were devastated as well. It was a terrible event for all of us. My world just fell apart." ~A grandchild

A SHATTERED CIRCLE

Many families have been through a tragic experience of one sort or another. My family is no exception. My father was born into a large family in 1933 in Veracruz, Mexico. He was the eleventh child with two brothers and eight sisters. When he was three months old, an influenza epidemic came through the area and his six-year-old sister died. She was the youngest girl and this was a devastating loss to the family. When he was three years old, his mother suddenly and unexpectedly died in the process of giving birth to her fourth son. The infant died as well. This new loss sent the family into overwhelming grief and led to utter catastrophe as members of the family were sent in all directions. His father also fell into a terrible grief, and overwhelmed with all the kids and family responsibilities, he farmed many of the kids out to relatives. My father wound up being sent by himself to live with an aunt and his paternal grandparents. His aunt had three children of her own, but they were grown by then. She was not interested in raising any more kids and was very irritated to have him around. Fortunately, his grandfather took the grief stricken, lost child under his wings, even taking him to work with him at times. He was a night watchman at a silk factory or plantation and my father remembers his grandfather pouring two mugs of coffee, adding a bit of whiskey to each, and handing one to him. Off to work they went, in the humid, cold, dark of the early morning hours. With the cold air in his face and the hot mug in his hands this little boy felt really big and grown up walking next to his grandfather, who walked with a confident swagger, carrying a large rifle on his shoulder.

The next year, when my father was four years old, his grandmother died. That left him with just his abusive aunt and his grandfather. A year later, when he was five years old, his grandfather died. When that happened his father came to live there with eight of his nine living siblings. Included in this family grouping was his oldest sister, and her two daughters, one his age and the other an infant. When he was six years old, the baby died of unknown causes. Although he is now eighty years old, my father still remembers looking into that crib and seeing the baby lying there cold and white and still, and a shiver runs down his spine. That is a lot of loss and grief and trauma for the first six years of life. These types of experiences in childhood shape our brains and our hearts and create the attachment styles we will continue to use for the rest of our lives.

My father's story is pretty dramatic, but it is not the worst story that I have heard. And fortunately it has a good ending as my father really understands the value of honesty, hard work, and close relationships and has had a wonderful life since all that happened. He has raised four children, has had four of his grandchildren living with him at one time or another, and is now enjoying his first three great-grandchildren, all adorable little girls. He owns his own business and still works full time and enjoys life with my mother. Just over a week ago, we had 21 people in the room where I now sit in front of the fire editing this chapter. We were all here to celebrate his eightieth birthday. All of his children and all but two of his grandchildren were here. It was a wonderful time and we crowded around and lit candles and sang happy birthday. Later we shared with him our best memories and what he has meant to us. From a childhood of trauma, grief, and loss, he has received about the best gift a man can hope to achieve in life. That gift is to be surrounded by generations of people that love you and take the time to tell you that and to celebrate you with love. That gift is to be able to look back and see that you loved much, that you lived with courage, and that you gave it your all.

DYING FOR LOVE

I am pretty sure that when you were raising your children you had no idea that you would also be raising your grandchildren. You probably never anticipated that tragedy might strike at your family and extend your parenting years. And no matter how much you love your grandchildren you likely did not hope that they would not have parents able to do it themselves. Personally, I LOVED being a mom. Yes, it was hard at times. Being a single mom I had a lot on my plate, ALL of the time. But I loved it! And I LOVE being a grandmother. It is probably one of the best things that has ever happened to me. However, if my grandchildren needed to come and live with me full time that would mean something terrible had happened to their parents, my kids. This has not happened to me, but I have been honored to experience this journey with many courageous grandfamilies who are going through it. When it comes to a relationship with your grandchildren, this one tragic event changes everything.

Kids who have been through an experience that removes their parents from that primary role have nearly always been through some kind of loss, neglect, or abuse constituting trauma. Because of this, you are now dealing with grandchildren who likely have much different problems and needs than your children had when you were raising them. Keeping that in mind, you will need many more powerful tools to do the job of raising your grandchildren. In order to understand what loss, trauma, neglect, or abuse really mean to a child, we must first understand what children ideally need in order to develop into mature, well-adjusted adults who are responsible, contributing members of society. I chose to use the framework of Healing Circles to describe what children need in order to thrive in spite of the reality of life trauma. These Healing Circles, which you as a grandparent have already begun to create, are made up of:

1. Safety, structure, and basic needs
2. Family traditions
3. Rules, authority agreements and non-toxic relationships

Love and joy must be contained within these circles or they will lack healing power. There simply is no greater power than the constant radiation of your love. You can make the greatest difference through your unconditional love that no one else may be in a position to offer your grandchild. Even when you can't feel it in the moment, miracles can and do happen through your dedication and love. Your joy feels like love to children and when they see joy in your eyes as you look at them, they feel your love deeply. Knowing how to create these circles, keeping yourself inside of them, and continuously drawing the children in with you, is the work of healing the lives of your grandchildren and giving them hope for the future. If they experience themselves as a joy to you, they can themselves become a joy to the universe! Empathy is the main ingredient that will allow you to offer them the kind of unconditional love that they need. Empathy grows with seeking to understand another and learning to look at the world through their eyes. This is much easier for us to do when we understand the impact that trauma and neglect have on children. In order to understand the magnitude of the impact, we must talk more specifically about what they need. So "let's start at the very beginning. It's a very good place to start."

One contributor to our emotional and physical well-being throughout life is the quality of the relationship between the birth father and the birth mother during pregnancy. Babies need parents who are in a loving and supportive relationship, and who are happy to be adding a baby to the family picture. Our greatest need is to belong to a family who offers unconditional love. That is, love that is not tied to appearance, performance, intelligence, charm, behaviors, or any other abilities or accomplishments. **We need to be loved just because we are.** This is the most basic, fundamental need of all humans.

We now have indisputable evidence that our brains are wired by our interactions with the environment starting from the moment of conception. A mother's thoughts and feelings toward her unborn baby directly affect the emotional health of the child. When these thoughts and feelings are loving and joyful, they set the stage for a sense of security and well-being that last a lifetime. In fact, how a mother feels about childbearing has a measurable impact on the sexual attitudes that the child develops in adulthood. A positive attitude about childbearing leads to a mature and healthy attitude toward sex.

The ideal setting then, for a child to experience healthy development, would be:

- Physically and emotionally available mother and father
- To receive love from parents and to be able to express it
- To feel heard, noticed, valued and responded to
- To hear words of encouragement and support
- To be celebrated for achievements
- Honesty and truth expressed at their level of understanding
- Predictably positive outcomes
- Conflicts resolved without use of force or anger
- Frequent safe and nurturing touch
- Promises kept (a word is as good as a promise to a child)
- Plenty of joy, laughter, and time for free play
- A sense of safety and comfort
- Regular focused attention and engagement from parents
- Training in self-control and decision-making
- Safety to express wants and needs
- A responsible provider
- Age appropriate independence

You may be reading this and thinking, "Oh my! I did not get all that when I was a child!" If you did not get your needs met when you were a child, you will enjoy chapter six which addresses your needs as a grandparent and as a person. The rest of the topics will be covered in other chapters, as far as how to make sure you are giving your grandchildren what they need to develop properly. When we do not get our needs met in childhood, we can spend the rest of our lives seeking that sense of love and belonging that seems to elude us. If you did not get what you needed, chances are you did not parent your children from a place of fullness, and now they are not able to give your grandchildren what they need. This is about generational family patterns that all families pass down. This is not a reason to blame our parents either, because they gave us what they had. We each give what we have to give and that is the human condition. Welcome to Planet Earth!

THE NO BLAME ZONE

This is not a time to blame yourself for the problems your children face either. Please do not read that into what I am saying. I don't want blame to be any part of this book. My idea is that we all seek understanding and are changed by it. If you are blaming yourself or someone else, if you are carrying guilt for the past, we will be dealing later with how to let go of that as well. So drop the blame game and do your best not to pick it up again.

Let's face it, there are no perfect parents. Not me, not you, not your parents. Good enough, maybe, but not perfect. And fortunately, research has shown that good enough is good enough! The hopeful news about all this is that even when really bad things have happened to mess up the wiring of our hearts and brains, we can be rewired. Your grandchildren can have hope of a good life even if really terrible things have already happened to them. Although we all struggle with propensities throughout life, they do not have to define us or determine our destiny. There is much that remains in our control throughout life and the purpose of this book is to put the tools in your hands to help yourself, your grandchildren, and your family to recover from your own family tragedies. But before we get to that, let's discover what happens for children when they are victims of loss, abuse, neglect, or other traumatic events.

CHILDREN SUFFER

Just because we grow up and manage to live our adult lives, even successfully as my father has done, does not mean that we don't carry these heartaches and experiences with us, sometimes for a very long time. Some people carry them for life. They impact us deeply, even those experiences that occurred before we are born. When a pregnant mother is not in a loving or supportive relationship, stress inevitably sets in as she faces the task of raising baby alone. A cascade of hormones such as cortisol and adrenaline are secreted in the mother's system during experiences of emotional stress. These hormones feed directly into the unborn infant, creating a climate of stress matching the mother's stress levels. Babies feel what mothers feel and after birth continue to be very sensitive to mother's every emotional nuance. There are few things more stressful to a mother than a troubled relationship with her husband or partner. Consequently, one of the most dangerous influences to the emotional and physical health of a child is a father who neglects or abuses his wife.

Some babies are actually born already in a state of depression or anxiety due to the emotional state of the mother during pregnancy. This is most likely to happen when a mother is not happy about being pregnant and resents the pregnancy. The unborn can sense this rejection and often these pregnancies will result in miscarriage. Some are born already traumatized due to domestic violence, sexual assault or other factors. Many babies have pre-birth exposure to drugs and alcohol. Our early life experiences weigh in very heavily on how our emotions and character are formed. The first 5 years appear to be the most important and children have very specific needs, which, if not met, may continue to haunt them for the rest of their lives. Personality disorders, such as Borderline, Narcissism, Histrionic, Dependent, and Obsessive-Compulsive, to name just a few, have roots in interrupted attachment. But not all children with adverse early life experiences develop these disorders. Many, like my father, go on to live highly functional lives. Part of understanding the problem is seeing hope for a solution, which I hope this book will be for many.

When a family tragedy has taken place and a circle is shattered, it is often the tendency of the adults to minimize or misunderstand the impact to children. Sometimes they may think a child is too young to understand what is going on, so they don't talk to them about it or help them go through a grieving process of their own. Sometimes they think a teenager is old enough to be able to understand and handle it on their own. Sometimes adults are too preoccupied with their own overwhelming emotions that they are not able to attend to the emotions of a child. Sometimes adults say too much about details that kids don't need to hear or that are harmful to them, and sometimes no one talks to them about it at all.

It can be hard to know exactly how to approach each child, consider their age, maturity level, and needs, and know just what to say. Any time there has been a family tragedy of some kind, it is safe to assume that ALL kids are having a hard time dealing with it. Some kids who are having a hard time dealing with it act up in different ways, and some kids deal with it by behaving better because they don't want to add stress to adults they see are also struggling. Some kids will become the "parents" of these struggling adults in their attempts to fix everything for the people they love. So whether the children and teens in your care are acting up or not, assume they are having a hard time and that they need to go through their own process of healing and recovery if they have sustained a loss.

A PAST & PRESENT VIEW OF TREATMENT

Tonight I took a break from writing to watch the 1975 movie, *One Flew Over the Cuckoo's Nest*. It reminded me that not long ago they were still treating mental illness with electroconvulsive therapy (shock treatments) and lobotomy (an invasive treatment or surgery to disable a part of the brain.) In fact, lobotomies were performed in the U.S., U.K. and many other countries clear into the 1980s. They were used as a treatment for mental illnesses such as schizophrenia, chronic depression, and sometimes for treating social or behavior problems. Lobotomies were performed in order to eliminate problem emotions and help a person to calm down. Some of these treatments were successful in that endeavor but lobotomy as a treatment method was outlawed because many were either unsuccessful or fatal. In the 1960s, which was certainly in my lifetime, a twelve-year-old boy by the name of Howard Dully was lobotomized because his stepmother said he was out of control. Her specific complaints were that he was defiant, did not want to go to bed and he daydreamed—not uncommon behaviors in a child who had lost his mother to cancer when he was five years old and was now the victim of an abusive stepmother.

Today, these same clinical goals are accomplished in a less drastic, more temporary way with chemical drugs that are given to children to subdue their problem behaviors. A mother called me recently trying to find some way to help her son that did not involve medication. He told her that his ADHD medication was helping him stay out of trouble in school, but he said it was mainly because he no longer cared about anything. That made it easy for him to just sit there and do what he was told. He did not care enough to ask questions, interrupt, or get out of his chair unless he was told too. But neither did he care about the things he had been excited and passionate about before. He described it as though he had been cut off from his very self. Many people who experienced lobotomies described the same kind of feelings. I mention this because many of the symptoms of trauma in children are the same as symptoms of ADHD. This leads to frequent misdiagnosis of ADHD and the administration of drugs that will not help a child deal with tragedy and resolve the emotional impact of their shattered circles.

It was not many years ago even professionals thought that children are resilient and that they bounce back even when terrible things happen. Now we know that is not true. In fact, it was just in the 1980s that Post Traumatic Stress Disorder (PTSD) was even considered a condition or diagnosis. It was used to describe soldiers returning from traumatic war experiences, formerly referred to as "shell shocked." But the same symptoms that plagued these unfortunate veterans were soon noticed in other adult survivors of rape, accidents, injuries, and other natural disasters. Then people began to notice that children also had these same symptoms of flashbacks of the traumatic event; nightmares and other sleep problems; extreme anxiety, and an exaggerated startle response. Now we know that children suffer much more than adults from PTSD. In fact the earlier in life the trauma occurs, the greater the harmful impact. The brains of babies are like little sponges soaking up everything in their environment, with no way to make meaning for themselves. Their meaning comes through interpretations of the reactions of the adults around them.

Children are forming the foundational ideas and emotional processes that will govern their relationships, thoughts, ideas, and reactions for the rest of their lives. The first five years are critical and are rightly called "the formative years." But clear on up through age twelve, issues of attachment, loss, and grief continue to be critical. Please don't despair at this point. This book is about regaining hope that comes through understanding and a clear path to healing. One of the most common problems for early trauma and attachment issues is that the symptoms can look like other disorders. Many children are misdiagnosed and are treated for the wrong condition. Lack of understanding and appropriate methods for dealing with their actual conditions only make the problems worse, driving the pain deeper into the souls of these children.

CAUSES OF TRAUMA

Most often, children will survive their traumatic events and make it through to adulthood. However, we know that the majority of people who are in prison experienced childhood trauma and never had the help they needed to heal the wound. Eventually that unresolved trauma became the fuel that caused them to hurt others. In fact, more than 90% of incarcerated people have a history of childhood trauma. As a grandparent raising your grandchild after a family tragedy of some sort, you are now the one in the position to create the Healing Circles that will help your grandchildren to recover and thrive. Post Traumatic Growth is even more common than Post Traumatic Stress Disorder, so don't lose heart. Gaining knowledge, which you are doing right now, is the first step in helping your grandchildren. Here is a partial list of events which many children have experienced as traumatizing:

- Divorce or parental separation, including dual-parent-working households
- Parent absence due to military deployment
- Death of a family member or a family pet
- Drug and alcohol abuse by parents (and related activities)
- Being removed from abusive parents by police or other social service workers
- Incarceration of parents
- Witnessing domestic violence
- Serious illness, accident, or natural disaster
- Difficult delivery (i.e. forceps, umbilical cord around the neck, Cesarean births)
- Multiple caregivers in the first few years of life
- Multiple foster care placements

- A move away from home community or school friends, especially frequent moves
- Unstable family or home environment
- <u>Emotional abuse (examples)</u>:

  o Overly protective, overly permissive, or negligent parenting
  o Criticism, sarcasm, teasing, and ridicule of the child or others
  o Hostile or aggressive actions toward child or others in the child's presence
  o Rejection, manipulation, or guilt tripping
  o Emotional unavailability due to (partial list):

  - Stress
  - Addictions
  - Depression
  - Being overwhelmed with personal problems
  - Electronic activities
  - Illness (mental or physical)

  o Bullying at school or at home, including racial discrimination
  o Thoughts and feelings of child are discounted
  o Domestic violence in presence of child
  o Obedience demanded without relationship
  o Being made fun of for body size, shape, or functions
  o Embarrassing behavior of parents (addictions, incarcerations, poverty, etc.)
  o Neglect, either physical or emotional
  o Being compared to others
  o Mixed messages and moral dilemmas

o Dishonest and misleading communication

o Denial of child's reality (he does not see/feel what he saw or feels)

o Refusal to communicate or angry threats

o Conditional love (You will be loved when you do what I want)

o An apathetic parent (does not appear to care about the child)

Physical abuse:

o Kicking, biting, burning, beating, or otherwise doing harm to a child

o Isolation, overuse of grounding and restriction

o Refusing food, sleep, safety, medical care

o Destroying or getting rid of child's possessions

Spiritual abuse:

o Scripture used in order to force parent's will on the child

o Moralizing of behavioral issues

o Legalism and perfectionism as means of being "saved"

o Male privilege or chauvinistic attitudes

Sexual abuse: (any sexual act by an adult or older child with a child)

o Sexual looks, touching, or sexual statements of any kind

o Exposing children to adult nudity, pornography, or sexual activity

o Encouraging masturbation or taking sexual pictures

<u>Intellectual abuse:</u>

- o   Lack of respect for a child's intellectual interests
- o   Ridicule of another's ideas and opinions
- o   Calling names like "stupid" or "idiot"
- o   Focusing on educational weaknesses and failures
- o   Unrealistic or developmentally inappropriate intellectual expectations
- o   Not honoring a child's unique learning style
- o   Lack of intellectual stimulations

Before you throw your hands up and say, "Woe is me! Too much damage has already been done!" let me share the good news that it is <u>the response of caring adults</u> during and after the trauma that can make all the difference in the world for the children. The outcome CAN be good if a child has the follow-up care they need, and your grandchildren have YOU, so that offers a lot of hope. With the support, encouragement, and love of consistent caregivers following a traumatic event, your grandchild can become resilient and experience Post Traumatic Growth rather than Post Traumatic Stress Disorder.

How Kids Feel

When bad things like this happen to children it brings up a lot of terrible feelings that they do not know how to express or process. Here is a short list of some of the very common feelings that kids have when they have experienced trauma, loss, or neglect:

*	Helpless	*	Unlovable
*	Unloved	*	Hopeless

* Terrified
* Worthless
* Filled with shame
* Self-loathing
* Anxious
* Unsafe
* Powerless
* Angry
* Like a failure
* Forgotten
* Deserving of abuse
* Alone in their pain
* Afraid or scared
* Ashamed
* Guilty "It's my fault"
* Rejected
* Responsible for causing it
* Responsible for fixing it
* Abandoned
* Insecure
* Stressed
* Confused
* Depressed
* "I am bad"
* Misunderstood
* Unheard and Invisible
* Jealous or envious

The more of these feelings they have combined, the more you are likely to see behaviors or symptoms of trauma. Tuning in to your grandchild's feelings when dealing with problem behaviors will go a lot further toward solving the problem and helping them calm down than reacting to their behavior. Try to figure out which of these feelings are behind the behavior that you are seeing. Ask questions and help them to label their feelings so that they can talk about them and express them. It is the unexpressed painful emotions that lead to all kinds of mental illness. Knowing how to appropriately express emotion, both negative and positive, is a learned behavior. You can teach them by role modeling appropriate expression, just be sure not to overwhelm kids with your own emotions, or to use them as your emotional support. Adults need other adults for emotional support, never kids.

Symptoms of Trauma

Here are some typical ways that children react to trauma:

- Openly rebellious or hostile
- Impulsive off-the-wall behaviors and easily frustrated
- Aggressive behavior and frequent tantrums
- Impaired attachment
- Eating disorders or self-harm behaviors
- Poor hygiene habits
- Disorganization
- May eat too fast, have a loss of appetite, or hoard food
- Easily intimidated by others (the "scared rabbit" syndrome)
- Mood swings
- Isolating or withdrawing from family and friends
- Depression
- Trouble falling asleep, staying asleep and nightmares or night-terrors
- Blames others or asks "Why me?"—Victim mentality
- Refuses to take responsibility for own behavior
- Hair pulling, nail biting, or skin picking
- Consistent disobedience
- Restless behaviors (often diagnosed ADHD)
- Bed wetting, or daytime wetting and soiling
- Constipation or regression in toilet training
- Bullies others
- Developmental delays and memory problems that lead to "story telling"
- Sexual promiscuity or inappropriate sexual behavior
- Self-harm behaviors (partial list):

- Head banging
- Biting self
- Scratching and picking at skin
- Hair pulling
- Punching things
- Cutting

Children's bodies and minds are consumed with trying to help them survive and there is no energy or capacity left in the system for learning. Due to memory impairment and hypervigilance to threats, children often remember things differently than calm adults in the room do. When this happens they are often accused of lying. It is important for caregivers to let go of "the truth" because if a child perceived it, then they received it, whatever it was. They will not be able to let go of their perception of an experience until they have been fully heard and have expressed all of their emotions surrounding the event. Once they have been able to do that, they can hear other versions and consider them. Please be aware that children are often not able to tell their stories by talking them out. Younger or developmentally delayed children tell their stories best by playing them out or acting them out.

Terror is the word that most describes the depth of feeling that leads children to the behaviors that these children are often most known for. Terror is a generalized reaction to trauma and is largely unidentified by both parents and professionals. Terror in children has not been studied much, but we do know that it distorts a child's identity and leaves a sense of guilt with a child that adults generally do not understand. Recently I was working with a boy who saw his father handcuffed and taken to prison when he was four. By the age of twelve he had still not seen him again and had no idea why he was arrested. After several years of abuse and neglect, including starvation, he was taken from his mother and raised by his grandmother. After a few years with her, his behavior became too much for grandmother to manage and he was put into foster care.

After a particularly bad day in which he had assaulted a couple of his peers and broken some equipment in the house, he admitted that he wished he had been taken to jail. He felt he belonged there. After a few more questions, it came out that he felt it was his fault that his father went to jail; his fault that his (drug addicted) mother could not handle him; his fault that his younger siblings had also started getting into trouble; and somehow that his best friend was being bullied, which he had nothing to do with. He felt that he should be taking the punishment for all of them. He believed that he was the worst person in the world. This is common to traumatized children. I have heard this story over and over, just slightly different versions of it.

Judith Hermann describes it like this, "traumatized people feel utterly abandoned, utterly alone, cast out of the human and divine systems of care and protection that sustain life. Thereafter, a sense of alienation, of disconnection, pervades every relationship, from the most intimate familial bonds to the most abstract affiliations of community and religion." Traumatic experiences are events in time, but the long-lasting damage is done by what is permanently altered in the mind. Children in the midst of a terrifying experience do not know what to do. They are too scared to think, to cry, sometimes almost too scared to breath. They are too surprised and overwhelmed and sometimes as Lenore Terr says, they "feel lucky not to die with a crazy heart rhythm or a burst blood vessel." Children in these unexpected circumstances don't know what to do except what they are told and may go on acting like normal. If you look in their faces, you will rarely see the horror and the fear. You will more likely see a blank, dazed face, grave and immobile. These events damage the foundational beliefs of a child's life and if the damage done during these events is not attended to, the child will carry the fears, beliefs and trauma throughout life.

A note of caution: *many times* grief and trauma responses in children are **misdiagnosed** as ADHD, Conduct Disorder, Depression, etc. The reason is that children often express their pain in ways that are difficult for adults to interpret. What looks like bad behavior to some, may simply be a symptom of grief or trauma. A label of ADHD should not be placed on any child without extensive testing by a qualified professional who *specializes in ADHD evaluation and treatment*, such as a psychiatrist, psychologist, or a neurodevelopmental pediatrician. A thorough evaluation should include:

- Two visits to the doctor, totaling a couple of hours at least
- A complete history from birth to present that includes physical, social and emotional history, and family dynamics
- A verbal interview with the child's school teacher
- A physical exam including neurological issues and coordination
- ADHD questionnaires such as the Conners' Rating Scale

Too many children are diagnosed and medicated after a 15-minute interview; it is impossible to truly diagnose ADHD without more extensive evaluation.

Can't Stop Crying-Grief

Whereas trauma leads to feelings of terror, grief leaves children with a deep sense of sadness. Grieving children, even if they are angry, are generally not violent. They do not suffer from the identity distortion so common to trauma. Their pain is related to their loss, not to an overwhelming sense of fear, anguish of soul, and hopelessness. Loss of parents is one of the common problems grandchildren being raised by grandparents are dealing with. Whether the parents have died or are gone due to incarceration, mental illness, or other reasons, both grandparents and grandchildren will be dealing with grief. In the midst of your own grief, it can be easy to lose sight of the fact that your grandchildren are suffering intensely. They don't usually show their grief simply by crying. Children six years of age and younger do not understand the permanence of death and when they have lost someone they love they may show their grief in some of the following ways:

- Feel abandoned or rejected (Why would she go to heaven and not want to be with me?)
- May be afraid of being alone or away from people they love
- Often have trouble sleeping alone
- May act out through disobedience, tantrums, pretend, or fantasy play
- May begin wetting the bed or develop eating problems
- Generally will not talk about it; under two may not talk at all
- May dream about the deceased

Children aged seven to twelve years old are beginning to understand the permanence of death, but still hope that death or significant loss it can be reversed. Even in cases of amicable divorce, children in this age group may entertain ideas or fantasies of their parents getting back together again. At this age they may show grief by:

- Wanting to withdraw or isolate
- Becoming overly compliant or by beginning to act out
- Having trouble concentrating at school
- An inability to stay on task or follow directions
- Being afraid of dying themselves
- Wanting to be with those they believe can protect them from death

Children of all ages, including teenagers, may:

- Cry a lot or at unexpected times
- Over-react to little things
- Become very angry or destructive
- Become irritable or forgetful
- Get stomach pain, headaches, or other minor illnesses
- Regress to younger stages of development
- Need more affection and become clingy
- Become lethargic or sleep more than usual

Children are trying to make sense of the loss and develop their own meanings about death. You can help them by listening, by telling the truth at their age level, and by anticipating that they will likely need to go back to the event at different ages or stages to get more information. At these times, they may need to grieve again due to a different understanding of their own loss. Grieving is a family event and should be shared openly. If you are grieving your grandchildren will feel that whether you talk about it or not. Sharing your own grief with your grandchildren can bring healing and bonding to both of you as long as you are careful not to overwhelm them with your emotions. If you avoid your own grief and always put on a "brave face" you may be giving them the message that it is not okay for them to feel the way they do. Just be sure that your adult needs are met through adult relationships, not through your grandchildren, and that the sharing you do benefits them and does not further harm or burden them. It should lead them to greater understanding and should role model healthy grieving for them.

I highly recommend grief groups or grief camps for children (and grandparents) who have suffered the loss of a close family member. When children have the chance to hear from other children who have also lost a parent, they will not feel so alone. Feeling heard and understood is very important to the process of healing and groups offer the opportunity to experience both. Check with a local social service agency, your family therapist, pediatrician, or social worker to find a grief group in your area. Most communities have them.

It is also very important for children to be included in the funerals or other rituals of death offered for close family members. If appropriate they should even be included in planning the service and encouraged to participate in it. Experiencing the loss and then having no ritual for grieving and sayi; g good bye makes it harder for children to experience the finality of death and gain closure. If your grandchild already missed an important funeral or was too young to remember, it may be helpful for them to be able to see pictures or hear stories about the person lost and the funeral event. Always ask children if they want to see these types of pictures before bringing them out and be open to their questions or their need to talk.

One of the problems that often comes up is the unbalanced picture of the deceased that usually occurs at funerals, especially during the eulogy and personal tributes. Often you hear only the positive aspects of a person and children will need a more truthful review of a person's life. Just be careful not to swing the other way and neglect to mention positive traits and stories from the life of a parent who may have died as a result of drugs or criminal activity. Every person has some good qualities and children will feel better hearing good about their parents, especially if you can help them see those same great qualities in themselves.

Children may also be grieving over losses that are not related to death. Sometimes a loss is experienced as an "ambiguous loss" because there is no conversation, no ritual, and no recognition of the loss. For example, separation from a sibling; a move away from a family pet or close friend; the loss of function or lifestyle due to an injury or illness. Ambiguous loss can be the hardest to grieve because no one notices with you how much it hurts. Simply notice with a child what hurts and how they feel in any moment of pain—and that feels like a gift to them. Also be sure to share with teachers and daycare providers that your grandchild is grieving so that they will be more understanding when they see symptoms of grief and not immediately assume "poor choices," "attention seeking," or any of the other labels that children often get when they are in pain. If your grandchild seems stuck in their grief and pain, please seek counseling by a professional with specialized training in childhood grief.

Never Enough-Neglect

Children experience neglect when their parents do not provide adequately or consistently for their physical, mental, and emotional needs. Food, shelter, clean water, and protection, along with kindness, love and attentiveness, are the most basic of needs. Children desperately need loving touch (i.e. hugs, rocking, holding) at age appropriate levels. Lack of education, medical care, relationships, physical exercise, and other types of stimulation in their environment also falls under the category of neglect.

Drug and alcohol addiction, mental illness, and poverty are the most common causes of neglect. Without intervention children can experience long-term debilitating effects to their emotional, mental and behavioral development. Here are some behavioral problems you might expect if your grandchild was neglected:

- Poor hygiene habits
- Lack of everyday knowledge or skills—such as not knowing how to do chores
- Difficulties with school, may be way behind
- Severe anxiety or depression
- Lack of interest in play
- Lethargic or they may sleep more than usual
- Lack of friends and social skills
- May withdraw, isolate, or avoid people
- Greedy and impulsive
- Stealing and hoarding food
- A tendency to steal shiny things

- Lack of emotional attachment to caregiver or easy, indiscriminate attachment to anyone
- Sexually active
- Abuse of drugs or alcohol
- Do not care about physical appearance
- Acting as though there is never enough, even when there is

Due to developmental imbalances in the brain, neglected children really do not have the same choices that normally developed children have. They have a much more limited range of options available to them until they get the help and the healing that they need.

Shame on You!

Most children who have been neglected or abused suffer from a toxic form of shame, which is basically a feeling of being unlovable, of being intrinsically bad, or not deserving of good things. It is often confused with guilt, which is the discomfort a person with a conscience feels when they have done something wrong or hurt someone in some way. Guilt is attached to a specific behavior or attitude, which can usually be fixed or forgiven. But shame has a way of sticking to the soul and draining hope and confidence right out of a person and sometimes a whole family. Shame is very much about feelings of not belonging and not deserving, of being defective, and just never good enough. Shame grows from the messages we receive from parents and other authority figures that tell us that for some reason we are not quite all right. Other factors that may cause feelings of shame for both you and your grandchildren might be: having family members who are incarcerated; mental illness in the family; or extreme poverty. Shame can spring forth from the messages that troubled children routinely hear every day, such as:

- Don't be angry or upset (like happy is the only emotion that's okay)
- Don't cry or express other negative feelings
- Be nice and avoid conflict
- Don't do as I do. Do as I say
- Obey without questioning
- Be successful in school, behaviorally and academically
- Keep our family secrets and don't betray us
- Always stay in control
- Always look good and behave perfectly

Family secrets are especially shaming, both to those who know the secret and those who do not. Don't take this as permission to begin to broadcast all the family secrets that you know. There are some secrets that need to be told to specific others because they become toxic to the family system and to individual family members when they are kept. Toxic secrets that should be told to your grandchildren are secrets that other people know but that the child does not know. For example: If a parent has an embarrassing or life threatening condition including cancer or a drug or alcohol addiction; if there is known abuse in the child's past; if there is a family history of trauma; or if a child might hear about the secret from someone outside the immediate family. These types of secrets should be told to the children in age appropriate ways so as not to overwhelm them.

If there are other types of family secrets that would hurt others if they were made public, they should only be discussed with a therapist or other person who is safe to tell, such as a close and trusted friend. If you are not sure who to let in on family secrets, or how to tell children about them, please talk to a family therapist who can help you decide who, when and how to tell.

Some shaming family events are not secrets at all, and these can cause tremendous harm to children. Grandparents with incarcerated adult children may be struggling with their own sense of shame. One grandmother shared this with me:

> *"Due to her drug addiction, my daughter wound up with seven felony accounts. The kids would get up in the morning and see their mom on the news in court looking scared to death. Seeing that scared them too and then they had to go to school with everyone knowing what was going on. The humiliation, shame and trauma that these kids go through is horrendous. It is not in the past, they live it every day. Their entire living every day is altered by this trauma. Trauma causes the flight/fight response and they are going through that every day plus carrying that shame around with them wherever they go."*

It is easy to see why these kids are so drawn to drugs and alcohol. Drug and alcohol addictions, obesity, and criminal behavior have all been linked in many studies to unresolved childhood trauma. It is very painful and takes a lot of effort just to get through the day when you are filled with toxic shame. Any escape from that feels heaven sent. Shame is very hard to get rid of and sometimes entire family systems are built around protecting a collective sense of shame. Neglected children struggle with shame because their experience in life has given them the message that they do not have the right to exist. Children who have been abused struggle the most with shame, especially victims of sexual abuse. Families that have secrets are guarding their shame and passing it on to the next generation. Shame is deepened and created by:

- Negligent parenting
- Addicted or incarcerated parents
- Over controlling parents
- Enmeshed family systems
- Abuse—emotional, physical or sexual

Children that have shame often display it through:

- Low self-esteem
- Social anxiety or acute shyness
- Perfectionism
- Addictions and compulsive behaviors
- People pleasing
- Withdrawal and isolation
- Anger or rage
- Contempt, resentment or by bullying others
- Compulsive behaviors

Sometimes children that are suffering appear to be very compliant and easy to manage. This does not mean they are not suffering on the inside. This is the kind of suffering that often goes unnoticed and unresolved.

Living in Fear-Domestic Violence

Honestly, the word "fear" does not fully describe how children feel when violence is going on in their home. "Terrified" is much closer to it. And they don't have to see it or hear it to be affected. If domestic violence has occurred in a family, the children are victims of it whether they have witnessed the actual violence or not. Domestic violence is not just about physical assault. It is also about an attitude of arrogance and disrespect, and often includes verbal degradation, humiliation, and other kinds of bullying. The longer a child spends in this environment, the harder it will be for them to experience life and relationships as safe. It is very painful for children to see their mother's being hurt or humiliated in any way. Their desire to help and rescue is in direct opposition to their own feelings of fear and guilt. Children will be affected in different ways. Some of them become violent themselves and others become chronic the victims of disrespect, bullying or violent behavior of others. Extreme cases of domestic violence will call for some extremely compassionate and loving interventions given consistently over a long period of time. When a parent or caregiver is unsafe and a child experiences the repercussions of domestic violence, expect to see some of the following difficulties:

- Aggressive, antisocial behavior
- Poor social relationships in general
- Angry and violent behavior
- Difficulty in school and impaired cognitive development
- Limited problem solving or conflict resolution skills
- Disobedience and oppositional behavior
- Depression and anxiety
- Fear and withdrawal

There are many protective or redeeming factors that can help children who have been exposed to domestic violence to be resilient and to not follow in the footsteps of their abusive parent. One is having a consistent, supportive relationship with a non-abusing caregiver, such as yourself. You bring hope into your grandchild's life by being safe and supportive. When children witness their caregivers being kind and compassionate and generous with others, it produces these same wonderful traits in them. If your grandchildren have come from families with domestic violence issues, I highly recommend Lundy Bancroft's books listed in the back of this book because it is excellent and I cannot possibly include enough here to do this topic justice. It is one of the most difficult family systems to treat. Bancroft has done extensive work and research with families in domestic violence and I am not aware of any resources that are more thorough and helpful in this specific area.

THE BRAIN ON TRAUMA AND NEGLECT

By understanding the impact of these difficult childhood experiences you are better prepared to deal with their symptoms of pain and brokenness. The specifics of how to deal with and help a child who has experienced domestic violence and other traumatic incidents will be covered in later chapters. The purpose of this chapter is simply to help you understand your grandchild and their symptoms. Not understanding generally causes the adults in a child's life to be more judgmental and punitive of these emotional and behavioral symptoms of trauma and stress. Understanding leads to greater compassion and opens doors to responding in ways that will be healing for the child.

Dr. Bruce Perry, a neuropsychiatrist in Houston, Texas, has done extensive research and work on early brain development in children of trauma. He states:

> *"By the age of two and a half, approximately 85 percent of the baby's neurological growth is complete, meaning the foundation of their brain's capacity is in place. By age three, the child's brain is 90 percent of its completed adult size. Think of it in terms of nutrition. If a baby is not fed consistent, predictable messages of love and communication, then those areas of the brain shut down and the child's capacity to function later in life is compromised."*

Our brains continue growing throughout our lives and it is our relationships and experiences in life that promote this growth. At the same time, the brain "trims away" any parts of the brain that are not being used. Neglect, abuse, and other types of trauma impair healthy brain development because the brain's resources are hijacked to deal with trauma and stress. Let me explain.

A brain consists of four basic parts, divided into two specific centers:

Decision-Making Center

1. The **Cortical System**—Responsible for logic, planning, and reasoning
2. The **Limbic System**—The center of feelings and emotions

Emergency Response Center

3. The **Midbrain**—The emergency system that responds to threats to our safety

4. The **Brainstem**—Responsible for body functions that we are not necessarily aware of, such as heartbeat, breathing, and digestion

The <u>Cortical/Limbic</u> part of the brain, which is the **Decision-Making Center**, is twice the size of the <u>Midbrain/Brainstem</u>, the **Emergency Response Center** in a normal, well developed person. When we tell children to "think before you act" we are asking them to engage the **Decision-Making Center** to override or control their **Emergency Responses**, which are generally known as the fight, flight, or freeze mode.

In a healthy brain this may at times be challenging, but it is generally doable under normal circumstances. You might want to put a bookmark on this page, or if you are like me, bend the corner of the page down so you can easily refer to it. These brain centers will be referred to in subsequent chapters.

A traumatized child develops a hypervigilant, over-active **Emergency Response Center**. This means that they will be more reactive and more impulsive than their non-traumatized peers even though their **Decision-Making Center** is likely to be normally developed.

These children exhibit anxiety, poor emotional control, and hyperactivity. They also have trouble understanding or expressing their emotions. When we talk about emergency response in this instance, do not picture an ambulance coming in for a rescue. Think more of all hell breaking loose inside a child's mind and body. It is more like a bomb just dropped or like they are falling into a black hole from which they have no hope of surviving. This emergency response feels like the end of the world to a traumatized child. They feel as though they are literally fighting for their life. That is why it often takes several adults to control a small child who has "flipped out." From his perspective, this child may be fighting for his life.

A neglected child on the other hand, will have an under-developed **Decision-Making Center**, which also gives the **Emergency Response Center** too much power, although by different means. Do not underestimate the impact of neglect on a child.

For example, many children who have often been left hungry for extended periods develop habits of hoarding food. It is significant enough of a problem that there is an actual diagnosis now for hoarding. Children will steal and lie and become very manipulative, sneaky, or angry if anyone gets in the way of them getting food and hiding it. Once again, it can feel like a matter of life or death to this child because they once felt they were going to die from hunger. They do not have the ability to overcome their fear of starvation until they have had the long-term, consistent caregiving that includes sufficient food on a regular basis, and the ability to easily get to food between meals. It can be very difficult to deal with a child that is stealing and lying to get food and "shiny" things, but it does not come from the child being "bad." It comes from serious and chronic neglect.

A child who is both traumatized and neglected receives a double whammy. With a hypervigilant, over-active **Emergency Response Center** AND an under-developed **Decision-Making Center** it is easy to see why they have severe behavior problems. It is like trying to drive downhill in a semi-truck with motorcycle brakes. When you reach the intersection at the bottom of the hill, you are in trouble! In a child, the difference between the amount of power, and the ability to control it, is called "acting out." But the child is not really being disobedient, defiant, attention seeking, or "bad," they simply do not have the means to do what is expected of them, even if they want to.

Even if she wants desperately to please the adult, she is not capable of pulling it off. This is why the normal, traditional parenting methods do not work with these kids. They need to be guided in the right direction by methods that take into account the compromised development of their brains. The parenting methods that work so well with children whose brains are healthy and fully developed only make things worse for traumatized and neglected kids because they increase the amount of stress and pressure that <u>activate</u> the **Emergency Response Center** at a very time when they have <u>no access to</u> the **Decision-Making Center**. We must use special methods for dealing with this kind of child. The powerful parenting method that I most recommend is the Nurtured Heart Approach®, which you will see mentioned several times in this book. The reasons that I recommend it are also scattered throughout the book to show why the stance that the Nurtured Heart Approach® takes is such an important one.

In his book *From Fear to Love*, Dr. Bryan Post goes into much more detail on the processes and development of the brain. I believe that understanding the root of problem behaviors in your grandchild can go a long way toward helping you offer empathy and understanding. Without coming from a place of empathy and engaging principles of love, it is impossible to help a traumatized child fully heal. Knowing that your grandchild is not "out to get you," "trying to manipulate," or "attention seeking," (like that's a bad thing), can help you to avoid taking their attitudes, behaviors, and reactions personally. Understanding the underlying issues will help you change parenting habits that are long ingrained. While these parenting habits may work just fine with a normal child, they will not work well with a traumatized child.

A universal identifying sign of trauma is hypervigilance and anxiety in the traumatized person, especially when they are in situations that are likely to trigger a trauma response. This trauma based hypervigilance looks like hyperactive behavior and inattentiveness in children. It is not that the child can't focus, it is that they are focusing so much on what they are afraid *might* happen, that they have no energy left to focus on what the adult expects, requests, or demands. Children are often considered lazy, hyperactive, distractible, defiant, manipulative or controlling; when really the problem is that they are traumatized. Many children, especially children who have lost or been removed from their parents, are **misdiagnosed with ADD/ADHD**. When this happens, and they are medicated for ADD/ADHD, it is no wonder the medication does not work.

ANTICIPATING TRAUMA SYMPTOMS

In the chapters to follow, you will find many great tools for helping your grandchildren recover from their traumatic past. In the meantime, here are a few things to keep in mind as you see many of the symptoms of trauma manifested in your grandchild:

- Don't take it personally when your grandchild acts out—it's not about you

- Avoid over-reacting as this may be threatening or frightening to the child and make problems worse
- Avoid any aggressive behaviors and avoid raising your voice. Speak softly and be kind
- If a child needs to be redirected from inappropriate behavior, touch their hand or shoulder gently, get on their eye level, make eye contact, then give simple directions in a calm voice
- Help a child express the emotions behind the behavior and offer understanding
- Do something with them to help them calm down, such as take a walk, breathe deeply, "Let's both count to 10," etc., or gently remind them to use coping techniques
- Let them know that they are safe and loved and that you are there for them
- Notice their good behaviors, and even more important, notice their neutral behaviors as this lets them know they are worthy of love just as they are (not achievement based)
- Manage your own emotions and give yourself a time out if you need it so that you can remain calm for the child

I worked with a nine year old boy who had been terribly abused and neglected by his mother for his entire life. He had developed Post Traumatic Stress Disorder from the extreme physical and emotional abuse that she had heaped on him. A few weeks before I met him, his grandparents had received full custody of him. A few months after living with his loving grandparents, he experienced a triggering event. He was getting ready for school and could not find his shoes. Grandmother came to help him and in her exasperation, at one point she grabbed his shoulders and got close to his face to get his attention and to scold him. For him, this was a triggering event that brought an instant flashback. He reported to me, "It reminded me of when my mother used to grab me, push me up against the wall, smash me in the nose, and spank me really hard. I actually thought I was back with my mother."

I asked him what he did when he got reminded of all that. He told me that he fell on the floor and started crying and screaming. Then I asked him what his grandmother did when he fell on the floor crying and screaming. His response melted my heart. "She sat down on the floor with me and we cried together and hugged for about an hour." This is a grandmother that understood his past and how it affected him. She did not take his behavior as manipulative, over-reactive, or oppositional. She quickly moved closer to him right where he was, joined him in his terror, and turned the event into a powerful healing moment. She helped him get from his most terrifying place, back to a place of love and joy. She will have to do this many more times before this young boy's brain has been rewired so that he can take himself back to love and joy when he is reminded of that dark past. But I have no doubt that she and her husband will do it.

STRUCTURE AND NURTURING

Understanding your grandchild's experience when their lives have been shattered, and providing a safe and structured environment are some of the first and most critical steps in helping your grandchild to begin the process of healing and growth. Nurturing, empathy, and joy are also critical ingredients, and there is much more that can be done to unbreak little hearts and rewire young brains. The good news is that the human brain has something called *neuroplasticity*. That's a long word and I don't like long words, but it means that throughout your life your brain is capable of being rewired and becoming healthier. So here is a new title for you, you are no longer just a grandparent, you are also a neuroplastician! Put that after your name next time you sign something and feel the pride that comes with one of the most important occupations available on Planet Earth! You have the power to help rewire your grandchild's brain and help them to overcome the tremendous challenges that they are facing. Now you just need to know how to do it!

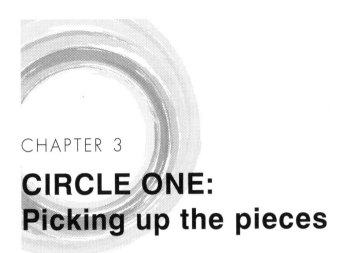

CHAPTER 3

CIRCLE ONE:
Picking up the pieces

"What I remember most about my grandmother is that
she was always there for me making sure I was safe.
Teaching me to pray, cook and stay true to myself. She
dropped whatever she was doing to make sure she
was there for her grandkids. She was my comfort and
stability . . . . my everything.

My world was so crazy back then and things were
always changing and she was the one person I could
share everything with." ~A grandchild

When a family is shattered by an event of such magnitude that parents
are no longer able to take care of their children, it can take a while for
the dust to settle and for everyone to take on new roles. But when a
family tragedy occurs, there are some things that can be done right
away that will make the transition to a new family structure easier
and more conducive to healing for the children. The first ring of the

Healing Circles is based on providing Safety, Basic Needs, and Structure for you and for the children. Keeping a safe, structured, and normally-functioning home environment can go a long way toward helping children become more resilient and thrive in spite of any kind of tragedy, neglect or abuse they may have experienced. As you find yourself picking up the pieces of your lives, here are some things that will help you to move forward in creating a new family structure that will promote Post Traumatic Growth and prevent Post Traumatic Stress Disorder from making itself an unwelcomed guest in your home.

SAFETY FIRST

There are times when the family tragedy involves drugs, alcohol, criminal activity, and/or abuse. There can be many people involved, some who are not safe for the kids and may even become threatening to the grandparents taking care of the kids. In any situation, **creating safety is always your most important concern.** If safety is an issue for your family, do the following right away to improve the safety factor for your home and grandchildren:

- Inform your local police and your neighbors about the situation and ask for their help in keeping alert to any signs of danger.
- Change locks on your doors and make sure all windows cannot be opened from the outside, but CAN be opened from the inside. Modern windows often have security features but you can always wedge wooden dowels in the window track to keep them from opening wide enough for someone to gain entrance. These are very inexpensive at Home Depot or Lowes and they will even cut them the right length for you free of

charge. Measure the window track and subtract 3-4 inches so you can let fresh air in without compromising safety.

- Make sure your front door has a peephole. If you do not have the tools to install one yourself, find someone in your circle of friends who can either do it for you or recommend a trusted handyman.

- Get a restraining order if you need to and carry it with you at all times. Also be sure that the school and daycare provider have a copy of it and are aware of the situation.

- Get legal guardianship of children if that will help.

- If sexual or physical abuse has taken place or is suspected, get professional help immediately. Children recover much more quickly if caring adults do not guilt them, but instead believe them and move quickly to keep them safe and provide counseling specific to their abuse. Be sure your counselor specializes in the type of abuse your child has suffered. Remember that <u>witnessing</u> domestic violence or other forms of abuse and sexual behavior is emotionally abusive to children.

- Have a code word that only you and your grandkids know so if they are in trouble they can indicate that to you without anyone else knowing. Choose a word that you don't usually use, but that is common enough to not raise red flags. My kids used the word "meatballs." That worked fine for us because we were vegetarian and never ate meatballs. Be creative and remind your grandkids often enough so that they will remember if they ever need it.

- Teach children to make important calls and help them memorize numbers. If they are very young, learning a song with the number in it may help.

- If you are concerned about intruders who are familiar to your home, rearrange the furniture to disorient them in the dark. Noise will alert you that someone is there. Hide sharp knives or other weapons where children and strangers will not have easy access to them.
- Install exterior lights that come on when they sense movement.
- Consider getting a dog. They are great alert systems and can also provide a great deal of comfort and joy to you and your grandchildren.

Children in these situations often have a great deal of fear and anxiety and likely have already been through a lot. Communicate to them that you know their situation has been scary and sometimes dangerous, but now you are here and you are keeping them safe. Remind them frequently that they are safe now. Do not allow this communication to be lip services only. Make sure that you deliver on this promise to the very best of your ability. Talk to them about the safety measures you are taking around the house and allow them to be part of making safety changes so that they feel included. This will also open the door for them to express their fears to you any time they do not feel safe.

If you are feeling unsafe or endangered at any time, do not hesitate to call the police. **Safety is always the very first consideration if you have to prioritize needs.** As much as you love your adult children, if they are causing an unsafe environment for your grandchildren, your first and most grave responsibility is to the grandchildren now in your care. If you have to decide between safety of children and safety of adults, act first in behalf of the children. Do not, for love or money, jeopardize the safety of a child for the sake of an adult. If you can provide safety for both, all the better. If your adult children are breaking the law and endangering others, it is an act of great love to turn them in to proper authorities and help them to be held accountable for their actions. This can be <u>extremely difficult</u> when it is your own child but to not do so is to be part of the problem. Once safety is established, it is time to take care of the practicalities of daily life.

TRYING TO FILL OUR BELLIES

My mom finally brought us some bread and peanut butter. I was 9 and older than my sisters, so she told me to fix us each a sandwich and then she left again. So I made sandwiches and we ate them, but we were so hungry that I made another, and then another and another. We just kept eating until it was all gone. When she got home and saw the food was all gone she got really mad and beat me, really hard. I don't understand why, because we were really hungry and we were just trying to fill our bellies." ~by a child taken from abusive mother, now being raised by grandparents

When your grandchildren arrive in your home, chances are that at least some of their basic needs have not been met in a consistent way. Alcoholic or drug abusing parents are not known for placing a great priority on the medical needs or the eating and sleeping habits of their children. I have talked to many children that were moved from hotel to hotel by their parents and also experienced homelessness before being rescued. Many of them have not been in school or have been moved from school to school making their educational foundation weak and shaky. Whatever condition you find your grandchildren in, once their safety is assured, you will begin to provide their most basic needs.

Food

Food is one of the first basic needs that you will have to address and is also one of the most powerful bonding tools that you have available to you. We will cover that aspect of mealtime in detail in a subsequent chapter. Right now though, you are simply facing a survival need.

Sooner or later your grandchildren are going to have to understand that the rules and eating habits they had before they came to live with you do not get to come with them. It will be much harder to change if you start out letting them demand what they want. In fact, catering to their whims in the beginning and then trying to change later will be much more difficult. Let them know right from the get-go that "This is how we eat in our home." Taking a stand like this, even though they may complain vehemently in the beginning, shows them that you are strong enough to give them the safety and structure that they have been lacking and that you are not a push over. They need to see your strength, especially if they have lived in an environment where they had to provide their own strength in order to survive.

This should <u>not</u> be done in an intense, punitive way. Food is nothing to shout and yell over. Just let them know that the meal you prepare is the meal they'll eat, PERIOD. If you don't provide a smorgasbord at each meal, made up of the foods they demand, eventually they will become hungry enough to eat something. They WILL get used to it and eventually learn to like fruits, vegetables, meatloaf and other healthy foods. In France when a child does not like a food, the adults tell them something along the lines "You just haven't tried it enough times to develop a taste for it. Today, just taste it." Ask them to just taste new things each time and eventually most children will find a wide variety of foods that they like. Eating one pea may not seem like a significant accomplishment, but each time a child eats one pea, they are that much closer to liking it. If you become punitive or forceful with them on each food item, it makes it more likely that they will hate that food for the rest of their lives because they will associate it with a very bad time. So be gentle and kind but firm. Being strict is not the same thing as being mean. And remember, humor that does not shame anyone goes a long way in creating positive connections.

One reason that it is important to put some thought into the nutrition and eating habits of your grandchildren is that there seems to be a sharply increased rate of food sensitivities among children compared to when you and I were growing up. Pesticides, preservatives, and other environmental changes are partly to blame. Many of the behavior problems that children have are from food allergies or sensitivities, or from too much sugar or other sweeteners. The more natural a diet you can provide, the better off your grandchildren will be, in a number of ways. Dr. Sandy Newmark, in his book *ADHD Without Drugs*, devotes a couple of chapters to the importance of proper nutrition for children with ADHD behaviors. In fact he states that a lack of good nutrition is one of the single largest contributing factors to children's lack of ability to concentrate and pay attention.

On top of everything else you have to do right now, I imagine that changing eating habits may seem overwhelming. And to teach your grandchildren healthy eating habits, you may have to change your own. To make this a little easier and quicker for yourself, check out Missy Chase Lapine's *Sneaky Chef* books. (See Recommended Reading section in the back of this book.) I noticed on Amazon.com's reviews of her books that some people who use her books buy the organic baby food in jars to "sneak" healthy vegetables into recipes or packaged meals. What a great idea if you don't have time to puree your vegies for children who refuse to eat them. Consider this a gift to yourself, one that will give you improved health and increased energy, which you will definitely need to raise your grandchildren!

Menus

I highly recommend planning a weekly menu and posting it on the front of the refrigerator. Keep your meals simple and nutritious. Include lots of fruits and vegetables and, as much as possible, foods that the kids do like, assuming they like some healthy food. Do not keep foods in your pantry or your refrigerator that you do not want the kids to eat. This will eliminate a lot of whining. No one will be tempted to eat what is not there. If you like ice cream or other treats, start using them for special events, not for every day at home. Of course, you can have a "special event" on a weekly basis or as often as you decide! You give your grandchildren a huge gift for life by helping them to develop good eating habits.

Kids like to know what to expect as much as possible, especially kids who have lived in a lot of chaos. For example, you can fix the same simple meals each week and make a fun name for that night, such as:

- Sunday Leftover Frenzy
- Mashed Potato Monday

- Taco Tuesday
- Wednesday Spaghetti & Family Night
- Chow Mein Thursday
- Friday Fish Fry
- Saturday Pizza Party

These are just some simple examples, but be creative and use whatever fits your style of eating. This will go a long way toward providing simple structure while eliminating that stress and fuss about "what's for supper tonight?" Here again, it is good to allow children to help choose menu items that they enjoy. On the other hand, you may be a stay-at-home grandma that loves to cook wonderful meals, and good for you! That is certainly a gift to your grandchildren and a wonderful heritage to pass on. Please invite me over when I visit your town!

When including the family in planning the menu, you might want to provide a list of nutritious foods for them to choose from. If you don't have one, you can search online for *Healthy Eating Plate* and *Healthy Eating Pyramid* to find out what Harvard University's School of Public Health has put together based on the most current scientific studies of what we all need to be most healthy. I found it at http://www.hsph. harvard.edu/nutritionsource/what-should-you-eat/pyramid/

When my kids were little I let them pick out their own cereal when they went shopping with me. I just gave them one rule: It has to have 9 or less grams of sugar per serving. That's pretty limiting, but it gives them a choice, a guideline and a challenge. You can decide on the guidelines that you want to give, then stick to them.

Snacks

If your grandchildren need snacks, make them healthy, whole food snacks and not processed junk food. A quick search on the Internet under "healthy kids snacks" may pull up all kinds of fancy and attractive things you can prepare for the kids if you are an inspired stay-at-home grandma with plenty of time on your hands. However, if you are like me, you might be closer to tossing a kid an apple and saying, "You're hungry? Here. Eat this." If you are short on time and the kids need a snack try some of these quick and easy healthy snacks:

- Fresh fruits of just about any kind
- Frozen fruit bars (Real fruit, homemade or store-bought)
- Frozen blueberries or peas
- Cheese sticks
- Celery sticks with cream cheese or peanut butter
- Nuts and raisins or trail-mix
- Crackers and cheese (real cheese, not the kind that squirts out of a bottle)
- Bagel with cream cheese
- Yogurt (which they now make in snack packaging)
- Frozen grapes (cut in half or smaller for young children to avoid choking hazards)
- Popcorn and apples
- Granola bars (Not chocolate filled! Watch sugar content on these.)

These are just a few simple ideas which are easy for you and much healthier for kids. If it has sugar or preservatives in it, it is probably not a healthy snack. If you can't pronounce the ingredients, it's likely not good for the kids.

Shopping

Once you have your menu planned out for the week, use that to make up a master grocery shopping list that you can either photocopy or print up each week. When it's time to go shopping cross everything off the list that you have plenty of already and then get what you need. Having a list will help you to avoid purchasing those items that you and your grandchildren would be better off not eating at all or at least eating rarely. It also makes it much easier to stick to your plan. If you don't bring it home, no one will eat it!

If possible, schedule your shopping trips during the week at times when you are not hungry. If that's not possible, go ahead and grab something quick as you head into the store, eat it immediately as you start your shopping to remove some of that hunger intensity. Grab an apple from the produce section, or a small bag of nuts or trail mix from the checkout line. Eat the snack before beginning your shopping. You'll be sated while shopping and less likely to buy on empty-stomach-impulse. Be sure you hand the wrapper to the checker and pay for it before you leave the store!

Sleep

Many traumatized children have sleep problems. They may not be able to fall asleep or they may have trouble staying asleep. Some children have nightmares or night-terrors and some kids wet the bed. Some kids even sleep walk or thrash around the bed so much they fall out of it. Sleeping problems can make it hard for kids to get up in the morning and may cause them to be irritable during the day. Current research on sleep shows that sufficient sleep and good sleep are critical to physical, mental, and emotional health. Children's sleep problems often mean that grandparents also have interrupted sleep and consequently may struggle with exhaustion and irritability. To be our best selves, good sleep habits are a must.

It will likely take a while before children can get to a normal and healthy sleep pattern, but there are some things you can do to help them along the way. Start by having a scheduled bed time and time to get up in the morning, even on weekends. In general, our needs for sleep vary widely. Some people, even as children, need only 6 hours of sleep, while other people feel better if they've had 10. Pay attention to your grandchildren's needs and adjust your schedule.

My son could not have naps from about the age of 2 ½ on because even a 10 minute nap would have him wide awake until 2am. For a single, working mom this was a disaster that became dangerous. I woke up at two in the morning one time and smelled something burning or melting—I wasn't sure. I jumped up to investigate and found him cooking potatoes in the living room! He had found a large electric skillet and put it on the couch since the counters were too high for him. He plugged it in, turned it on, filled it with potatoes and was kneeling by the couch watching it. He was just three years old at the time. The couch was a bit melted but no further harm was done. It was one of many incidents that occurred before I was able to convince the babysitter that he really should not have a nap.

My daughter on the other hand, took daily naps until she went to school. So each child is different and there are no hard and fast rules. In general, infants start out sleeping about 16 hours per 24 hour period and gradually taper down to 8 or 9 hours by the time they are twelve.

All children need routines they can count on, but children of trauma need them even more. Because nighttime may have been a stressful time in the past, having a good bedtime routine is very important for helping to relieve anxiety and bring them back to feeling calm and connected. Never leave a child of trauma in bed with a ruptured relationship between you and them. This concept will be discussed further in a later chapter.) Do your best to provide a bedtime routine that is basically the same every night and that leaves them feeling loved and connected.

The more chaotic and stressful the day was, the more important the bedtime routine is. Doing the same thing every night helps them gain the sense that they are safe and that you are a strong and comforting parent. A good bedtime routine for young children should be at least fifteen minutes long and longer if possible. Following are some ideas for activities you might want to include in your bedtime routine. Pick and choose those that help calm your child and leave all of you feeling close and happy at the end of the day.

- A bedtime snack—Although bedtime is not a good time for a big meal, you never want to send a child to bed hungry ESPECIALLY if they are victims of neglect and have experienced periods where they did not get enough food. In general, carbohydrates with calcium and tryptophan are the best thing to eat just before bed but remember, this is just a SNACK, not a meal so offer small portions. Here are some snacks that can help children fall and stay asleep better:

- o Milk, hot or cold
- o Cereal
- o Toast or bagel
- o Peanut butter and honey sandwich
- o Turkey sandwich
- o Mashed potatoes
- o Macaroni and cheese
- o Rice (try with milk and a sprinkle of sugar and cinnamon or with a little chicken)
- o Scrambled eggs
- o Yogurt with granola
- o Crackers and cheese
- o Apple slices with cheese
- o Boiled egg

- Wash hands and face and brush teeth
- Take a warm bath—both relaxing and as an added bonus, it gets the dirt off!
- Get into pajamas—be sure pajamas are comfortable, not tight, and weather appropriate
- A gentle massage. Even just rubbing a child's head or feet can help them relax and sleep better
- Listen to relaxing music
- Do a jigsaw puzzle together
- Rock and sing
- Draw and color

- Read books together—children learn to read naturally when they sit can sit in your lap or close to you while you read. An additional benefit is that kids who are read to during childhood develop a love of reading and continue this great habit throughout life.
- Talk about the day and about tomorrow—this can be a really great opportunity to listen to your grandchild and find out what he is worried about or excited about. Always end these little chats on a positive note. Especially on bad days, hope for a better tomorrow is a bedtime gift.
- Sing—make up happy songs about what you did that day or what you will do tomorrow
- A bedtime stuffed animal is really helpful to many kids, or a real pet they can sleep with (obviously not a fish, a hippopotamus, or a bird)

The main idea of the routine is that you are totally focused on the kids for this period of time and that they go to bed clean, happy, and feeling connected to you. Sorry, this will not cure all the problems in life, but it will really help. Even older kids enjoy the routine of some bedtime rituals. They will let you know when they are too old for rocking for example. Right before bed is one of the best times to talk to kids, as long as the conversation is relaxed and loving and does not escalate into arguments or tears. You can always say, "We will talk about that in the morning. I need some time to think about it." But if you say that, be sure to talk about it the next morning.

I know that it can be terribly frustrating to deal with kids with sleep problems. If you are exhausted and upset with them, keep that to yourself as much as you possibly can. By the end of the book you will have more tools for dealing with some of these problems. If getting to sleep and staying asleep are big problems with your grandchildren and you need more information, I recommend Elizabeth Pantley's *No-Cry Sleep Solution* books for both babies and toddlers/preschoolers.

Medical Care

Children who come from homes where they were abused or neglected often have not had their medical and dental needs taken care of. Your grandchildren may have come with some really urgent problems that you must attend to immediately. If finances are an issue, ask your local Children's Services agency to get them on a medical assistance program or find a community medical center with programs for at-risk children. Do this as soon as you possibly can. Legal or guardianship advice is outside the scope of this book, but I want you to be aware that this is one area which, if neglected, can cause legal problems for you, not to mention the fact that unattended medical problems can escalate and become serious if not dealt with.

One great thing about the Internet is that you can do a lot of research both on medical services and on specific health problems. There are many conditions that you can take care of with simple home remedies, but knowing which conditions fall in that category and which require professional medical care is important.

School or Daycare

Choosing a school or daycare for your grandchildren may be simple or it may be complicated. You will likely need some kind of guardianship papers giving you permission to enroll a child in school or other programs. Once you have what you need, it is time to find the right place. If they are going into the public school system then it should be pretty straight-forward. However, troubled children, and children that are behind in their studies, are often moved into special programs where they are with other troubled children. Studies show that this has a detrimental effect on them as they can easily learn more bad habits and socially unacceptable behaviors from kids even more troubled than they are.

If you are looking for a daycare center or a private school for your grandchildren, here are some great steps to take in deciding where to send the kids:

- Try asking neighbors or friends in the area who have children. Call pediatricians' offices or social service agencies for lists or referrals. You can also call most churches for information about programs they run or church members who either have daycare centers or are willing to watch children in their homes.
- Figure out the best location, whether close to home or work
- Will your child be better off in a small, private setting or will a larger group setting do?
- You can go to www.childcareaware.com or call their hotline (800-424-2246) for a free child care search in your area.
- Get as much information as you can over the phone or Internet regarding fees, hours, vacations, and schedules. It is also important to ask what their policies are on discipline, feeding, and nap time.

- Ask the school or daycare center if they are equipped to handle the types of problems your grandchild has and if not, they may be able to refer you to one that does.

- Visit the daycare or school. You need to meet the people and ask any other questions that you have. Ask for a complete tour of the place and then tune in to your gut feeling. Don't ignore any uneasy feelings. Ask more questions if you need to until you are comfortable that you have found the right place for your kids.

- Make sure they do not use television or other electronics as a babysitter and that children have plenty of time for free play with friends, especially up through age 5. Avoid any school or daycare setting that does not have generous recess time.

- Be sure to get references whenever possible from other parents whose children are there. If you must, sit in the parking lot during pick up time and approach a couple of friendly, unhurried parents to get their opinions about the place or just watch to see if the children coming out look happy or anxious and upset.

Once you have decided on the right place, there are some things you can do to make this transition easier for reluctant children or for children with separation anxiety or other trauma related disorders. Some children find just changing schools traumatic all by itself and it will make it even more difficult if they have been through many other changes recently. Here are some things you can do to help:

- Give the child as much advance notice as possible and allow him to ask questions

- Make as many short visits as you reasonably can before the big start date
- Do not push the child into contact he is not ready for. Just make your polite introductions and model good social behavior
- Remain positive about this change without discounting the fearful feelings the child may have. You can say something like, "I can see that you are feeling very frightened about going to a new place and making new friends. It may be hard at first because it's so new, but you will make many new good friends and learn to enjoy a new school."
- Get on the same sleep and meal schedule that they will be on at school as soon as you can so that you will not add physical adjustment on top of everything else.
- Help them choose their clothes for that first day the night before and plan the lunch you will pack. Leave the fewest possible decisions to that morning as the child may be stressed and you may find yourself reacting to their stress and resistance with your own anxiety about how it is going to go. Do everything you can to remain understanding and positive
- Remind your child about the schedule of their first day at school or daycare and what time you will be back to pick them up. For highly anxious kids, it often helps if you give them something of yours that appears to be valuable, like a watch or other piece of jewelry (choose one you won't mind losing). This gives them the sense that you will indeed be back for your possession and this small act may help them calm down.
- Arrive early enough on the first day that you will have time to stay with the child for a while, if they want you to. Older children might find your presence even more stressful and embarrassing. Respect that and don't take it personally.

- If your child is crying and you really must leave, give them a big hug and remind them that you will be back. Tell them you know it is hard right now, but they will be okay in a few minutes and have a fun day with their new friends. Be sure to call within a couple of hours if there has been a particularly emotional parting to make sure that your grandchild is doing better. You may need help from understanding teachers or staff to make these transitions easier. Do not under any circumstances scold the child or get angry with them about their fears and anxieties. Remain calm and loving but firm. This may be hard, but you can do it.

- If such problems continue to happen for more than a week or two, check to see if there is something going on at the school or daycare that is causing additional trauma and stress. Notice the behavior of the other children. Do not be afraid to ask direct and open questions of the care providers. They should be forthcoming with their answers if there is not a problem—as long as you don't come across as Medusa or Attila the Hun! The most common reason for kids refusing to go to school is that they are being bullied or are feeling unsafe there.

- Talk to teachers or daycare providers about child's history so they will have more understanding of behaviors and school performance. If they are not sympathetic to the issues, you might consider seeking another environment for your grandchild. Work to keep open communication between home and school. Consider using the credit system outlined in the *Nurtured Heart Approach®*, including the daily reports from the teacher.

Some schools and daycare centers do very well with compliant children but have no idea how to handle children of trauma who often act out. If you continue to have problems with your grandchild's adjustment to the new setting, look for alternatives.

Exercise

Daily exercise is extremely important for anyone experiencing anxiety, depression, anger, or trauma. Fun exercise can also be a wonderful family bonding time. If you are already an active person this should not be hard for you. You may already have a long list of your own of things you can't wait to do with your grandchildren. However, if like many others, you have settled into a routine that includes veg'ing out in front of the tube for several hours a day, you can improve your life as well as the kids. Here are some ideas to get everyone moving:

- Take a daily after-dinner walk. You can meet the neighbors and get good exercise at the same time
- Garden or do yard work. Your yard will be a lot more fun to play and picnic in if it is well manicured and kids can help (even if they pretend they don't like it)
- Play outside games such as tag or hide & seek with small children
- Teach your grandchildren the "old-fashioned" games you played when you were a kid
- Shoot some hoops—you'll remember why you loved it so much 45 years ago
- Crank up the tunes and dance! This is completely free and you don't have to go anywhere. It also brings a lot of joy in the music and movement and it can be done on rainy days

- If you can't go outside because of weather, consider getting a game console such as the Nintendo Wii or Xbox Kinect that allows you to be very active in your living room. Avoid using it when it is wonderful outside; there is no replacement for fresh air and sunshine.
- Run, hike, swim, ride bikes
- Just get out and DO SOMETHING—you all need it!

Exercise effectively relieves symptoms of both depression and anxiety. Stress melts away, enabling you and your grandchildren to cope more effectively with all the stuff that life is throwing at you right now. It takes your mind away from your problems and also boosts your immune system. It can also be a wonderful bonding time for your new family system.

PROVIDE STRUCTURE

Children of trauma need to have a balanced environment that is both highly nurturing and highly structured. Think KIND and firm. I put kind first for a reason. You must be kind and loving while providing a structured home or it will trigger the fears that already plague them. Calmness is another really great quality to have when dealing with your troubled grandchildren. Especially during episodes of acting out, the kindness and structure become even more important.

Due to the circumstances that your grandchildren have been through, they may have a hard time developing trust in you, their caregiver. Up until now, their chaotic environment has virtually saturated them with fear and that is the lens through which they now see the world.

What they need most is safety and love, which cannot be experienced without structure provided by someone whose eyes communicate deep love and caring. This is the only environment which can produce the kind of deep and long lasting healing I know you long to provide for your precious grandchildren.

Structure helps children of trauma to feel safe, but structure without love feels like unloving punishment—not what the child of trauma needs. We will go into a lot more detail on how to provide the love and nurturing they need to heal, but structure comes first as it provides the framework that sustains the love and nurturing, so we will start here with a VERY LOUD note of caution that structure MUST be delivered in a loving manner. Structure provided in a loving manner communicates something crucial, "I care about you and I am strong enough to handle and fix the bad stuff that has happened for you." Structure is provided through routines, schedules, with clear rules and limits.

Routines and the Family Schedule

Structure means a consistent routine and a schedule for the family that is as consistent as possible while allowing for reasonable flexibility. An important part of early intervention for children of trauma is to allow them to provide input into planning how their day will go. Grandparents and children (if they are old enough) need to work together to set up a schedule of regular, age-appropriate daily activities in regards to basic physical needs. We will cover other activities later.

Daily routines are one way that structure helps both children and adults to set their body clocks and routines also help to reduce stress and offer a sense of control over the environment. Incorporating times to shower, brush teeth, etc., teaches good hygiene habits. Each child should know what time they need to get up and what they need to accomplish before heading off to school or daycare each day. They should know what is expected when they come home, and what to expect from you. Keeping schedules posted gives everyone a way to get back on track when things get chaotic. The more you can do to reduce chaos and keep structure, the less stress and the more harmony you can create in your home.

One of the first things that you can do is get some kind of **daily calendar or planner** that you can carry with you at all times. If you do not already have one, you can pick one up relatively inexpensively at most stores that carry office supply. A nice selection of calendars and organizers, is available at www.theorganizedparent.com.

Look at several types of calendars and see which one makes the most sense to you, keeping in mind that you want to end up with something that provides plenty of room to keep a record of calls made and other conversations and important data you will need to keep track of for legal matters or for communicating with schools, medical providers, and social service personnel. Also keep a record of the behavior and emotional patterns of your grandchildren. This will help a great deal when talking to medical, legal, and social service professionals that you will be interacting with. These patterns can help you and others to understand their trauma response triggers and provide greater safety for the child. If you notice that certain people or activities cause an increase in problem emotions or behaviors you can take steps to limit their exposure and help them get the support they need.

Some pointers for creating your family schedule:

- Call a family meeting and let everyone who is old enough to speak know that their input is important. As you listen to each person be sure to note what is important to them

- Write ideas and needs down as each person talks so that you won't forget or lose track of input. This allows everyone to feel heard even if you can't do everything mentioned

- Write down all of the activities that need to be done in a week

- In addition to your planner that you will carry with you, create a schedule to post in your home where everyone can see it; use a calendar, poster board, Excel spreadsheet or whatever works for you

- Some things to include on your family schedule are:

  o Bed times and rising times

  o Meal times

  o School

  o Laundry, housecleaning, and chores

  o Church and religious activities

  o Exercise

  o Medical and dental appointments

  o Extracurricular activities

  o TV/gaming/computer/texting/phone time. (More info in chapter titled *Plugged In*)

- Follow the schedule for a week and then have another family meeting to see if it is working for everyone. Make any needed adjustments and then follow until it becomes second nature to the entire family.

- I recommend permanent weekly family meetings, which will be covered in detail in Chapter 4. Put "review schedule" on your meeting agenda and ask for input from everyone for upcoming projects, activities, holiday and vacation plans. Even young children can be included in these meetings if they are kept short, light, and on point.

Having daily and weekly schedules offers a way to pass on family values and beliefs and teaches kids to work together as a team. This also promotes feelings of belonging for the child; they can see they are part of the family and that they are helping to accomplish shared goals. Regular routines will decrease anxiety and increase feelings of security even in the midst of other changes occurring in the family.

Collect the important stuff:

You will need an **information binder** or folder of some kind in which to keep all important documents relating to the children in your care. Get everything you can from the parents or other legal guardians so that you will have it if anything comes up. You may need some of these papers in dealing with the school, in order to travel, for medical care, etc. If you do not have a handy way to organize and quickly access all important documents it will add lots of unnecessary time and energy to the long list of tasks that you need to do. This one thing will go a long way towards reducing your stress and empowering you to communicate quickly and effectively with the right people in a timely manner. How many times do people wait in long lines only to be sent back home for papers they did not have? Don't let this happen to you. You do not need the stress or the lost time involved in these avoidable incidents. Be prepared with the correct documents for every conversation by having your calendar/planner and your information binder handy at all times.

Here is a list of documents to have in your possession:

- Contact list including local police, crisis help line, family members, school, attorney, children's friends, doctors, counselors, and anyone else that you may need to interact with
- Birth certificates, social security cards, immigration papers, and passports
- School records
- Medical, dental, and immunization records
- Information and identification for Insurance, Medicaid, or Aid to Families with Dependent Children, etc.
- Divorce and custody papers, guardianship and other court orders or other legal documentation
- Current photos of children, both close up of face and full body
- Photos of potential abusers, as well as identifying information such as address, phone, date of birth, employer, etc., if available

You may want to do as I do and carry a large purse that is big enough to hold a file folder and a planner. That way I am never caught without them. Perhaps you are technically savvy and are able to use the calendar on your smart phone in order to keep track of all appointments and details. If so, be sure you have a live system that backs itself up continually. It is really devastating to have all your plans in life disappear when you drop your phone and it breaks. I know because I've done it! Once is enough to learn the lesson for life.

LIFE WITH PURPOSE

I learned in my fourteen years as a single parent that every moment counts and if you don't get organized, life can quickly turn to overwhelming chaos. If you just take fifteen minutes early in the morning to plan your day, go over appointments, create a list of things to-do and things to take with you, you can save hours of frustration and stress later in the day. You might be in survival mode, but you and your grandchildren can certainly thrive rather than flounder. Living life on purpose keeps you from becoming reactive and living on the defense. You are worth taking that time for and you can do it over an early morning cup of coffee or tea before waking the kids. A special "you time!"

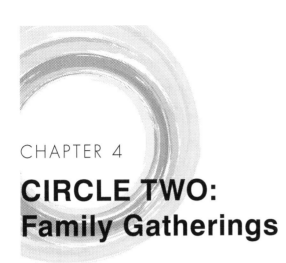

CHAPTER 4

CIRCLE TWO:
Family Gatherings

"This was a crazy Christmas. I ordered several of these one piece pajamas with feet and hood in them and drop drawers in the back. I bought one for each of the boys and the females had flannel pajamas. For Christmas we were all there and all the boys (including 2 exchange students) wore these pajamas. And they all embraced this tradition of the new pajamas on Christmas Eve.

My granddaughter got a Nerf gun. She had another gun too so she got them both and started shooting the boys. Then I gave the boys Nerf guns so they were running all over the house shooting guns in their PJs. Even my grandson, who as 18 at the time, said that he had fun."

~ A grandmother

When I was little we lived at the base of the foothills that overlook Los Angeles. My parents used to get us all bathed and in our pajamas on

Friday evenings and pile us all in the back seat of the old convertible my Dad was so proud of. He would drive us up higher in the hills where we could look down and see the splendor of the city lights as they sparkled below. I was six years old the last time we did that, before we moved up north. But I will never forget that family tradition. We talked about it recently as a family and I felt the happiness and the closeness all over again. Routines around regularly scheduled family activities help build strong family relationships and make up the second ring of our Healing Circles.

As a single mom, I used to take my kids out for dinner every Friday night. My main reason was I was just too tired to cook and I wanted to relax and enjoy some time with them. As they got older, they were encouraged to invite friends along. This allowed me to also develop a friendship with their friends and I was much more aware of what was going on in their lives as a result of it. This became one of our best family times because we would sit around the table at Spaghetti Factory for a couple of hours, eating, talking and laughing. We all look back on those happy times and when we get together we still try to plan a dinner out, preferable at Spaghetti Factory.

On Sunday nights, we had pizza and then watched a fun (clean) comedy show that came on every Sunday evening. We all watched it together and laughed together. Laughing and sharing good food and fun activities helps to create solid relationships, leading to feelings of love and safety for kids. Daniel J. Siegel, an MD in Psychiatry, has done a lot of work on interpersonal neurobiology primarily with children and adolescents and families. In his book *The Developing Mind*, he states that children's minds are shaped by the repeated patterns of interactions with primary caregivers. One of the most telling indicators of healthy, positive attachments between children and their caregivers is how those caregivers tell the stories of their own childhoods. If you are raising grandchildren who have already been negatively influenced by the attitudes and stories of parents who feel bitter about their childhoods, the good news is that our minds appear to be developing throughout our lives and can always be influenced by the relationships and experiences in the present.

FAMILY STORIES

Remember: it is not what has happened to us, but <u>what we believe about what has happened</u>, that continues to affect us the most. Children with caregivers in their lives, who can tell positive stories even about negative things that happen, fare better than those with caregivers who remember events and tell stories from a negative stance. Some therapists use what is called "Narrative Therapy," where they listen to people's stories and help them to retell the story from a positive angle. Families who are active together and who have rich traditions have a lot more stories. When they get together they usually have wonderful "Remember when...?" fests along with good food, laughter, and opportunities to make new memories. Even unfortunate family vacations can be fodder for great stories later on.

An example of making a positive meaning out of what could be a terribly hurtful reality came recently from a ten-year-old boy. I met him when he came with his grandmother to a Nurtured Heart Approach® class that I was teaching. I asked him if he had any brothers and sisters, to which he answered, "Yes, I have four, but they are all half-brothers and sisters. I don't get to live with any of them because they either live with our mom or their dad, or they are grown up already." "Oh," I said. "That's too bad." I was thinking how I would have missed my siblings. "No, it's okay," he responded. "I get to live with my Grandma and my Grandpa and my dad is there a lot, so I am the lucky one." Wow! I was happily surprised to hear his positive attitude and felt a little bad that I had assumed he would view this experience negatively. I learned later that his mother was extremely negligent, leaving him with various adults, some that she barely knew. Her drugs and party life were more important to her. When this little boy was two years old, he came to live with his grandparents and called every woman he met "Mommy." He did not know who his real mother was so he did not miss her. He has a good life now with people that love him and are there for him every single day. He's right—he is the lucky one.

Your grandchildren are lucky too, because they have you and obviously you care deeply about them and are willing to expend considerable time and effort making the best life for them that you possibly can. The fact that you are reading this book confirms this, and gives me hope that you will pass the important habit of learning on to your grandchildren. There are many activities you can pass on, some for learning, some for fun and laughter, some for reaching out to your community, and some just because that's the way you do it! Having those family stories and a positive family identity is very important for kids, and good family activities and traditions contribute considerably to building resilience in your children. Think right now about some of the family activities and traditions that you already have. Reflect on how they got started and how they impact your family.

If there is a drug and alcohol problem in your family, or there has been one in the last two or three generations, it is possible that family activities and traditions have been lost to the disease of addiction. If that has happened in your family, do not despair. A sense of connectedness can be created or re-established at any age and now is as good a time as any to begin developing meaningful family patterns in activities, traditions, and connecting experiences. The more that you can do together as a family, the closer the bond will be, assuming the relational interactions are positive. If family relationships are toxic to children, there are no activities or traditions that can help to heal them until those relationships become safe. Depending on the quality of the relationships, family activities can either be rich bonding experiences, or they can multiply the amount of abuse and trauma the children experience.

As you think about the kind of activities and traditions that you want to develop for your new family grouping, keep in mind the interests and abilities of each member, what is available in your area, seasons and holidays, and keep it age appropriate.

FAMILY MEALS

We have known for decades that family mealtime is one of the most important activities of happy and successful families. I was fortunate to grow up in a family that shared at least one big family meal at the dinner table every day. That meal often included my grandmother who lived nearby, and friends of mine, or of my siblings. We often invited guests or friends to eat with us. Our mealtimes were happy times and there was generally lots of laughter mixed in with the food. I followed this same tradition when raising my kids. There have been many meals in our family that lasted 2 hours or longer, simply because we were having so much fun we all forgot to get up and leave the table when we were done eating.

The Relationships

Some families add mealtime activities such as the one that my bonus child, Erica, shared with me. At one of her family homes they go around the table and each share their "high" and "low" moments from the day. This allows them to all be in on what is going well in each other's lives and celebrate successes together. It also allows them to share in the disappointments and help to bear each other's burdens. Mealtimes are also good times to teach table manners. Rules should be different for everyday meals, formal dinners, picnics, etc. Kids do not grow up knowing how to have good table manners. They need to be taught, not by being chastised when they are messing up, but by seeing the right example and by being recognized when they are being polite and well-mannered. You might want to have a formal dinner every now and then and have everyone dress up just so that you can teach formal manners. When prom time rolls around, your kids will appreciate knowing what to do with all the forks. There are many good sources online and at your local library for teaching manners. If you don't know formal table manners yourself, this would make a great family activity as you all learn together.

A family meal should NEVER include the following:

- Television
- Books (except for sharing short excerpts for conversation starters)

- Games that keep meaningful conversations from happening
- Loud music
- Criticism and disrespect
- Anger or teasing
- Discussing stressful topics (save that for the family meeting or private conversations)
- Too many rules—especially "Children should be seen and not heard"
- Complete lack of rules or manners
- Rude and crude behavior
- Arguing and fighting

These behaviors do not prepare children to reach their potential in life and can cause health problems if family members are trying to eat with their stomachs all tied up in knots. Mealtime is a great time to share positive feedback for behaviors you would like to see repeated. It is also a great place to teach basic nutritional and health habits to your children. Families who have family meals are less likely to eat junk food and fast food. Degenerative diseases are primarily caused by poor lifestyle choices. Good eating habits are one of the most important things you can pass on to your children. You will be adding good quality years to their lives.

Having this daily routine also gives kids from chaotic or traumatic backgrounds the structure and predictability that helps them to regain normalcy. Kids who have been raised by parents with drug and alcohol problems often have not had regular meals. Many have gone hungry for long periods of time because their parents were not tuned in to their needs. This one daily habit can make a HUGE difference to a child. My son once told me that he felt the most loved when he saw me in the kitchen cooking. I have heard the same sentiment expressed by grown men to their wives. Many men, like both my husband and my father, also love to cook and to be involved with what happens in the kitchen. Cooking and eating can be wonderfully warm and bonding activities for families.

The Food

If you do not like to cook, or you feel too busy and stressed out to worry about a family dinner every night then you might be surprised to find out that a study done at Brigham Young University showed that parents also receive a positive benefit from family dinners. Having regular family dinnertime actually reduces the stress of a long work day, which leads parents to feel more successful, both at work and in their marriage. It also contributes to parents feeling closer to their children. So if you are a grandparent who is working and raising your grandchildren, there is something in it for you too.

One way to make this job easier is to plan your menu ahead. When I was raising my kids as a single mom I kept an easy one-week menu planner on the front of the refrigerator. If it was Sunday night we had homemade pizza and salad, Monday night it was spaghetti, salad and mixed vegetables, Tuesday night, tacos, etc. You get the idea. My one rule was that it had to be easy enough for me to get dinner on the table within thirty minutes of walking into the house. Discuss favorite foods at a family meeting and have kids choose the foods they like from a list of healthy choices. Then make a simple weekly menu that everyone can enjoy, that's easy to prepare, and that is healthy. To make things even easier, make up a grocery list so that each week you can check to see what you are out of to prepare your week's worth of meals. If you have picky eaters do not prepare separate meals for them. Simply applaud any efforts they make to try new foods and to make any healthy choices. Let them know that they don't like it because they have not tried it enough times. Encourage just one bite, but never force-feed a child or punish them for not "cleaning the plate." Include something healthy that they like in each meal and encourage them to try new things. Do this without making mealtime a stressful fiasco.

When my children were babies, I carried them on my hip as I cooked in the kitchen or sat them up on the counter next to where I was working if I could do so safely. When they got older, they often stood on a chair to help prepare simple foods or to wash the dishes. They loved this! You can have each family member who is old enough be responsible for making dinner one night a week. I did this when my kids were teenagers.

One of the family activities we enjoy the most is cooking together. One year, after my daughter married, we decided to cook together one night each week. We would pick a new recipe each Thursday evening that neither of us had ever tried before. We cooked up some really wonderful foods that we will never forget. We tried recipes from all over the world. My husband's daughter says she loves to make cupcakes once in a while with her sister and her mother, and she loves macaroni and cheese, so we enjoy finding new recipes for that.

At age 6 my son started making our spaghetti sauce from scratch. I even made him a little chef's apron that said "Chef Boy 'R Michael" on the front. He wore it quite proudly and he still likes to cook with and for his wife. The kitchen can be one of the best places in the house where some of your best memories are made. The great thing about cooking is that the worst thing that can generally happen is that something might get burned or become inedible for some other reason. Keep something in the freezer or pantry that you can prepare quickly just in case! That way you don't have to micro-manage or get all hysterical when someone messes up.

One time I baked my favorite casserole because we had company coming over. When the first person bit into it, she spit it out and exclaimed, "Oh my, this is SO SALTY!" I tasted it and sure enough, it was way too salty to eat. To this day I do not know what happened— although I have my suspicions . . . We had to throw it out and fifteen minutes later I had hot spaghetti on the table. Yes, I poured the sauce out of a jar, but we enjoyed it all the same. Eating healthy doesn't have to be hard, but you do have to plan ahead. You will feel so much better once you are organized and you are serving healthy meals to your family on a regular basis.

The Habit

If your grandchildren are resistant to this idea in the beginning, don't be discouraged. What may start out as a restrictive chore will become one of their favorite times in the day. For kids who are not used to it, expect up to a month for them to turn things around. Your kindness and calmness throughout the transition will help. The more often you have family dinner, the more value each member of the family gains from it. Having family dinner less than three times per week will lead to less satisfaction. So shoot for every day and allow for some flexibility on time. Some families, like ours when my parents had four teenagers in high school, will have the big family meal for lunch or for breakfast because it is just too hard to get everyone home at the same time together in the evening when each person is headed in a different direction.

FAMILY MEETINGS

Family meetings are important for all families but they are even more important for kids who are struggling emotionally and for kids who have come from a chaotic environment or any environment where their needs were not met or they felt at the mercy of a stressful situation. During family meetings everyone should have a voice and should be able to contribute their ideas to the decisions being made. Grandparents and parents are still the final decision makers, but it is much easier for kids to handle decisions made by others when they feel that they have been heard and considered in the process. The purpose of the meetings is never to chastise anyone, or to offer verdicts over decisions made outside of the family meeting. A family meeting is a place where everyone is heard. I like the word "collaborative" because it means that we are all working together toward common goals and everyone is valued for their ideas and opinions.

I remember one family meeting that occurred at the dinner table when I was about 13 years old. There was an announcement made at church that there was to be a weekend "Family Snow Camp" up near Lake Tahoe. I wanted very badly to go and began right away begging my parents to take the family. At first my dad said, "No, we can't afford it," but then he decided that we should all discuss it in a family meeting. All six of us gathered around the table and we discussed how much it would cost for the camp, the drive, the snow clothes we would all need, etc. My mom added it all up on a piece of paper. Then my dad told us what our budget was for family events and asked each of us what we were willing to give up in order to have enough money for the whole family to go to Family Snow Camp. By the end of the family meeting we had figured out a way to make it happen without creating a financial crisis. We went and we had a wonderful time. I still have many good memories from that weekend.

When I was raising my kids we had frequent family meetings. For a while we even had weekly meetings. The kids were on credit systems of some kind during much of their growing up years and so weekly meetings were a time to square up, pay allowance, discuss schedules, plan vacations or holidays, and resolve problems of various kinds and other concerns brought to the meeting by family members. I recommend you keep a specially designated notebook for your family meetings in a place where everyone can get to it. Everyone in the family can write down items that they would like to discuss in the next family meeting as it comes to mind. Even young children can contribute as they come to understand the process. Notes can be made in the notebook regarding decisions reached or contracts made during meetings. Each meeting should have an agenda, which might include any of the following:

- An opening exercise that will build good will and positive attitude to start out the meeting. Some examples:

  Choose a word from the Values list you will find if you flip ahead in the book a couple of pages. Share a definition and an example. Have each person share a time when they used that value or saw someone else use it in the past week.

Each person shares something good that happened to them in the last week and why they think it went well using a value word from your list of family values.

"I was promoted at work this week because I was persistent and worked really hard to master the new technology that was brought in six months ago."

"I made a new friend at school this week because I was compassionate and helped the new girl find her classroom when she was lost."

"I got good grades on my report card because I listened in class and turned in all my homework."

"My friend sent me a birthday card and a gift certificate because she is really thoughtful and generous."

- Spiritual Focus: If you practice a religion or acknowledge a Higher Power this is a good time to connect through a brief prayer or reading to emphasize the spiritual nature of family connectedness. Keep it short and authentic. If your family is musical, you might want to pick a special song to start out your meeting.

- Schedules/Holidays: Go over weekly schedule and any upcoming holidays, vacations, or other special events. If there are conflicts, such as two kids going to different events at the same time, try to find solutions that work well for everyone.

- Family Concerns: This is the time to bring up items that have been listed in the notebook. This may include decisions that need to be made. Be sure that everyone has an opportunity to talk without interruption on any topic that will affect them directly or indirectly. If you have family members that tend to filibuster, you can use a timer and put time limits on everyone. But be fair and use the timer on everyone if you are going to use it. You might find that you are long-winded too!

- Go over the credit system if you are using one and update scoring/points. Pay out allowance if any is due. (Never use a credit system that takes points away. It is punitive and way too discouraging for some kids).

- Open Forum: Does anyone have any other concerns that have not been addressed?

- Closing Exercise: Give each person get a turn to have two other family members appreciate them for something done well in the past week. For example:

"I was really proud of how you handled your disappointment when the field trip you were looking forward to was cancelled because of the weather."

"I really appreciated your help yesterday when I got stuck with my math homework and you took the time to explain it to me."

"I loved what you made for dinner tonight. Thank you for working so hard to keep our family healthy."

"I noticed that you tried two new foods this week that you didn't think you would like. You were adventuresome and you made a really healthy choice even though it was not what you wanted."

If your family tends to be long winded and you are short on time, it is okay to set time limits on each topic as well as on each person and the entire meeting. Be reasonable both ways and consider the age and ability of your kids to sit still. Most family meetings can happen in less than thirty minutes. If you decide to have weekly family meetings, you might want to make a Family Night out of it and have dinner first and games after. Whatever you do, keep the kids involved and keep it positive and you won't have trouble keeping them engaged. Kids love to be part of the process of solving family problems. It makes them feel mature to be part of the discussion. Even very young children may surprise you with their ability to comprehend and contribute. If you find you are being too serious as a family, consider starting with a short family comedy like "I Love Lucy" or something else that produces good clean laughter. If you are not sure about appropriateness, check your shows and movies out at www.pluggedin.com and you can avoid having to shut off the TV in the middle of a program when you find it is inappropriate.

How you work together to resolve family problems or conflicts will set your grandchildren up for life with a model that they can follow. If fighting breaks out, do not shut things down. Take a breather and ask everyone to commit to staying with the process until any conflicts are worked out. If necessary, have everyone take 10 minutes to journal what they are feeling and thinking so that the negative energy can be diffused before you start the discussion up again. Family fighting is generally very stressful for children and teenagers, even those that appear to be calm. The best family fights are those that end with resolution and reconciliation, not because someone strong-armed the rest of the family, but because an actual agreement was made.

Do not be afraid to bring up hard topics in your family meetings. When you are afraid to talk about problems it makes them seem even more frightening to children. Silence encourages kids to make up their own meanings for events, which we all do when we don't know facts. Your grandchildren need your help to interpret the family problems in ways that let them know they are not at fault, they are loved, and they are worthy of love. Often kids will blame themselves for their parents' problems. Always tell the truth at the appropriate level of detail for the age of the child. Show respect to those who have been incarcerated, negligent, abusive, and/ or addicted, but don't be afraid to say the truth either. Do not pretend that nothing is wrong when something **is** wrong. Watch for emotional displays from the kids and try to understand what triggers them. Ask if you don't know. Many times kids who are hurting will say they are fine and that nothing is wrong, simply because they do not want to put more stress on already burdened grandparents or parents. But they do not need the burden of being the strong one in the family. When young children grow up in closed, secretive environments it can be very hard for them to change these habits and become teens or adults who know how to talk openly about their feelings and problems. You can help them by labeling emotions that they appear to be experiencing and by telling them the truth about the "who, where, what, why and when" in their world. The unknown and the unpredictable exacerbate the fear and the behavior problems they are having.

FAMILY WORSHIP

Whether you are religious or not, there are activities your family can do together that are spiritual in the sense that they help you focus on higher values. Here is a list of some of the values that you can focus on together to strengthen your internal compasses as individuals, and your cohesiveness as a family.

- Gratitude
- Generosity
- Service
- Honesty
- Hope for the future
- Taking responsibility for your part
- Openness
- Understanding and acceptance
- Restraint
- Patience
- Accountability
- Humility
- Empathy
- Delayed gratification
- Self-discipline
- Forgiveness
- Courage
- Faith
- Hope
- Love
- Compassion
- Commitment

Families who have a habit of being together and reading, praying, singing, sharing gratitude, etc., on a daily basis are generally much closer than families who do not. Passing on family values and beliefs should not happen randomly and by chance. It should be done on purpose and consistently over time. Many families who go to church together each week do not talk openly about their spiritual beliefs and do not read the Bible or other spiritual writings together. Many children grow up not knowing the true beliefs of their parents, and not caring.

Here are several activities that might spiritually benefit your family, regardless of your religious views or practices.

Reading good books that teach values is something that you can do as part of a bedtime routine. My mother read to me and my siblings every evening before bedtime. I did the same with my kids. Somewhere in middle school, my daughter decided to start reading to me. She would climb up in bed next to me and read out loud until I fell asleep or it was time for her to go to bed. Spencer and Ann Donegan Johnson wrote a series of 45 books altogether, called the *Value Tales Series*. These are wonderful books that I highly recommend. They are no longer in print, but used sets can be purchased online. Each book takes 15-20 minutes to read through and they each teach a different value lesson using the biographical story of a historical figure. My kids loved the books and would beg for different ones to be read over and over and over again. The stories are all about people who made significant contributions to our world after overcoming obstacles to reach their goals or realize their dreams. There are many other good books which also teach life lessons to kids and perhaps your family already has their favorites.

Singing together as a family is fun and has the added benefit of lifting depression, regulating heart rate and breathing, and being just plain fun. Listening to music can also be a great way to shrug off the blues. My kids and I used to listen to Paul Simon's *Graceland* CD while cleaning the house. It energized us and made it seem like fun. We listened to contemporary Christian music in the car sometimes and sang as loudly as we could. It just feels good to sing! Be sure that whatever music you listen to with your grandchildren reflects the values that you wish to teach them, but don't be too strict on style of music other than that. You might be surprised how much you enjoy new styles of music once you get used to them, and they will be thrilled to have such cool grandparents! Be as willing to learn from them as you want them to be to learn from you. I believe that my two kids taught me much more about love and life than I ever taught them. They are still teaching me today! And they introduced me to all kinds of music I would never have tuned in to on my own.

Community service is another great way to have fun with your grandchildren at the same time that you are teaching them values. Whether you choose to volunteer every Thanksgiving at a soup kitchen or sign up for a community trail clean-up day, you'll have a new family experience to talk about for years to come. Here are some other ideas for community service projects:

- Take food to shut-ins
- Play cards with nursing home residence or sing to them
- Do yard work for disabled or elderly person in your neighborhood
- Pick up litter in your neighborhood or at a local park
- Plant wildflowers where other people can enjoy them
- Collect coats or stuffed animals for a homeless shelter
- Make surprise packages and see if you can deliver them without being caught
- Bake cookies to take to neighbors you have not met
- Write letters to soldiers
- Help tutor a younger child
- Read a book to a blind person
- Make care packages to keep in the car to hand out to the homeless rather than cash. Include toothbrush/paste, socks, food bar, soap, etc.

- Take dog bones to the dogs at a local animal shelter (my daughter loved doing this)
- Organize a "Formal Dinner Event" for the kids and their peers. Teach them proper manners for setting up and attending a formal dinner. For information on etiquette, have them search for it online or get a book at the library
- Write thank you cards and hand deliver them to people that you forgot to thank

The main thing is, *just do it!* Kids feel better about themselves when they are helping others. If your kids seem depressed, help them do something kind for someone else and it will give their spirits a lift.

Practicing gratitude is one of the most beneficial, inexpensive, easy-to-use natural supplements you can possibly use to add happiness and years to your life. Appreciating the simple pleasures of life is a wonderful place to start. Gratitude heals because it acknowledges what **is** rather than bemoaning what **is not**. The more time you spend in moments of gratitude, the less time you spend pitying yourself or resenting others. This will be a very important skill for your family as you move forward. Instilling the habits of gratitude in your children can help them get through many rough times ahead. In addition to letting the kids know how grateful you are that they are a part of your life, you can share with them specifically what they are doing that you are most grateful for. This can change their view of themselves and help them to live out of their strengths rather than their weaknesses. Try adding the "3 Good Things" exercise to your daily family dinner. Let each person share the three things they are most grateful for that day.

Going to church or another place of worship together as a family has many benefits. Research consistently shows that people who attend religious or spiritual services on a regular, weekly basis are happier than those who do not. Research done by Duke University, Indiana University, Barna Research Group, University of Michigan, Pew, Gallup, Centers for Disease Control, and National Institute for Healthcare Research all agree on this. In addition to being happier, active church participation offers the following benefits:

- Increased life span
- Reduced alcohol, drug, and tobacco use
- Lower suicide risk
- 70% faster recovery from depression
- Significantly reduced crime rates
- Improved school performance
- More caring adults in a child's life
- Higher values instilled
- Reduced rebelliousness
- Less binge drinking in college
- Greater chances for a happy life

If you have a church or synagogue that you already attend, reach out to others who can offer support as you raise your grandchildren. Getting together after church with other families can broaden the number of great people in your circle and you will have more fun. Be selective and choose people that share your value system, who are loving and not judgmental, to become close friends with. If you are a single grandparent, finding intact families that you can be friends with will give your child the opportunity to have the influence of adults from both genders to influence them.

If you do not have a church and you would like to, or you are attending a one that is not supportive or does not meet your needs at this time, here are some things to consider while looking for your new church home:

- Shared belief system. Most churches have some unique beliefs; be sure that the most important beliefs you have are reflected in the church you attend
- Age appropriate activities for you and your grandchildren
- Size: Large enough to offer a selection of programs, small enough to be personal
- Formal vs. casual church attire
- Traditional vs. contemporary services
- Style of music—Remember to consider the tastes and needs of your grandchildren. Hymns might be good for you, but kids may need something different that speaks to them. Don't criticize their taste in music, but do guide their choices in terms of appropriate lyrics.
- Close enough to home to make an easy commute
- Can you make friends there? That may be the most important question. People usually stay more involved in church, and enjoy it more, if they can make at least five or six friends there. This is especially true of teenagers. If you or your grandchildren can't make friends anywhere, get a family therapist. It may not be the church.

Visit several churches and when you find one you think you might like to make your church home, attend several times before joining up. Keep in mind that no church is perfect and that you do not have to be perfect to attend.

Keeping promises is one of the most important things you can do to build trust and consistency. If you promise to take the kids out for ice cream if they help with the yard work, then be sure that you do it, even if you are tired, even if it is late. Getting to bed on time is not as important as keeping your promises. Kids need to know they can count on their caregivers. If you promise a consequence, deliver on that promise every time, unless you realize that it was not a fair consequence to begin with. Then you need to make an apology and explain the change, not just let it slide hoping the kids will not notice. I cannot stress this enough, especially in working with troubled kids who have already been through so much disappointment and betrayal. They may be especially sensitive to unfairness and afraid to trust. You cannot afford to create the kind of break in trust that occurs with breaking promises, which is a common source of rebelliousness. Be careful to not make promises that you cannot keep in the first place, but once you make one, do your absolute best to keep it.

FAMILY ACTIVITIES

Family meetings and family worship are excellent activities, but there are an unlimited number of other activities that families can enjoy together. Family activities are very unique to each family and should include and/or expand the abilities and interests of each family member. For example, if you have one child (like my daughter) that thinks she must have a metal detector to be happy, and one that loves to dance, throw pottery, play competitive sports, or any number of other activities, do your best to include time for each of them to pursue their dreams in such a way that the family can stay involved. Planning your family activities is an excellent topic for family meetings. Make sure that everyone is included in the discussion; go around the table and have everyone contribute their ideas. Other considerations are ages, fitness levels, climate and season, budget, and time available. You will save yourself some money if you rent equipment the first few times you try an activity to make sure you really do like it.

All children need time to play. Play is their work and children of trauma and chaos, neglect, and/or abuse may need to be taught how to play and have fun. Non-structured, non-competitive play and imaginative play are very healthy for kids. When families can have joy and laughter in free play together, more healing may happen than in an intensive therapy program. Family activities can help to build stronger connections and increase the sense of belonging as members experience being supported and understood by one another. Family activities can be geared around physical activity, spiritual activity or around learning something new. Below are some ideas for low cost activities that you can do with the whole family. I also encourage you to include other families, relatives, and friends. The larger the supportive community in a child's life, the better their chance for a great future. At the same time, the larger the support group surrounding you, the better off you will be as you parent your grandchildren.

- Plant a small garden from seeds. Have each person choose one or more type of seeds to plant and then be responsible for the care of that part of the garden. Perhaps you can make bouquets or salads or your whole dinner from the garden.
- Go on a nature walk and have each person bring back one thing they found and then share with each other a life lesson that can be learned from that item.

- Go to a nearby park and have a picnic or a weenie roast. Throw Frisbees or have a family baseball game.
- Feed the ducks whenever you have stale bread or crackers
- Get a map of the night sky and go outside at night to see how many constellations you can find.
- Play charades or have the kids put on an improv drama show for the adults. Most kids LOVE to put on shows and have the approving attention of adults.
- Visit art galleries and museums
- Have a yard clean-up day. Rake up leaves and jump in the piles. Children love to throw the leaves up in the air and dance and squeal. Reward the labor with a family movie and pizza afterward.
- Try to visit every park within thirty minutes of your home
- Play games like tug-of-war, horseshoes, badminton, hide-and-seek or active indoor games such as Ping-Pong (one of the best activities for the brain), hula hoop, or Nerf ball
- Play board games that encourage interaction and getting to know each other better or just plain laughter. Everyone feels better after playing a game the makes you laugh.
- Go miniature golfing
- Bake bread and give some to the neighbors or eat it yourself!
- Get a beach ball and play outside in the rain. See how long you can keep it in the air.
- Climb trees, watch clouds, press flowers, make mud pies, and build sand castles.
- Set up a back yard fire pit so you can roast marshmallows and tell stories about how different the world was when you were a kid. (Check with the fire marshal for local fire code on backyard burning first)

- Take the President's Family Fitness Award. https://www.presidentschallenge.org/
- Take turns sharing your most embarrassing moments, or the accomplishments you are most proud of

Creative activities that are especially helpful to troubled kids are music, dance, puppets, making collages, woodworking, auto mechanics, painting, clay, creative writing, or story writing. There are many others that are also beneficial. These types of activities allow kids to express their pent-up emotions in healthy ways and also give them some sense of control over their lives. Any activity that is unstructured has the potential to allow a child to come up with their own ideas, make their own choices and decisions, and thereby gain a greater sense of control and confidence. Resist your urge to monitor and instruct every moment of a child's life. They need times of free expression. Always look for opportunities to simply notice what they are doing or how they appear to be feeling. Let them know that you really notice them and that you care, without correcting or directing their behavior.

I think you get the idea that there are an unlimited number of activities you and your grandchildren can do together. If you run short on inspiration, call your friends and relatives and ask them for their favorite family activities and traditions. The main idea is to have fun as a family and get off the couch! Couch potatoes do not thrive or flourish in life. You and your grandchildren deserve better. If you are watching more than 10 hours of TV per week consider that too much. I think less than five hours a week would be better. I don't watch TV at all. Don't be a spectator, living your life vicariously. You are much better off to buy a video camera and make a video of a vibrant life, right there in your own home. Your relationships will become much more alive and the grandkids will have wonderful memories to last them the rest of their lives and to pass on to the next generation.

FAMILY VACATIONS

Vacations can be long or short; far away or close by; expensive or free; and anywhere in between. If you can't afford your dream vacation, don't let that keep you from having any vacations. Stay within your budget so that you don't regret taking a vacation and double your stress when you get back trying to catch up on everything, including more bills. Whatever your budget, you can have wonderful, fun vacations, and even the things that seemed awful at the time can make for good stories for the rest of your life. We will never let my brother forget the time we were waiting for the parental units to get the car loaded up at the hotel. We were all dressed up because we were going to go to church and then head down to see some relatives in a different town directly after. While waiting we sat in some chairs around a table by the pool. When we were all ready to go my brother scooted his chair back to get up and the back legs of the chair went over the edge of the pool and he flipped over backwards into the shocking cold water. I can still remember the dollar bills that were in his pocket drying in the back window of the car. Of course my parents had to unpack his suitcase and take the time for him to change and figure out what to do with all the wet clothes. Some 40 years later, I still remember the surprised expression on his face as he flipped backwards—and it makes me laugh every time!

Because I don't watch TV and I love to be out doing stuff, to me, every weekend is an opportunity for a mini-vacation. When my kids were growing up I usually had weekends booked for two or three months out. That's how active I like to be. And I like to plan ahead. This may not match your style at all, but do—in your own style—think and plan ahead to take time out as a family, and also some time away from the kids. If you can't manage a month of vacation time every year, try for two weeks or two one-week vacations. If you can't do a whole week, go for a weekend. If you can't manage a weekend, you might consider changing your life up a bit. That's like saying you can't eat Pop-Tarts for breakfast (which I do not recommend!) because you don't have time to cook them in the microwave for the recommended three seconds. If this is you, you might want to consider getting help. Vacations are very important to your health and happiness and to your family's relational health.

Here are some vacation ideas just to prime your pump. Let this short guide get you started thinking about what it is you really want to do. Make this thetopic of a family meeting or discussion at dinner time: "What is your dream vacation?" or "What vacation would you like to take this year considering our budget and time constraints?" Let all members of the family have an opportunity to state their ideas. Sometimes it is a really "bad" idea that sparks the next really great idea, so don't consider anything invalid in terms of brainstorming.

Vacation ideas:

Weekenders

- Spend an entire weekend exploring the largest city in your area. Go to the Chamber of Commerce and get information about the city. Explore historic landmarks. Try to find out how the city got started and what it is most known for. Then explore like tourists.

- A weekend at the beach, either camping or staying at a hotel, can be incredibly rejuvenating. So whether you take the whole family, or use this idea to rejuvenate your tired self, try it. Even if the closest beach is at the side of a lake or river, being near the water can be calming and restful. Build sand castles, beachcomb, and see who can find the most unique items. Explore tide pools or search for hidden creeks and waterfalls.
- Is it fall? Spend a weekend doing fall activities. Find a nearby fall festival area. Get your faces painted, eat caramel apples, take a hay ride, and pick pumpkins. Try making pumpkin pie out of real, fresh pumpkins. Make enough to share with friends and neighbors.
- Have a stay at home movie marathon weekend. Watch everyone's favorite movie all in one weekend, or watch a series. Of course I only recommend healthy, family friendly movies, but there are many to choose from. Check www.pluggedin.com if you are not sure if a movie is appropriate.
- Go camping. This is an opportunity to be completely unplugged for a weekend or for several days. Camping sets everyone free from all the burdens of life and allows you to rest in a completely different way.

Vacations:

- Consider an organized family summer camp and also summer camps for the kids. This will give you time off from the daily parenting and will give them experiences they will remember for years to come.

- State parks are wonderful places to vacation if you are on a tight budget. If you do not like to camp you can often find cabins or yurts that are very inexpensive.
- Some of the best vacations are to visit relatives out of town. Often you can save yourself the resort or hotel bill by staying in their homes. Staying in touch with extended family can be a very important healing and bonding time as kids are able to see themselves as part of a much bigger picture and feel connected to more caring people who will be in their lives for a very long time.
- Traveling by train can be an exciting adventure all by itself. Add a destination that the whole family can enjoy and you have a winner!
- If you have energetic teenagers, a working dude ranch might just be the answer.
- Over the river and through the woods . . . send them to their other grandparents' home for a few weeks in the summer. For some families this is possible and will be welcomed by the other grandparents who may be feeling left out or guilty. Give yourself a break—a vacation at home.

I am sure that there are at least a million other ideas for family vacations. There are probably whole books written on it, so make this a family project and find the right vacation for your family.

FAMILY DATES

One of the most important ideas that I came across while raising my kids, was the idea of having a separate weekly date with each of my children. When you are always together as a family, you can have wonderful times. But there is just something extra special that happens when you are alone with a child. These dates should be on a regular basis so that kids have something to look forward to. Of course you might miss a week now and then, but there must be an important reason and an explanation every time you miss so that your grandchild knows you are thinking of them and that your time together is important to you too. This does not have to be expensive. For quite a while, I took my daughter to the donut shop early on Sunday morning while her brother was sleeping in. Then she loved to go to the local humane society with a box of doggy bones and feed the dogs through the fence. She got a lot of joy out of this weekly routine and it was our special time. At that time, my son was into collecting baseball cards, so when she was at her music lesson, I would take him to Taco Bell for dinner and then to the baseball card shop where he could buy one or two packets of cards. You could even have your date night right there at home. Maybe you can work every week on a special scrapbook or a quilt or model cars or watching a special TV show. My husband and his daughter had a standing date each week to watch *American Idol* from their special TV chairs while eating their favorite dinner that they cooked together.

If your grandchildren have incarcerated parents this might be something good to center your date night around. You can put together a photo album or scrap book of the good times they have had together in the past to preserve those memories. You can help them to write letters to send if they are far away, or take them for regular family visits. It is important to be honest but respectful in your interactions with kids regarding the incarceration and reasons for it.

If a child has lost his or her parents to death or another tragedy, creating the scrapbook can be very healing for them as well. Regular visits to the cemetery can also be helpful for some children, but probably not every week. Parents who are away on military duty should also be remembered on a regular basis and efforts made to communicate with them regularly. For distant family, learning to Skype, Face Time, or use some other type of personal video conferencing is wonderful for kids and their parents. Skype is available for free on the Internet or on many smart phones. You can check into it at www.skype.com

FAMILY TRADITIONS

Any family activity that is repeated regularly can become a family tradition. According to Daniel J. Siegel in his book, *The Developing Mind*, it is the repeated patterns of their experiences with caregivers that become embedded in their memories, directly shaping their view of family and of themselves. Don't let the most repeated patterns be the scolding and continuous criticism that many troubled kids receive on a daily basis. The most repeated patterns should be patterns of love and joy and having fun family times together. Traditions can be daily, like reading stories together just before bedtime, or yearly like an annual trip to the beach with cousins for the 4th of July. It can be using the "You are special!" red plate for breakfast on a birthday morning. It can be waffles or pancakes every Sunday morning. It can be going out for coffee or going to cut the Christmas tree every year on the

Sunday after Thanksgiving. My daughter remembers one tradition that my parents had with her. She spent most summers of her childhood with them and each year they would take her to a nice department store and buy her a pretty dress. She said that being remembered this way meant more to her than the dress itself. She knew she had stayed on their minds and in their hearts since the last summer and they remembered about the special dress shopping trip.

Families typically have traditions around holidays, birthdays, and other special events. Family traditions are the strongest reinforcements of what it means to be family. They are what keep your kids coming back to visit year after year. For me it was my grandmother's stew and dumplings; strawberries with as much sugar as I wanted on top; the amazing sewing and craft projects she always had going; and the way she smiled proudly at me, just because I was there, that kept me excited about going back to Grandma's house. Now, when my kids come to visit me, they usually ask for my special potato soup, biscuits and gravy, gingerbread boys at Christmas, and a trip to Spaghetti Factory on Friday night. Starting rich family traditions that keep the family coming together for good, healthy, fun times, long after you are gone, will have a positive impact on your family for many generations.

CHAPTER 5

CIRCLE THREE: You Are Not the Boss of Me!

"When I saw my daughter's life getting out of control with her meth addiction, I thought I could love her through it, logic her out of it, or something. I thought there had to be something I could do to fix it. For over seven years I tried everything and FINALLY realized there was nothing I could do or say to change her. I finally had no choice but to let her go. It was an extremely painful process of grieving the loss of my adult child. It was like she was dead. I could not see that things would ever get better or that we would ever have a relationship again."

~ A Mother Raising her Granddaughter

"Having my mom there taking care of my daughter when I was out drugging was a fallback plan. I was just thinking 'I can do what I want because she will always be there. Anyway, you owe me this because you let me down when I was a kid. So prove you can do it right now.'

It made it easier for me to stay in the drug world. I regret
it all now and I guess that thinking was sub-conscious,
but I definitely used it to the fullest. The turning point
came for me when mom cut me off when I was in jail.
She just left me there and I realized I would have to step
up. Since then I have made an effort to have clean time."
~ A Meth Addict Adult Child

WHO'S IN CHARGE?

The Healing Circles are all dependent upon each other in order for the love and joy contained inside to bring about optimum healing. This outer circle gives clarity, shape, and structure to the other circles and helps you to know who is in the Healing Circle and who is not. This circle is made up of Authority Agreements, Rules and Values, and Non-toxic Relationships.

If you are raising your grandchildren either full or part time, then when they are with you, YOU are in charge. That means more than just keeping them happy and safe. That means training them for a life of usefulness, responsibility, connection, and respect. There are three common situations for grandparents raising grandchildren and no matter which of these you are in, you will be in charge of the kids at least some of the time.

Changing Guard

<u>When grandparents have full legal custody and the parents are out of the picture completely</u> there is little question as to who holds

authority over the children, and these kids are generally more willing to accept grandparent's authority. Although this is sometimes the simplest scenario, it can also be the hardest if both grandparents and grandchildren are dealing with grief and loss issues. If this is your situation, you are in charge and the fact that you are reading this book shows that you realize what a huge responsibility it is.

Revolving Doors

<u>When grandparents have full legal custody or guardianship of their grandchildren, but the parents come and go from the child's life</u> due to drug and alcohol addiction, illness, poverty, and other issues, questions often come up about who is in charge when both are present. This can create a lot of conflict between grandparents and parents and can also cause confusion and resentment in the children. In any situation where the grandparents have custody or guardianship, they have the right to determine rules and structure for the family. But even that is subject to court orders and visitation orders which are the ultimate authority over the amount and level of involvement of the parents. Then you have parents who disregard court orders and make things even harder.

The well-being and best interest of the child should always be primary and it is appropriate for the grandparents to exert their authority over the parents when necessary for the benefit of their grandchildren but only after trying to work it out amicably. The problem with this is that often both parents and grandchildren may be pressuring you about something and you may get a lot of heat from both sides. It is often wise to engage the help of a social worker or family therapist who can offer professional advice and clarify what the needs of the children are.

In extreme cases it may even be necessary to go back to the courts to get court orders that do a better job at protecting the interests of the children. If you do not feel confident about your position, or conflict and resentments are escalating, seek outside help and do not risk making things worse for yourself or your grandchildren. Any time you feel that you or your grandchildren may be in danger, seek outside help.

When parents are still involved, or perhaps come and go from the child's life, sticking to the family schedule and including the parents in that, will help to keep kids on track and add a sense of normalcy and security. Allowing parents to come and go and disrupt the routine will add to the feeling of being out of control that children in these situations often struggle with. Be in charge and insist on keeping a structured life for the kids as much as possible. Having said that, don't be ridiculously inflexible. There are always good reasons that come up from time to time to deviate from a well-planned schedule, but this should be the exception and not the rule.

Shared Authority

> *"Some of the dynamics with mom have been good. Co-raising a kid has forced us to buck up and put our differences aside to work things out together. She actually listened to me and applied what I said and started being stricter—more like a mom instead of like a friend or a "Disneyland Mommy." We do not let my daughter play us against each other on issues. We keep communicating to make sure she doesn't get away with manipulating us."*
> *~A part-time mother*

<u>When parents have legal custody of their children, but grandparents are doing all or much of the actual care:</u> This is a set-up for all kinds of problems if there are not established rules and agreements regarding authority issues. It is very important for parents and grandparents to have continuing discussions and agreements on the rules and responsibilities and who is to enforce them. Use of written contracts, schedules, and chore/responsibility lists will help you solidify the agreements. Have both grandparents and parents sign them and keep them posted so you can refer to them when necessary. When everyone signs the contract it gives you a point to go back to and minimizes blaming or playing victim while giving the children something to rely on. When this does not happen, children of all ages know where the weaknesses in the system are and use that knowledge to get what they want. This is one area that can become the best training ground for manipulative behaviors.

If parents and grandparents cannot come to agreements and the parents have legal authority, you as the grandparents may be placed in the awkward position of needing to decide what you are willing to offer in terms of help and of learning to say "no." Deciding what you are willing to do and sticking to it are two different things. The desire to provide love, safety, and structure for your grandchildren can be one of the greatest areas of sacrifice from you as a grandparent. You must either stand by quietly and watch or be willing to risk conflict. Either way, you should be the one to decide what goes on in your own home and which services you offer in terms of help and care.

The Temptation to Compensate

One of the worst possible scenarios is when a child has one overly or abusive strict caregiver AND one overly permissive caregiver. It doesn't matter who plays what role, this system teaches very harmful attitudes and behaviors to kids. It is far better to work towards an agreement so that the child will have consistency. Perhaps both of you will have to compromise. Sometimes that is not possible, and in those cases you must at least be consistent with yourself and not polarize with the other person and parent in a reactive stance against them.

For example, if you think that the other parenting figure is too strict, or if you are feeling sorry for what a hard time your grandchildren have been through, **do not compensate** by being overly permissive. Getting caught in the bind of being the "Disneyland mommy" is very bad for kids. This is often a temptation for either the grandparent or the parent when both are involved in the raising of the children. But it teaches children how to be manipulative and gives them a sense of entitlement and disrespect for authority.

You may feel that you want to make them happy and give them everything they missed out on, or anything that would help them forget their pain. But heading down this road, while it feels right in the moment, can lead you to a situation where you have a teenager that you cannot handle. I am confident you do not want to end up with a teenager who comes and goes as they please all hours of the day or night or who punches holes in your walls when you restrict electronic use.

I spoke to a grandmother recently who is helping her son-in-law to raise her two grandchildren because her daughter, (their mother) died when the youngest one was only eight months old. She admitted to me that one of her biggest problems is her tendency to want to do too much and give too much because of the grief she still carries over the loss of her daughter. She wants to somehow make up for that loss and any regrets she has.

Her son-in-law complains that she is spoiling the kids and sabotaging his efforts to create the structure and discipline he feels they need. She thinks he is too strict and tells him so in front of the kids. This undermines his authority and causes the kids to become rebellious with him and not respect the rules that he has in his home. The more rebellious they get, the more Grandma believes it is his strict rules and inflexible attitude and the more she undermines his authority in the presence of the kids. The more they misbehave, the stricter he gets. She was not able to see that she was causing even more of the rebellion than Dad because she basically told the kids their dad was being unfair and that they did not have to obey his rules. They are now seeking residential placement for the fourteen-year-old boy because neither of them can control him. It is not so much the "too strict" or the "too permissive" that is the problem here. It is the inconsistency and the playing against each other's authority that is causing the problems. Now no one has authority. If you find yourself in this situation with the parent of your child, be sure that you are not doing anything to undermine the authority they have and take steps to limit any undermining that they are doing of you. (See Toxic Relationships)

RULES AND VALUES

A home without rules and values is like a schoolyard with no fence and no teachers next to a railroad track. Some children will get outside of the schoolyard and be in danger while some will huddle close to the building because they do not feel safe. Rules help children feel safe; and values tell them who they are. Teaching rules and passing on values will help our children grow into responsible adults who contribute positively to their community, and that is one of the main goals of parenting. How rules and values are communicated has always been just as important as the content. But with traumatized children, the how, or the relationship and the communication is the most important part.

Let Me Make This Very Clear

Rules should be very clear and they should not change based on whims. It is not necessary to post the rules on the wall for the kids. But you might want to post them somewhere for you so that you follow the same rules every day. Rules that change based on the stress level or mood of the caregiver are very confusing for kids. It is like trying to hit a moving target and causes them to live in fear and anxiety rather than joy and confidence. Eventually, fear will give way to anger, and anxiety may give way to people pleasing. Children who become people pleasers may not cause much trouble, but they are suffering on the inside, probably more than the children that are acting out. All children really need to know what to expect, and not suddenly be in trouble for something they could not anticipate. When the rules make sense and they are consistent, it helps kids feel safe and cared for rather than resentful and controlled. Rules that seem fair are also much easier to follow than rules that seem arbitrary or unfair. It is good to explain the reasons for your rules and always deliver them in a kind but firm tone. While consistency is very important, remember that rules are never more important than relationships.

When a child is having behavior problems or temper tantrums, remain calm yourself so that you can give them more of what they need to calm down and make the right choices. An out of control parent cannot control a child. You may be able to get some temporary cooperation, but no lasting positive change comes from that. The more upset children become, the less chance they have of doing the right thing. Remaining calm and in control of yourself during those times is very important. In his book *The Great Behavior Breakdown*, Dr. Bryan Post discusses many of the behavior challenges that children of trauma experience. I highly recommend his books if your grandchildren have behavior problems such as lying, stealing, self-mutilation, aggression, defiance, hoarding or gorging food, lack of personal hygiene, clinging and whining, poor social skills, masturbation and other sexualized behaviors. When children are acting out of the Emergency Response Center of their brain, lectures, logic and reason will not work with them. Yelling, criticizing, lecturing, or threatening will further shut down the Decision-Making Center and cause the children to have an even harder time controlling themselves.

Making mistakes and poor choices does not need to be met with anger and hostility. Making mistakes and poor choices is normal for children of trauma. Expect it and don't get all excited. Your negative excitement over their problem behaviors make it likely that more problem behaviors will follow. Remember their brain development does not support great choices right now.

Doable Requests

Another important guideline is to make your rules, expectations, and requests doable. When you ask a child to do or not do something that seems impossible to them, they get very discouraged and may give up on trying. For example, I have seen parents yelling at a child to "Stop crying!" At that moment, it may be impossible for the child to stop crying and the parent's demands just make it even more difficult. Another example is to tell a child to "clean your room" when it is very messy. I remember going through this with my daughter one time when she was young. She could not manage the instruction, "Clean your room," so I broke it up into manageable tasks, each one given when the last one was done:

1. "Throw all the trash in this waste basket."
2. "Okay, now put all the dirty clothes in this hamper."
3. "Done? Good, then put all your toys in the toy box."

And so on . . . Breaking larger projects down into individual tasks help children master big projects and when they are able to do that, it builds their confidence. Eventually they will be able to clean by themselves. This method also gives you many more opportunities to recognize and appreciate their efforts and success in following instructions and accomplishing goals.

Please Pass the Values

When we fast forward in our minds to view our children as adults and raising their own children, one of the concerns we have is making sure that our family values are passed on to future generations. We want to know that we are really teaching honesty, respect, generosity, compassion, and other values we hold dear. This is too important to be left to chance, but sadly that is how it happens in many families.

Consider teaching family values on purpose. Perhaps at your family meetings or family dinners you can bring a value such as "generosity" and have everyone share what it means to them and how they have used it or seen someone else use it. Then during the next week you can watch for acts of generosity in each family member. Look for movement in the right direction, progress, efforts. Don't wait for a perfectly mature display. Let them know that you just saw them being generous and then write it down so you will remember to share it with the whole family at the next family meeting. Try to notice this value in each person, even if there is only a shred of it displayed. Shine your light on that shred and you will watch it grow into a fully developed value trait. Pass your values to future generations on purpose. Do not highlight moments of failure to display values, for example: "Here you go, lying again. How can I ever trust you when you lie all the time?" Teach them only by being honest yourself, by creating safety for them, and by highlighting those moments of honesty and other values. Highlighting moments of failure is too discouraging for children who are struggling emotionally or behaviorally. It makes it even more scary for them, and fear is always at the root of lying. Teach them by modeling the desired behavior and by highlighting their efforts to pattern themselves after you.

Here is a list of values that you might choose from. Pick one each week to focus on and do your best to demonstrate them in your life. Remember that <u>children learn more by imitating their role models than they do from lectures or punishment.</u> Of course this is a partial list and you may come up with many more. That would be a fun family activity.

- Patience
- Tolerance
- Integrity
- Helpfulness
- Leadership
- Persistence
- Courage
- Independence
- Cooperative
- Concise
- Genuine
- Caring
- Focused
- Creative
- Curious
- Open-minded
- Confidence
- Love to learn
- Aware
- A good friend
- Imaginative
- Trustworthy
- Responsible
- Driven
- Contentedness
- Peaceful
- Joyful
- Committed
- Loyal
- In tune with others
- Observant
- Love beauty
- Seeking excellence
- Hopeful
- Sense of humor
- Spiritual
- Loving
- Compassionate
- Empathetic
- Self-Controlled
- Humble
- Fair
- Understanding
- Polite
- Industrious
- Friendly
- Outgoing
- Tolerant of others
- Punctual
- Obedient
- Peacemaker
- Caring
- Clean/good hygiene
- Sincere
- Healthy
- Determined
- Hardworking
- Thoughtful
- Well mannered
- Cooperative
- Forgiving
- Grateful
- Generous
- Energetic
- Organized
- Diligent

Relationship Rules

No matter how much is said about the importance of rules and values, the best way to pass them on to your grandchildren is through role-modeling and the quality of your relationship with them. Managing a child's behavior during the time that they are with you is not the same thing as bringing about deep, internal healing and transformation. Obedience in the moment may be important, but what counts even more is that your grandchildren grow up and continue living out the values and rules that you taught them even when you are not around to remind them. What counts is that they are living right even when no one is looking. When children have a positive, strong relationship with an adult that truly loves them and sees what is beautiful in them, it really changes how they see themselves. When you are kind to them, compassionate, empathetic and caring, it changes them. When they see a valued and beautiful reflection of themselves in your eyes they in turn become kind, compassionate, empathetic, caring people and they too can make a positive difference in the world.

The lesson that we often miss in our efforts to discipline children and to keep them on the right track is that we—that's you and me—are what they want and need more than any other thing on earth. According to the *Nurtured Heart Approach®*, parents are the children's favorite toy. All children are dependent on loving and caring adults in their life whom they can count on to always bring them back into the Healing Circles. They see themselves reflected through your eyes. What kind of picture are you giving them? What they want and crave the most is for us to understand them and meet their emotional need for unconditional empathy and love.

Eye contact is critically important and they should see love and joy when they look into your eyes. Developmentally, this is what the brain, the heart, and the physical system of the human needs. Healing of their brain can only come when they have someone consistently empathetic, firm and kind to rely on. These qualities along with laughter and joy are like healing salve to their little hearts. A harsh and punitive attitude will drive them farther away from an ability to use the Decision-Making Center of their brain and from fully developing it. It will keep them hypervigilant in using the Emergency Response Center, causing it to grow ever stronger.

Unresolved childhood trauma is at the root of much of what is wrong in the world today. There is evidence mounting that violence, obesity, addictions, and all kinds of health problems are rooted in unresolved early childhood trauma. You now have the power to make a difference for someone who may not have anyone else to depend on. That makes you pretty important, especially since no one can love them like you do. What does unresolved trauma mean? It is any trauma that is left unattended. Trauma leaves its mark by changing the way the brain is wired and by breaking hearts. Brains can be rewired and hearts can heal. That's what the circles are all about. Creating the appropriate environment allows children to resolve their trauma. In addition, seeking the help of professional trauma therapists that are trained to work with kids would be very helpful.

AUTHORITY AGREEMENTS

Ongoing family conflict and drama is not a healing environment and children only learn great conflict resolution skills when they see them being used by the adults in their lives. Yelling, screaming, threatening, banging doors, kicking, slapping, or cussing do not belong in the Healing Circles. Shaming, guilt-tripping, lying, and manipulative behaviors of all kind do not belong in the Healing Circles either, even though they can be delivered with a smile and a warm tone. Honest, open, kind but firm communication will help children to feel safe. If you are having an ongoing conflict with your adult children regarding care of your grandchildren I recommend that you sit down with them and calmly but openly discuss your concerns if this is possible.

First, ask them about their thoughts, feelings, and experiences and really listen with the intent to understand their side before you offer yours. See if you can negotiate a fair compromise that works for everyone. If not, then you may have to offer firm limits as to what you are willing to do or tolerate in your home. Then create a written Authority Agreement that spells out specifically what each of you will be responsible for and when each of you will be in charge of the kids. In general, if the parents are around, they should be in charge if they are capable of that. Even if you are all living in the same house you should have some breaks, some time to revert to being a "grandparent," some time to take a bubble bath, go golfing, or to do whatever it is that spins your beanie.

Agreements and contracts might seem like something that is not very "family friendly" but what can really tear a family apart are misunderstandings, gifts of service offered in resentment, and long standing unresolved conflicts. Enabling behavior is a big part of the addiction process, and both enabling and addictive behaviors are passed down from generation to generation. Go back to the beginning of this chapter and re-read the quotes from a grandmother and her meth addicted daughter. Enabling and addictive behaviors are learned. Coupled with genetic tendencies and unresolved childhood trauma, enabling and addictive behaviors can be irresistible to your grandchildren, but you can help break that chain.

NON-TOXIC RELATIONSHIPS

It is impossible to control every person in a child's life and protect them from anyone that might hurt them in any way. In fact we are all guilty of hurting each other from time to time, even with the best of intentions. However, there are three or four types of people we all deal with, and in fact each of us fit in one of these categories ourselves. I first read about this in a book entitled *Bold Love* by Dan B. Allendar and Dr. Tremper Longman III. I read about it again more recently in a book by Dr. Henry Cloud called *Necessary Endings*. These two book titles are interesting because one focuses on how to love even the evil person, but for the purpose of redemption, and the other focuses on knowing when to end relationships with those who continue to do harm to you. Here are the four types of people Dr. Cloud and Allendar/Longman collectively talk about:

1. **The Wise**:

    a. Take personal responsibility for problems
    b. Empathize and care how their behavior affects others
    c. Appreciate feedback that helps them grow
    d. Show remorse
    e. Problem solve rather than blame
    f. Actively seek change that will make them better people

2. **The Simpleton**:

    a. Want what they don't have

    b. Are never completely satisfied

    c. Impatient about gaining satisfaction

    d. Naïve and gullible

    e. Has poor judgment and poor intuition leaving them vulnerable to dangerous relationships or situations

3. **The Foolish**:

    a. Displays hot anger over trivia

    b. Impulsive

    c. Takes no personal responsibility for problems

    d. Self-centered and arrogant

    e. Cannot handle feedback regarding his own imperfections

    f. Defensive, shifts blame, and minimizes when approached with problems

    g. Lacks empathy

    h. Has a victim mentality

    i. Always has to be right

    j. Black and white thinker

4. **The Evil**:

    a. A fool lacking empathy or shame

    b. Cold and unfeeling

    c. Puts blame on the innocent and takes no responsibility for his cruel actions

    d. Purposefully shames others

e. Removes all hope

f. Takes pleasure in causing others to fail

g. Sometimes charming and innocent acting.

In going through the list myself, I find that I am part wise, part simpleton and just a smidge foolish. All of us are made up of some unique combination of these four types and probably none of us are completely wise or completely evil. And probably none of us see ourselves as others who deal with us every day do. That's okay because most of us could not handle it! We might either be devastated or become conceited if we knew how others view us. It is easy to see in looking at these four types that the Evil person, and in fact all of us, are formed by our early relationships and experiences and those that follow. If you never receive empathy, you cannot possibly know how to show it. If you have been blamed for things as a child that you could not possibly control you may never learn to take any responsibility for your actions due to early feelings of powerlessness. If you have no hope, you can't give it or see it in others and if you feel ashamed, you will spread that to those around you. At some point, traumatized children grow up and then become responsible for finding what they need to heal and grow. But if no framework for that is laid, the chances are slim that it will happen, although it sometimes does occur that beauty rises unexpectedly from ashes.

I think we can picture the four types of people on a spectrum with truly wise people falling at one end, truly evil at the other and the rest of us somewhere in between. When we are in relationships with people who are mostly Wise or mostly Simpleton we can usually find ways to work through our disagreements and differences.

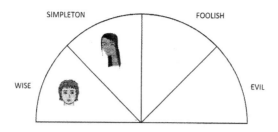

Toxic Relationships

If we are dealing with people who are too much on the Foolish end, it gets a little trickier and when we are dealing with the Evil, as Dr. Cloud says, we are going to need "lawyers, guns, and money."

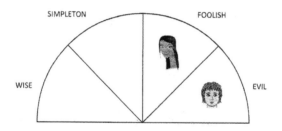

It can be really difficult to think that there are people out there who are truly evil. Unfortunately, those who are do not come equipped with a long red tail and a pitchfork. Instead, they usually look like charming or innocent people and, sadly, sometimes they are closely related to us. On the other hand, many of them are made evil by their addictions, not because they are truly evil at the core. Some addictions so take over a person's life that they will act with a complete lack of empathy or shame, be completely cold and unfeeling, blame the innocent, and take no responsibility for their own cruel or irresponsible actions. If it will get them their next fix they don't mind shaming others or causing them to fail. Their only concern is their next fix, not you, or their child.

If you are dealing with a person who is evil, either due to their deep-seated nature or due to an addiction, you may need to gather reliable resources together in order to protect yourself and your grandchildren. This could include police, attorneys, child protective services, restraining orders or whatever else it takes, but hopefully not guns!

Necessary Endings

In some of these cases, you will have to face the need for a necessary ending. Sometimes the law will take that out of your hands and may incarcerate your son or daughter. That does not stop you or your grandchildren from loving them and it may not stop you or the children from visiting them. But sometimes, you, along with your family counselor, social worker, attorney, friends, and family must make the painful decision to end a relationship with someone that you love. If this is your case, take heart because sometimes it is losing heart, giving up and ending the relationship that helps that person turn things around. Enabling on the other hand, allows them to continue their self-centered and evil lifestyle and to continue hurting others. There is no hope in that for them or for you.

There are also times when grandparents have to face situations in which they have to choose between their own children and their grandchildren in terms of who to care for. Sara was a 10-year-old girl I worked with for a couple of years who was placed in foster care when her grandmother chose to help her adult child, Sara's mother. Sara had been taken away from her mother due to issues of abuse and neglect and was not allowed to live in the same house with her. When grandmother chose the mom, Sara was taken out of the home and put in foster care. Her grandmother felt that someone else could love a child, but she was afraid that her own daughter would die if she left her out on the streets. Who would take her in?

Another grandmother who is raising her granddaughter, due to meth-addicted parents, put it this way,

> *"You have a child and you love them no matter what, for always. It is SO confusing to put the needs of the grandchild above the child and you have to break your own heart for the sake of the grandchild. So to think of my child having the experience of having the door shut in her face—by me—for the sake of the grandchild . . . How would you even fathom doing that? For me, being a grandmother raising a grandchild is so difficult because I have to let go of one to do the other. That is foreign to a mother."*

But her adult child, the meth addict, offers this advice: *"Parents need to know that cutting them off is what wakes them up. You will either be the death of him or you'll let go and offer hope for him to get out."*

It is called "letting go" and if you don't know how to do that now is a good time to learn. For this purpose I highly recommend daily journaling and daily reading of Melody Beatty's book *The Language of Letting Go*. It can change your life if you have an addict who keeps you all tied up in knots and playing into their games.

If you find yourself facing challenges similar to those of the grandmother quoted above, you know how gut wrenching these decisions can be. In this grandmother's case it turned out that the very act of letting go of her adult daughter was what started the process of her daughter's recovery. In Martin Seligman's book, *Flourishing,* flourishing is determined by measuring positive emotion, interest in life, having meaning or purpose, good self-esteem, optimism about the future, resilience (ability to bounce back after hardship), and the presence of positive relationships. You now have the opportunity to help your grandchildren to flourish and you may have to make some very painful choices in the process. It may be hard, but it will be worth it!

Who to Leave In—Who to Leave Out

Not all relationships can or should be restored. Some people are just unsafe and always will be. You should not feel guilty about ending your relationship with them or letting them go. Other times we must, for complicated reasons, have people in our lives that are unsafe. In those cases we need to have protective boundaries. For example, if your grandchild's father has molested the child, he may still have visitation rights, but his visitation must be supervised by the proper professionals.

Through your journaling you may be able to define the following three types of people:

- Those you should keep in your life
- Those you should dismiss from your life
- Those who must stay, but within strict guidelines for protection

You may find you need professional help to determine who fits in which category and to make the necessary changes. It can be very difficult to distance yourself from someone you love, depend on, or are accustomed to having around for one reason or another. Do not assume that abusers of children do not have any rights. And do not assume the abused children do not want to have a relationship with their abuser. I worked with one little girl who was removed from her home at age six because her step-dad was molesting her. The mother refused to get rid of him so the child had to be removed. When he died a couple of years later, the child was returned to her mother through a family reunification program. When mom continued to be negligent and physically abusive, she was taken from the home again. It was a couple of years later that I came into this child's life as her therapist. She expressed fear over her step-father's death and admitted that she missed him. She talked candidly about her mother beating her and she vividly remembered all the blood when she was beaten. But she clearly stated that she wanted a relationship with her mother and wants to visit her as often as possible. She longed for connection with her people. She did not care that their lives were in shambles.

I could go on and on with all the stories, but the bottom line is, no matter what the parents do, kids long for relationship with them. They crave love and acceptance from them. If you read Dave Pelzer's book, *A Child Called "It"*, you know that even though his mother horribly abused him his entire childhood, he never stopped trying to win her approval until she was dead. He was in his 30s by then. This is typical of many children who have been abused or abandoned.

Other children have such serious attachment issues that they appear to not care about others and do not try to attach to them. Indeed, the question of who to leave in and who to leave out when it comes to the Healing Circles of your grandchildren's lives is a complicated one. One 11-year-old boy that I spoke to said that he hates his mom because of all her lies, her destruction of his things, making stupid choices with men, and too many other problems to mention here. When they came to visit his grandparents, he refused to go back home with his mom. Fortunately, his grandparents went to bat for him and were able to get custody right away. He is much happier now and honestly, I think his grandfather, who is retired, is having a pretty good time too!

Each situation is different and there are no simple, easy answers or solutions. Your main job is to create the Healing Circles, get in them, get the kids in them with you, and keep the people out who try to shatter the circles. If parents cannot live in the framework of the Healing Circles, then either you have to set limits to minimize the damage they can do, or you will need to create a necessary ending. Some kids, after talking to parents on the phone or visiting them in jail or elsewhere will cry themselves to sleep or will have terrible stomach pains or migraine headaches. Other kids will act out horribly in school or withdraw and isolate. That could be because they miss them so much and want to be back with them. Or it could be that contact with the parent causes flashbacks or triggers emotions from past experiences. Then you need to be able to draw them out and find out what it is that they need. If you are unable to do this yourself, seek the help of a trained counselor or family therapist. No one should try to do this alone and seeking help is a sign of strength, courage, and wisdom. Reading this book is a sign of wisdom. Did you notice that? Remember, the wise take personal responsibility for problems; empathize and care how their behavior affects others; appreciate feedback that helps them to grow; problem solve rather than blame; actively seek change that will make them better people. I think that reading this book demonstrates that you are striving to be Wise.

Little Pitchers Have Big Ears

Children of trauma have over-active, hypervigilant Emergency Response Centers. They are always tuned in and instead of small "antennae" on their right shoulder, they have a huge "satellite receiver" above their heads. They watch and listen for everything. Think they are in bed asleep at night? Many of them lay awake listening for every little sound that will indicate what they are most afraid of. When discussing the child with others, do not recite their negative behaviors and talk about them negatively if there is any chance the child can hear. If you must talk about them, do it in a way that is respectful of the child. Hearing about themselves contributes to their identity development; they will become what they hear. Labels are very powerful and often they stick. Just as it is sometimes hard to take a sticker off of a package you buy in the store, it is hard for kids to shed ideas they obtain about themselves from things they have heard you say about them. This works the opposite way as well. If they overhear you saying wonderful, positive things about them, they will create a more positive identity for themselves. Your words make a difference, so make them count.

When talking about their parents, the same thing holds true. Do not paint bad pictures of their parents with your words. Even though there may be serious problems, they need to think the best possible about their parents. Do not lie. Do not keep secrets. Children have uncanny ways of knowing the truth.

"I felt I always knew that there was a secret they were keeping from me. They always said 'a mother is not one who gives birth, but the one who raises you.' They said it over and over. That was their way of letting me know that 'if you ever find out the truth, don't forget that your grandmother is the one that raised you and so is really your mother' even though she was not the one who gave birth to me. But hearing that also gave me the feeling that there was a secret. My final confirmation was when I was in the first grade and I learned to read and I found my birth certificate and read the names of the mother and grandparents and that was my final confirmation. I never talked to anyone or asked anyone about it. I just kept it to myself and knew inside 'this is the secret.' I wondered for a while about why my mom abandoned me and then I let it go and came back to 'my mother has been my grandmother who has taken care of me.' I let go of thinking about my bio mom so their idea of 'who cares for you is your mom' became my own truth. Then I let it go, left it there and lived my life not caring about that detail. I loved my grandma so much and I thought she was my mom. They had done a really good job at making me think that I didn't need anything or anyone else because my grandma was doing it all and I believed that.

Now that I think about it, I think I went through a short period of anger because they kept it a secret and nobody talked about it and helped me process it so I had to do it all by myself. I have done enough work on it now that

I think they were just ignorant and doing the best they knew how even though in the end it did not turn out to be the best thing for me. I wish someone would have talked to me and helped me to process all these things. I needed some support in that regard. As I found little things and big things out I needed help in processing it. That is the only thing. I would not change having grown up with my grandma and having the values she instilled in me. I am very glad it happened the way that it did."
~A grandchild

Children do not need all the details. But they do need to know the truth. It's not the facts that change, it's how we interpret them that matters to our grandchildren. It's the meaning we make of the facts that they carry with them. One little boy, who lives with his grandparents and his dad, was talking to an uncle about his biological mother. He was taken away from her because of extreme neglect when he was two. She was not around much because she just wanted to party and get lost in drugs. He was wondering why his mother does not love him and his uncle told him, "It's not that she doesn't love you. She does love you. She just doesn't know how to be a mommy." This child accepted that as his truth and was able to look at his situation without bitterness.

Assume they are always listening and choose your words carefully. Saying bad things about their parents will just upset most children who still love and need their parents, even if their lives are in shambles.

Bad-Mouthing

A temptation to both parents and grandparents, bad-mouthing each other is never a good idea. It hurts everyone, but the biggest victims are always the kids. It negatively impacts their own identity development. Here is a quote from one grandmother who has taken in two teenaged grandchildren.

> *"I have been called every name in the book. I have been accused of stealing the kids—like I wanted this. I am 73 years old and had open heart surgery a year ago. I wish I was in my cabin in the woods. I told my daughter that this is very hard for me and if she wants the best for her kids she can't trash talk me. But I know that she does and she calls me names that are not very nice. I know she resents that I am raising her kids but I am. It is court ordered. I told her that if she wants to do something positive for the kids that she will not downgrade me. I think she is getting better but she wanted to get even with me for 'taking the kids.' She needs to realize that she gave them to me by her behavior and I only ACCEPTED them from her. But I did not take them." ~A grandmother*

While you may be able to impact your adult child and their choice to bad-mouth you, you cannot control it. In his book *Divorce Poison,* Dr. Warshak recommends that parents (in your case 'grandparents') who are the subjects of bad-mouthing accept that the feelings your grandchildren express, even those of contempt and fear. You may know the source of those feelings, but if you become defensive and blaming of their parents, it will only drive a wedge deeper into your own relationship with your grandchildren. Instead, speak to the very real feelings that they are having in the moment. Be empathetic, realizing that they are the bigger victim in this. You know your motives in caring for your grandchildren are good and loving, so you do not have to defend yourself. Instead, use that same motive of care and love to be with your grandchild in their bad feelings. Offer an understanding listening ear and help them use words to describe how they really feel so that they know you understand. It may feel on the inside that you are agreeing with them, but in actuality you are treating them with respect because their feelings, regardless of the origin, are very real for them. Once they have expressed their feelings and have been *heard and understood*, the intensity of the feelings reduces and then you can talk things through calmly from a more balanced perspective.

Grandma Kate is a wonderful example of this. As they were getting ready to leave Jamie's court-ordered, weekly, supervised visitation at the library with his mother Juliet, he was crying and clinging to his mom. Kate heard her say quietly to him, "I want you to come home with me, but Grandma won't let you."

Kate bit her tongue and pressed her lips tightly together. She didn't want to say anything because she was afraid of what might come out of her mouth at that moment. She gave her daughter "the look." (You know the one I am talking about.) Later, in the car, Jamie yelled at her with tears streaming down his face, "You never let me go home to Mommy's house, and I want to go home!"

She wisely responded, "It sounds like you really miss your mommy and you are really angry that you don't get to spend more time at home with her." As he continued crying and fussing, she was able to offer more comfort and understanding, "It is really hard to be apart from your Mommy so much"; "I can see that you are really upset and disappointed that your time with Mommy ended so soon"; "It's hard to leave Mommy when you are not sure when you will see her again"; and so on.

There were many times that Juliet did not even show up at the library for visitation so it was hit or miss. Of course, as a drug addict, she is not going to take responsibility for the neglect and emotional abuse that she had inflicted on her son. She blames her mother because she is resentful and jealous of grandma's relationship with her son. Once the child is calm again, you can talk about some of the reasons for the court's involvement and let your grandchild know that you love them and want to keep them safe and take good care of them AND that you understand how hard it is to miss mommy or daddy.

It can be extremely difficult to stay positive about a son (in-law) or daughter (in law) who is making so many destructive choices, especially if they have neglected and abused their children. But keep in mind that children love their parents and are better off if they can view even the worst situations in some kind of positive light. Bad-mouthing their parents only hurts them more. A child's personal identity is formed in part by the image they hold in their mind of their parents. While you are in a primary parenting role this gives you great opportunity to become part of their identity as well, but their parents, if they spent any time with them, or hear about them, also contribute. No matter what the circumstances of the child's parents, talk about them through as positive and understanding a lens as you possibly can.

If you are tempted to talk negatively about the parents of your grandchildren, please consider the long-term damage that the child will sustain from hearing it. It is understandable that you may be very angry at them sometimes. The child knows that things are bad. Remember they probably lived in it and have a first-hand experience with their parents. If they have their own bad memories and feelings it will not be helpful for them to hear yours. Every person has some good qualities and you can always choose to highlight those offering an empathetic attitude for the others while not excusing or justifying bad behavior. Some grandparents have gone a long way toward creating a positive picture in their child's mind by telling funny stories about when their parents were growing up, stories from before the tragedy or addiction struck the family. This gives kids a bigger picture of their parents than just the problems. Even the worst parents have some good qualities. Be sure to discuss those along with your discussions of the problems. It will help your grandchildren to have a balanced view of life and to realize that ALL OF US are part good and part bad; part Wise, part Simpleton, part Foolish, and some of us, part Evil.

Dr. Richard A. Warshak also offers several questions as a test of your own motives when you are tempted to talk negatively to a child about their parent. There are most certainly things that you need to tell them, for example if a parent has gone to prison for 10 years, they will need to know about this. It will probably be prudent for young children not to watch their parents on the news if there is bad press going on, but they will need to know the truth and it will be much better if they hear it from you rather than from kids at school. Here are some of the questions that make up the Warshak test modified slightly for our purposes:

1. What is my real reason for revealing this information to my grandchild?
2. Are my grandchildren being harmed by the behavior I am about to criticize?
3. Are they being harmed by not having the information I am about to reveal?
4. How will it help them to hear what I am about to tell them?
5. Do the possible benefits of revealing this information outweigh the possible risks?

When you have to offer difficult news, do your best to be honest but shed a positive light on it. For example, instead of saying "Your dad is a useless, no-good, drug addict who can't hold a job for five days. Now he's in jail because he is a rotten thief and I hope you don't turn out to be like him," you could say, "Your dad is having problems keeping a job and I am glad that I can be here for you when you need someone. I hope he gets back on his feet because I know that he misses you. Right now he has to stay in jail for a while because he broke the law. Maybe he can get the help he needs to fix his life back up. In the meantime we are going to go visit him at the jail every Tuesday, just for a few minutes, so we can remind him that we still love him."

Keep in mind the needs of the child and remember they are listening to everything you say. When you are talking to other adults be very aware if they can hear you and make sure that what you are saying is going to be helpful and not hurtful for them. Remember that we all make mistakes and that we are all part Wise, part Simpleton, part Foolish and sometimes even part Evil. Your incarcerated or drug-addicted son or daughter is no different. Honor your grandchild, and their love and need for a connection and a positive picture of their parents. Do your best to be honest and sensitive at the same time.

The Tonic

If you and your adult children have already injured each other and your relationship is strained at best, there are some things you can do to help repair relationships, or at least stop injuring each other and the kids. You will need to take a long hard look at the whole situation and also ask close friends and family if they see ways that you are contributing to the problems with your adult children. If so, you make need to start by forgiving yourself.

I Forgive Me

Speaking of evil, you don't have to be Evil to make mistakes. If you believe that you have made mistakes the first time around in parenting and you are carrying a load of guilt for the problems that have led to you raising your grandchildren, here is what you can do to help yourself and the rest of your family.

1. **Own up.** Acknowledge to yourself the wrong that you did
2. **'Fess up.** Apologize to your adult child and be willing to change what you can change and be accountable. Keep it simple but be specific. You can say something like, "I have realized that I hurt you and made you feel like you were never good enough by expecting you to be perfect and correcting you all the time. I am sorry and I am going to try to focus now on what is good about you because there is so much that is. If I start being critical again, I would appreciate a reminder so

that I become more aware of how I am impacting you." Or, "I am sorry that when you were growing up I was not there for you. I realize now that I got caught up in my own experience and my own pain and I was not there to help you with yours. I have learned some better ways and I am changing. I hope you can forgive me and be patient as I learn to be different with you. I have always loved you, but want to be better at showing it." Ask them, "Is there anything else I should be apologizing for?" and be willing to hear it without being defensive.

3. **Move on.** Change your methods as needed and humbly take the resistance and disbelief that you may get in response. It sometimes takes a while for your adult child to believe and trust that you have really changed. That's okay. Time and patience with them and with yourself will get you all through.

4. **Be kind to yourself**, knowing that you did the best you could possibly do at the time.

5. **Forgive yourself.** Not forgiving yourself will keep the guilt and shame alive. Live without the guilt, moving forward the best that you can. There is a reason why you did what you did and whatever it is, there is forgiveness for you. If you believe in God or some other higher power, ask forgiveness and trust that it has been granted to you.

6. **Let go of it** and do not allow your kids or yourself to keep reminding you of past mistakes. If your adult child cannot let go and continues to remind you, you can simply respond with something like, "You are right. I did that and I am sorry. I already apologized and moved on. I hope you can forgive me and do the same. I love you either way." Do not give it energy, get defensive, or attack back.

7. **Be prepared**, once you become humble and safe, to hear from your kids exactly how hurt or angry they are. Do whatever it takes to not react and become defensive. If there is any way possible to delay your response until you have had the chance to process it, try to give yourself that opportunity. It will help you to do the right thing. Respond simply with something like, "I am glad that you are being honest with me about how I hurt you. I want to respond but I want to think this all through first. Can we talk about this again once I have had a chance to process it?" Schedule the time and make sure that you follow through. Remember that you are already forgiven by yourself and your Higher Power.

Once you have gone through all these steps you will have work to do in repairing the relationships that have suffered. If you slip up and react or fall into some of the same old hurtful habits, be kind and forgiving to yourself. Apologize and move on. Use journaling or other techniques to process your emotions and change your patterns.

I Forgive You

Whether a relationship needs to be restored or not, give yourself the gift of forgiveness. Other people benefit to be sure, but the one who forgives benefits the most. When you forgive wrongs done to you, you free yourself from the harmful impact of those events or actions. When you hang onto your anger it turns into bitterness. When you hang on to bitterness, regardless of how justified your anger was, you give whoever wronged you the power to continue to damage your life and the lives of those you love. Bitterness is very powerful. The only way to avoid becoming bitter over the bad things that happen to us is to forgive. Forgiveness is even more powerful than bitterness, so any time you choose to forgive, you are taking back the power from the one who harmed you.

If you have people in your life or in your past that you still get stirred up over, maybe you need to forgive them. If someone has abused you and you are still carrying that pain around, forgiveness will set you free. Your journaling will reveal what you need to be set free from. When you are ready, here are the steps to forgiving.

Decide to forgive. Forgive everyone involved. Forgive others and forgive yourself. Forgiving yourself might just be the hardest part. Starting with the decision that you want to be set free, and that you are willing to forgive as part of that process is the best place to start. Many people get so used to self-pity that they don't want to let go of it. Their bitterness is their best friend and they may leave it for a day or two, but then they change their mind and decide they cannot go on without it. I hope that is not you. I think the fact that you are still reading this and thinking deeply about it, maybe even thinking of a few people you would like to forgive and get freedom from, shows your true intention beginning to emerge. Grab that intention and hang onto it. Don't let it go! Make it your new best friend, your intention to forgive. If this is your intention, keep reading.

Congratulations! The fact that you are still reading means that **you are** already starting the process of forgiving! **You are** pursuing your conscious decision to forgive. Now that you've made that decision and started the process, let's start by talking about what forgiveness is NOT. Forgiveness is not the same as reconciliation. It is not about condoning or excusing wrong or hurtful behavior. It is not the same as forgetting either. Forgiveness must fully acknowledge the harm done and the full impact of that harm. Forgiveness does not forget, it remembers and makes the decision to let go. If there is no remembering, no acknowledgement of harm, forgiveness is empty.

To forgive is to **agree to let go of needing to take personal revenge** simply for the sake of hurting them back. It is an agreement with yourself to let go of the hurt and anger, or bitterness, rage, and hatred, if it has gone that far. Sometimes people need to be held accountable for their actions. Sometimes the legal authorities will have to be involved. But in this moment you are agreeing to let go of jealousy, bitterness, hatred, and need for revenge. These all poison your own soul. I have seen bitter people destroy relationships unrelated to the event over which they became bitter. Bitterness and hatred are choices a person makes that twists their own soul. These emotions might hurt the person that hurt you, but they will definitely hurt you more.

To really forgive someone who has hurt you or someone you love, write a letter, which you do not send, to the offending person. Let them know how they have hurt you, how that impacted your life. Write down everything that you can remember about what happened and how you felt at the time. Write about how you are feeling in the moment, just thinking about what happened. Write in the letter that you choose to forgive them, and that you are moving on with your life. End this letter by stating three things you are thankful for in regards to the situation. Read this letter out loud to someone you trust, such as a spouse, trusted friend, or counselor, but do not send the letter.

Get Closure. It might be a good idea to destroy all of your letters and notes that you wrote during the process of journaling or forgiving in order to avoid hurting others who might run across them. You might want to make some kind of closure ceremony out of it. I had a client one time that was recovering from a date-rape relationship. We used clay during therapy and she made a fish to represent her abuser out of the clay. At the end of her journaling and letter writing assignment I suggested that she read the letter to a trusted friend and then have a ceremony to really bring closure to it. She came back for a final session and told me about her closing ceremony. She involved her whole family and her new boyfriend in the event. She told everyone what had happened to her and what she was doing to get over it. She then read her final summary letter out loud to her parents only. After that they all had a pizza dinner outside by the fire pit where she burned all her journaling notes. She also burned all the pictures and cards and letters and other burnable memorabilia from that past hurtful relationship. She gave the rest of the stuff to her father to get rid of. Later she and her boyfriend went to the ocean and she threw the clay fish over the edge of a seaside cliff, into the ocean and it was over. She glowed as she told me about her experience. She really felt free after that and could enjoy her new relationship without any clutter in her heart.

Is there anything you are hanging onto as reminders of the loss or the pain that you endured? Maybe you have pictures or old letters or other memorabilia that serve as reminders of the pain. If it will help you, get rid of it. If it is something that might be important to others, consider giving it to them rather than destroying it, for example, family photos. Be sure you do not add further harm to others by destroying what they might value. And do not destroy what belongs to someone else.

If you are still feeling negative emotions about this person after writing the letter, realize that sometimes emotional healing does not come immediately with the act of forgiveness. This is a signal that you need to do more work in the emotional recovery area. Spend however long it takes writing about this during your journaling time. Remember, journaling must include what happened and how you felt to be effective. It should lead at some point to reduced negative emotions and the ability to be more honest and open with yourself and others about how you feel. It should lead to an increased awareness of your own self. It should include both old stuff and current stuff.

Some people believe that the past is behind you and you should leave it there. But the past is actually within you until you deal with the truth of it. If you pretend it didn't happen then it is highly unlikely you will forgive your offenders. You are worth fifteen minutes each day. So are the kids you love and care for. If you can't do it for you, do it for them. If your efforts on your own do not get you the freedom you need, please do yourself and your family a favor and get a good counselor or therapist who specializes in trauma work or family therapy to help you. You deserve to be free.

YOU ARE THE BOSS!

As grandparents, we are normally in a role of spoiling the children and sending them back home when they get tired and cranky. It is usually our job to have fun with them and their parent's job to raise them. However, when you are **raising** your grandchildren, your role changes to the parenting role and spoiling your grandchildren can easily lead to some unhappy surprises during the teen years, if not sooner. Of all the changes made, one of the most difficult adjustments might be to let go of that wonderful grandparenting space and become a parental authority figure instead.

As mentioned earlier, if you share parenting roles with your adult children, it will help the kids if you can all agree on rules and structure. But if you are unable to work this out with your adult children, you can let your grandchildren know that they do not get to bring any rules from their other home into your home that you object to. If so, when they arrive at your home, they may resent your rules, but you can let them know that the rules are going to stay and they will get used to it. For example, if they are plugged in to electronics all the time at their other home, it is perfectly okay for you to have a rule stating "No electronics at the table during dinner" and see that it is adhered to in your home. If they are used to eating individually whenever and wherever they please, and you prefer sit down meals, it is perfectly okay for you to enforce this in your own home. They may fuss at first, but they will get used to it. However, there is no reason to become like a drill sergeant about all this. You can and should be both **firm and kind** with the kids. Strict does not have to be mean and critical.

CHAPTER 6

Do the Hokey Pokey

"And I felt like my heart had been so thoroughly and irreparably broken that there could be no real joy again, that at best there might eventually be a little contentment. Everyone wanted me to get help and rejoin life, pick up the pieces and move on, and I tried to, I wanted to, but I just had to lie in the mud with my arms wrapped around myself, eyes closed, grieving, until I didn't have to anymore."

~ Anne Lamott, *Operating Instructions: A Journal of My Son's First Year*

"As my sufferings mounted I soon realized that there were two ways in which I could respond to my situation—either to react with bitterness or seek to transform the suffering into a creative force. I decided to follow the latter course."

~ Martin Luther King Jr.

"The soul is healed by being with children."

~ Fyodor Dostoyevsky

*"The human heart has a way of making itself large again
even after it's been broken into a million pieces."*
~ Robert James Waller, *The Bridges of Madison County*

*"You put your right hand in, you put your right hand out,
You put your right hand in and you shake it all about.
You do the hokey pokey and your turn yourself around.
That's what it's all about!"*
~Roland Lawrence LaPrise

When was the last time you went to the skating rink, got in a big circle with other skaters, and did the Hokey Pokey on 8 wheels? *"You put your left foot in. You put your left foot out. You put your left foot in and you shake it all around . . ."* It's been many years for me, but this chapter is about you getting in the healing circle so that you can draw your grandchildren into it with you. It may take a while. You may have to put your left foot in and then your right foot in and shake it all about. That's okay. Take your time, but do the Hokey Pokey and turn your whole self around as many times as you need to until you are all in the healing circle together. Joy is one of the most important healing ingredients available. When a family tragedy occurs, shattering the family Healing Circles, it feels sometimes as if joy has been sucked right out of your life and heart. Sometimes it is not about recovering from one tragedy, or forgiving one offense. Sometimes it is about ongoing problems and continuous disruptive and hurtful behaviors that weigh you down. Regardless of the type of pain and problems that you have in your life, there are ways to help yourself heal and move back into this place where joy can once again become part of most of your days.

I wish I could just say, "Here, take this little yellow pill and everything sad and complicated and painful in your life will be okay." But the truth is, there is no such pill. As much as I wish that this book contained a "magic bullet" or "Five Easy Steps," it does not. Life is often hard and sometimes unavoidably painful, but you can choose only that pain that leads to healing. The instructions put forward in this book are for those who are **courageous** and for those who are willing to fight for the lives of the children they **love**. These instructions may not all be easy, but they are worth taking because they will lead you and your family to a better future. Some of the sad, complicated, and painful things can be okay, and I hope this book helps you on your journey. There is a path to freedom, and that path is made by walking. I invite you to start taking steps on that path today and the next step is to take care of YOU so that you can take better care of your grandchildren.

Today I received a call from Sylvia who was desperately seeking help for her niece. She said her sister has abandoned her four children. One of them has been adopted out, two of them are living with their fathers, and Elizabeth, age fourteen, is living with her grandmother, the mom of Sylvia and her sister, Lorraine. Lorraine has been a crack cocaine addict for more than 20 years. She spends more time in jail than out. She frequently cries out to her family for help, but none of them lift a finger anymore because they have lost hope. All they can do is try to rally around her daughter, Elizabeth, and try to help her grow up somewhat normally. As she has gotten older, this has become more difficult. Sylvia was distraught because grandmother has not been able to provide adequate care for Elizabeth, even though she is trying. When Lorraine gets out of jail, she is clean and drug free so she comes to get her daughter. It is only a matter of time until she is back in with her regular drug crowd. It turns out that during the times

COURAGEOUS LOVE

she is with her mother Elizabeth has been sexually molested and raped repeatedly by the men that her mother hangs out with. When she comes back home to her grandmother she is obviously disturbed and begins acting out, being defiant, depressed, and withdrawn. She refuses to do chores or take care of her personal hygiene. She doesn't want to go to school. Grandmother then begins to punish her by taking away her good clothes, the only thing she has that matters to her. One time, she made Elizabeth sleep in the bathtub for a month because she was trying to get her to shower. It had become a standoff and Elizabeth won. For a month she won and went to school in ratty clothes without bathing even once. This caused social problems for her, creating even more withdrawal and isolation. No one is close to her right now. All of grandmother's attempts to get her to behave by punishing her have not worked. She has tried reasoning with her, bribing her, yelling at her, taking things away, grounding her, and has even beaten her. But that does not work either. Sylvia cries when she tells me what a charming and sweet girl Elizabeth is underneath the acting out and withdrawal. She feels she knows the real Elizabeth, but hasn't seen her for a few months. Now grandmother, overwhelmed and exhausted, wants Elizabeth gone but doesn't know where to send her. Sylvia admits that her mother sent both herself and her sister Lorraine from the house when they turned 16 because she couldn't handle them anymore. I asked what kind of childhood grandmother had and Sylvia just groans and says, "It was really bad." I had already guessed that.

Sylvia is unable to say that her grandmother is abusing Elizabeth. I voice it and ask her if anyone has called Children's Services to get support and training for the family. She says no one in the family will call for help because they do not want to put Elizabeth into "the system" and cause family problems. She is worried about upsetting everyone.

I am saddened by this answer. There are already family problems. Everyone is already upset. Not talking about the family problems, not seeking help, guarantees continued family problems. "A family is as sick as the secrets it keeps." This is an oft quoted statement which I believe to be true. When you have been part of a family system that keeps secrets, how do you begin to bring healthy change into your own life without tearing apart and destroying others? I think you begin by believing that help is there to be found, by believing that healing is possible for those who seek it, and by believing that hearts can be unbroken.

Although there are many grandparents raising grandchildren today, each story is different and unique. Some grandparents are having a wonderful second chance to raise a houseful of happy, well-adjusted kids and others are barely surviving a painful and chaotic experience with severely troubled children. Your story may not be as difficult as the one above. On the other hand, it may be even more complicated and painful. We included this chapter because every grandparent has a story of their own. How did you grow up? Were your needs met? Were you abandoned in some way? Was there abuse or addiction in the family you grew up in?

How did you learn to parent? How was parenting your children different than parenting your grandchildren is after so much has gone wrong? Chances are your childhood and your training has not prepared you for much of what you are dealing with today. Your parents did not have access to the information we have today about parenting and child development. Back then many kids just "grew themselves up" and that was considered normal.

In the field of marital and family therapy we talk about the *multigenerational transmission process*. This refers to learned family patterns that are passed down from generation to generation. The emotional system of a family refers to the ways they interact with each other, the parenting and relating styles, and the ways of coping with stress and anxiety. When this process is inadequate, it leads to individual dysfunctions. Consider schizophrenia for example. It is considered a disorder of the family's emotional system and not just one individual's illness. Other sad outcomes are the children who grow up without developing an intact sense of self and who operate as complete emotional appendages of others. The family processes that lead to these symptoms in an individual begin many generations earlier. This child does not just randomly appear in a family, but exists as an outcome of the multigenerational processes that existed before him.

Many outcomes, such as bipolar disorder, alcoholism, obsessive-compulsive disorder, depression, suicidal tendencies, borderline personality disorder, and many other psychiatric conditions, develop as a result of several generations of inadequate management of family anxiety. All of these disorders occur on a continuum of functionality, with some people experiencing one or two episodes in a lifetime while others are unable to function effectively throughout most of their lives. Many people believe that these illnesses "run in families" on a biological level. Although there may be genetic tendencies towards certain dysfunctions, it takes a family emotional process to push the individual to a seriously dysfunctional level.

To blame one member of the family for these kinds of family or individual problems is to give way too much credit to one person. Each time a baby is born, there are two family systems that come together, with everything that each one brings. As you think about and explore your own family roots, be as tolerant and understanding as you possibly can of yourself and others, remembering that all of us are wounded creatures, aching to belong and to have our deepest needs met. Most of us have had to do this with very little information and awareness, with inadequate guidance, and with role models who are struggling themselves. We have all made mistakes in parenting and in our other relationships, even the experts. My desire is that you will use any new insights you gain to make your family relationships more fulfilling and not to blame yourself or others.

This chapter is about helping you to get yourself into that circle, to get your joy back, and to put the Hokey Pokey back in your step! It will include an emotional recovery process that will help you to heal so that you can be emotionally available to meet the needs of your grandchildren as they deal with their own brokenness. Taking care of yourself will significantly reduce the amount of chaos and continuing pain that you have to deal with on a daily basis. This will set the stage for the most successful outcome for your new family. It will also bring emotional healing to others in your family and you will serve as a powerful role model for your grandchildren.

Realize that fear, stress, isolation, and not taking care of yourself are four factors that can take the biggest bite out of the quality and length of your life. One of my favorite quotes was written by Flavia Weedn. She said, *"If one dream should fall and break into a thousand pieces, never be afraid to pick one of those pieces up and begin again."* So today, I am inviting you to pick up one of those pieces. Start by taking these simple steps to healing yourself and to creating a healing relationship with the grandchildren you love. Unbreaking your own heart will empower you to unbreak the hearts of the children in your care. It is much easier to offer love from a place of strength and wholeness than from a place of weakness and brokenness.

When you take a trip in a commercial airline, they tell you that if they should lose cabin pressure an oxygen mask will fall down from the ceiling in front of you. They tell you to put on your own oxygen mask before trying to help another person so that you don't pass out. Think of this chapter as helping you to put your oxygen mask on so that you can be strong enough to help your grandchildren and possibly your children as well, if they are still in the picture. Here are five things you can do to take care of yourself and be the best grandparent you can be.

THERAPEUTIC JOURNALING

One of the best and most effective tools available in the field of psychotherapy is therapeutic journaling. I recommend it for two reasons: one because it is so effective and two, because it can be done at no cost.

One reason that journaling is so important is that when you write it uses different parts of the brain than when you simply think or talk. When you think or talk, you only have access to the conscious part of your mind. This is about awareness. What you are aware of is called "conscious thought." Most people have only a small percentage, for example 10%, of conscious thought and emotion, which they are aware of. The other 90% is called the "sub-conscious" because it is below the conscious mind. What is in the sub-conscious mind is actually more powerful in controlling our thoughts, emotions, and behaviors than what is in the conscious mind. But we are not aware that it is there and this explains why we so often repeat patterns or habits that we do not like. We try to control on a conscious level what is being caused by the sub-conscious mind.

When we write, it allows what is in the subconscious mind to be expressed. As you see yourself writing it and you read it, what was in your sub-conscious mind becomes conscious as you are now aware of it. The more you are aware of your thoughts and emotions, the more control you can have of your life. It is when we become aware of our thoughts and emotions that we have the opportunity to examine them and decide if they are correct or not. This is our opportunity to replace lies with truth; to decide to forgive ourselves and others; to let go of old emotions that are no longer valid; and to change patterns that are keeping us stuck.

Expressive therapeutic journaling is different from "keeping a diary" and has been shown to have the following benefits:

- Significantly reduced trauma and grief symptoms
- Reduced intensity of painful emotions
- Improved health and immune function
- Freedom from obsessive thoughts and feelings
- Improved relationships
- Reduction in stress, anxiety, and depression
- Better sleep and improved ability to focus
- Improvement in verbal communication skills
- Clarification of personal thoughts and confusing situations
- Find creative solutions to problems

A Time and a Place

There are many ways to go about the process of journaling, but since I know that you are busy and private moments come at a premium, I am going to recommend that you begin your journaling time in increments of just 15-20 minutes per day. If you are really in severe stress or pain, or you are really serious about getting your emotional freedom, I recommend journaling for an hour each day. Here are some things you can do to make the most of this experience.

- <u>Do it at the same time every day</u> if possible. It should be a time when it is quiet and you are unlikely to experience interruptions. For me, that is early in the morning when everyone is still asleep. You can also do additional journaling whenever you feel really strong emotions about something that has just happened. You might want to carry a small notebook in your purse or pocket so that if you are waiting for something you can use that time to write.

- <u>Create a space for yourself</u>. For a couple of years, I used a card table placed either outside on the patio or by my fireplace. You might want to put a beautiful tablecloth on it with your favorite colors. I put pens and pencils in a small pot my daughter brought me from a trip to Italy. Brew up a cup of tea or coffee, or cut up a small bowl of fruit. Make this a time you look forward to because it is for you. Avoid snacking on junk food.

- <u>Keeping your journal electronically on your computer or in a cheap spiral notebook</u> will be the least expensive ways to journal. Spend more money on a good pen than on the paper you use. A good pen for journaling will have a good, easy flow and will not stick, smear on the paper, or wear out your hand.

Some of the more popular brands of journaling pens are Pilot and Uni-ball, and if you are really into color, you might want to try the Bic Mark-it 36 ULTRA Fine Point. Try several pens and decide which one you like the best. If your hand cramps up, you might notice that you are gripping your pen too tightly while writing. Try to relax your hand while you write and note whether the gripping might be an indication of the stress or pain in your emotions that need to be expressed.

- <u>Keep your journal private</u>. Many people worry about having their journals read by others in the family. If this is a big concern to you, you might want to burn or shred what you write each day, or hide/lock up your journal when you are not using it. If you are using your computer for journaling, try password protecting the file where you keep your journal entries or simply delete each entry without saving.

The only problem with destroying your journaling is that you cannot read back over it and experience the power of reading your own story, and you cannot re-examine your thoughts to see if they are based on truth, assumptions, or fears that you have. Still, it is best to make sure that you have enough safety and security around your journaling experience so your ability to express your thoughts and feelings is not inhibited by fear of discovery. You may be afraid that either you can be hurt or someone else could be hurt by reading your journal, and you may be correct. I usually write a warning in the front of each journal such as "STOP! THIS IS A PERSONAL JOURNAL AND IS NOT MEANT TO BE READ BY ANYONE OTHER THAN THE WRITER. PLEASE DO NOT CONTINUE READING. THOUGHTS EXPRESSED HERE MAY HAVE BEEN FLEETING

AND NOT HOW I REALLY FEEL. READING THEM MAY CAUSE GREAT HARM TO YOU OR TO A RELATIONSHIP THAT YOU CONSIDER VALUABLE."

The Journaling Process

Once you have set up the place to write, the time to write, and the appropriate tools, choose an event, particularly one accompanied by a surge of emotions and answer these questions about it:

Step 1: Acknowledge the hurt. Write about what happened and how you felt. There are no rules of grammar or punctuation. Just let your hand write whatever comes naturally. If you have trouble getting started, try starting with the words, "I am feeling/I felt really (emotions) when (what happened) because (what the experience meant to you)." Use present or past tense while writing. Tell your whole story. Include as many details as you can remember. You want to clear the "secrets" out of your sub-conscious mind. This is very important. If you do not acknowledge that something hurtful happened, you cannot move past it. You cannot forgive and heal from what you have not acknowledged.

Step 2: Identify similar circumstances from the past. Have you ever felt this way before? What was happening then? Is it a pattern? List all the times or situations you can think of that seem similar or related. Write about those.

Step 3: <u>Determine which feelings are from the past and which are from the present situation</u>. Notice how your body feels when you write about each one. Do you feel shaky, angry, embarrassed, scared, and sweaty? Is your heart pounding? Who are your strongest emotions directed at? Was there an original wound that the current situation is taking you back to? Is there a lie about you that you have accepted as the truth because of this situation? Is it hard to feel anger towards someone that you love or need? Are you afraid of losing a relationship by expressing your truth?

Step 4: <u>Allow yourself to really feel and accept your feelings</u>. All of your feelings are valid. They are there to tell you something important. What are they telling you about needs not met, feelings hurt, betrayals, etc.? Do not judge or blame yourself for having these feelings. Here is a list of common feeling words that might help you describe what you feel or felt. If you begin crying or have some other emotional reaction to reading one of these words, write it down. This emotion is telling you something about yourself and your truth. Follow the emotional trails to find the roots of your problems.

Abandoned	Don't care	Hurt	Sad
Afraid	Doubtful	Inadequate	Scared
Angry	Embarrassed	Insecure	Shocked
Anxious	Envious	Irritated	Silly
Ashamed	Exhausted	Jealous	Stupid
Awkward	Flustered	Left out	Suicidal

Betrayed	Foolish	Livid	Tempted
Beyond help	Forgotten	Lonely	Tense
Bored	Frustrated	Lost	Terrified
Confused	Furious	Neglected	Threatened
Cruel	Guilty	Nervous	Trapped
Crushed	Hateful	Numb	Uncomfortable
Depressed	Helpless	Out of Control	Unmet longings
Desperate	Homesick	Overwhelmed	Used
Devastated	Hopeless	Powerless	Weak
Disgusted	Horrified	Rejected	Withdrawn
Disrespected	Humiliated	Remorseful	Worried

Step 5: <u>See if you can come up with alternative reasons</u> for the other person's behavior or whatever happened, other than what you had originally interpreted. Could there have been anything going on that you did not see? What reason do you think others would give you for doing or saying what they did? Do you believe any of these other reasons? Why? Or why not? Have you blamed yourself for things done against you? Did someone say something that caused you to feel guilty or take the blame? What have you believed about yourself as a result? What have you believed about the other person? What would the other person say about the incident? Write a narrative from their perspective. What would people that love you say about the incident? Write a narrative from their perspective too.

Step 6: <u>Assess the long term impact</u>. What was the long term impact on my life of all or any of these related events? Did they really hurt me in the end? Did anything good come out of it? Does this person still have power over me? In what ways? Is there anything I can do differently to stop giving them this power over me? In what ways am I still living out of my pain or anger?

Step 7: <u>Find the lies. Find the truth</u>. Remember it is not what happens, but what we come to believe about what has happened that really harms us. Write down what you came to believe about yourself as a result of the incident or relationship. Then seek the truth about this. If you have a relationship with God or a Higher Power, ask for insight and wisdom to understand the truth. Once you find the truth, you can write this down somewhere and read it every morning upon waking and every night just before you go to sleep. In the beginning, reading this truth might cause you to feel angry or uncomfortable. But that is because your brain and your heart do not want to accept it. They accepted the lie a long time ago and now you have to make a new path in your brain. Keep reading it morning and night until you feel happy reading it and know that you really do now believe the truth—in your brain and in your heart. It is about making a new pathway that is deeper and wider than the old pathway that you no longer want to use.

Step 8: <u>Practice the</u> **<u>Three Things of Self Love, Gratitude and "What-Went-Well:"</u>** Each day, end your journaling experience by writing three good things about yourself that you have noticed in the last 24 hours. Don't feel that this is a prideful act. Look for character traits and values that you have exhibited during the day like courage, persistence, patience, love, honesty, generosity. True humility is simply being honest about who you are, it includes the warts AND the good stuff. Write 3 things that you are most thankful for. They can be simple things. Next write down three things that went well in your day. Then write what you believe to be the reason this went well.

According to Martin Seligman, bestselling author of the books *Authentic Happiness* and *Flourish*, doing this every day will help you to become more aware of the good things in life. He recommends that each of us savor what is good in life, much as we would a good wine or chocolate. He states that if you do this every day you will be happier and less depressed. He has tried it on thousands of people and it works. It is very simple so DO THIS DAILY. It won't cost you anything and you can't afford not to.

This morning I watched a very inspiring one-minute YouTube video posted on a friend's Facebook page. It is an excerpt of an interview of Alice Herz-Sommer, the oldest living Holocaust survivor, filmed in 2011. At that time, she was 109 year old. Although she lost most of her family during the Holocaust, she remains grateful every day of her life. She says, "I know about the bad things, but I look for beauty everywhere. She is thankful every day just to be alive, because she realizes how easily she could have had that taken away. She makes

sure to share love and joy and to laugh out loud, every day. She says, "How can a child not laugh when he sees his mother laughing?" This is the kind of wisdom it takes to live for more than a century and to make an incredible difference to others. This is something you can learn to do by purposefully practicing it every day. You can see the whole twelve-minute video is by going here https://www.youtube.com/watch?v=LManGeoEbDk.

If you feel you are stuck in your pain, or stuck in relationship patterns that are not working well for you, it is important to identify what you needed in the past that you did not get. If you are a victim of childhood abuse or neglect you will need to acknowledge not only the pain of that, but also the pain that caused the previous generation to pass that on to you. Your parents could not give what they did not have. Addictions, family patterns, and abusive cycles do not come out of nowhere. They are usually related to generational patterns that are passed down, just like eating habits and other family traditions. We learn from our families what is "normal" but that does not mean it is healthy. It was just the best they could do with what they had. It may not have been good; it may not have met your needs. That's okay. Acknowledge that, grieve your pain and losses, then decide to move on and have a better life in the future than you had in the past. Learn as Alice did to look back and see the beauty of what happened. This habit of looking back at all your experiences with gratitude, focusing on the beauty, is also a life habit that can be passed on to the next generation. In fact, it is one of the habits that turns out to make the most difference to children surviving trauma—to be able to look back on it and see the good. Practice it daily even if it is hard at first and in a later chapter we will talk about how to pass this habit on purposefully to your grandchildren.

Journaling Privately in Public

Expressing emotions while they are happening to you keeps you from hanging onto them and burying them inside where they grow and cause physical, emotional, and relational problems. The problem is that it is not always useful or appropriate to vent our emotions on the person nearby. There have been periods of my life when I was under such stress or emotional turmoil of some kind that I found I sometimes needed to journal in the moment when it was happening in order to endure it. Sometimes this would be at work or while sitting in a classroom. I came up with a system where I could vent all of my emotions, giving them full expression, and not hurt anyone or let anyone else in on my personal issue. I call this technique "speed journaling".

Earlier I mentioned that you could carry a small notebook in your purse. I have done this for years. It is handy to jot down names and phone numbers, reminders of things I need to do, things that people say that I don't want to forget, etc. This small notebook also doubles as a "to go journal." I have journaled in class, in meetings, in church, on a plane, in the car, and in many other places. When I need to do this when there are other people around that I don't want in on my angst, I journal privately by using a special type of writing that I came up with. I write in cursive but I don't put a space between words, I don't cross t's or dot i's. I shorten words by leaving out extra letters and instead of writing names I just use the first letter of the name, non-capitalized. It is like creating one-word paragraphs. Even I am unable to read it back later. I incorporated some of the shortcuts I learned in a speed writing class back in 1976. But you can make up your own style of private speed journaling. The trick is to write as fast as the thoughts are flying through your head and don't worry about what it looks like. In fact the sloppier the better because no one ever needs to read it again, even you. You are simply getting all your emotions out of you and onto paper which can be crumpled up and tossed. It works wonderfully and has helped me process a lot of emotions and also get to know myself better and has probably saved a lot of my important relationships! Here is an example of what mine looks like:

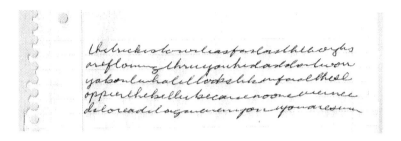

You probably did not recognize that I simply wrote a few lines from the previous paragraph. Now that you know, can you tell which four sentences I wrote? You might find this type of journaling useful when:

- Waiting for stressful appointments
- Sitting in a court room
- Waiting for someone in surgery or other crisis care at a hospital
- Directly after hearing bad news, especially if your grandchildren are the only people around to talk to. You don't ever want to vent to them
- Before, during or after difficult or emotional phone calls
- While watching a children's movie or sitting through story time at the library
- While kids are playing at the park (with one eye on the kids)

- Whenever you are feeling confused, angry, sad, or any other painful emotion in public
- If you are afraid that someone may find your journal and read it

Prayer Journaling

For praying people, there is an extra therapeutic benefit gained by pouring your heart out to God or Higher Power onto paper. To be able to express your heart's cry to someone more powerful than you, someone who has solutions to problems that you never thought of, is very comforting. It also allows God to speak to you and you may be surprised by some of the ideas that flow from your pen. Prayer journaling also helps people who are easily distracted to be more focused in their prayer. Your journal entry is just one long prayer or cry out to God. Always end with three things you are grateful for. God has thousands of ways of helping us and providing for us that we could never dream up on our own. Laying your troubles out to Him and asking for help can open the door to solutions and possibilities. Pray often and believe that miracles can happen.

SOCIAL CONNECTIONS

Because having your grandchildren in a primary position in your life changes your social status, it is crucial to be aware of the importance of social connections. People who are isolated from their family, peers and other caring adults put their mental and physical health at risk. It turns out that isolation is as bad for your health as smoking or obesity. The secret number for good health is to have at least six friends and the payoff for putting forth the effort it takes to find and maintain good friendships includes:

- A longer life and better health
- Less anxiety, stress, and depression
- Higher self-esteem, empathy, and trust

I think Brene Brown, a Professor at the University of Houston Graduate College of Social Work, said it well: *"A deep sense of love and belonging is an irresistible need of all people. We are biologically, cognitively, physically, and spiritually wired to love, to be loved, and to belong. When those needs are not met, we don't function as we were meant to. We break. We fall apart. We numb. We ache. We hurt others. We get sick."*

In order to have healthy relationships, a person must have the following skills:

- The ability to give and accept support
- The ability to honestly express thoughts, feelings, and needs
- Skills for managing conflict (which will always come up sooner or later)

You must also take the initiative to find friends. There are many good ways to do this and if you find that your old social network is no longer a good fit for you since you have kids, or that your social circle was too small to begin with, try meeting people in some of these ways:

- Family—make those bonds as strong and healthy as possible

- Grandparents as Parents support groups in your community or online. There is a good one at http://www.dailystrength. org/c/Grandparents-Raising-Children/forum
- At work (the number one place to make good friends)
- Church
- When volunteering (take your grandchildren; even toddlers can learn to help others)
- Neighbors (great source of help for small projects or thirty minutes of babysitting)
- Recreational activities such as taking the kids to the park or library
- Get a pet: Dogs, cats, birds or other animals create wonderful healing attachments with both adults and children. Pets often make it easier to start conversations with strangers
- Go to www.meetups.com and join some groups that are based on activities that you enjoy or that you would like to try (this is not a dating site)

If you are shy and have a hard time meeting people, don't worry; you can always look someone in the eyes and smile. A smile is one of the most powerful communications possible because it invites interaction and forms a positive connection. It's like silently inviting the other person to take the initiative to strike up a conversation with you.

MUSIC AND DANCE

Somewhere in my basement is a large box filled with cassette tapes (remember those?) from when my children were growing up. I don't know if I have anything to play them with anymore, but I cannot bear to part with them. We listened to music every day and even had special music for cleaning the house—Paul Simon's *Graceland* album. I am sure that I have at least one wonderful memory attached to each tape in the big box, which is why I cannot bear to part with them. Music is one of the most powerful forces available to us and it can increase your health and the quality of your life. Here is a partial list of the benefits of listening to music:

- Slow music can lower your stress level, blood pressure, and heart rate and help you sleep better
- Motivates you to exercise or helps you relax
- Music can help you express your feelings, both positive and negative
- Encouraging music can lift your mood to a more positive one and promote optimism
- Music used for worship can get you in touch with God
- It can reduce pain, both physical and emotional, by releasing endorphins (natural pain killers)
- Singing or listening to music can decrease cortisol levels, giving a boost to the immune system
- Music makes it easier to learn and may even increase IQ
- Easy listening music improves attention span and concentration
- Improves coordination and restores physical function
- Brings people together and promotes social connectedness

There are a lot of good reasons for listening to music. There are so many styles of music and you are the only one that knows which style of music helps you feel happy or relaxed or connected. It's a great way to create memories with your grandchildren at the same time that you are doing something good for you. The right kind of music also makes you want to dance and dancing has a lot of great health benefits as well. First of all, dancing is just plain fun and having fun is good for everyone, but it also:

- Increases flexibility, endurance and strength—a total body workout including lungs and heart
- Increases balance and strengthens bones
- Can be a social activity that will help you to meet other people
- Improves memory and thinking abilities
- Boosts the immune system
- Encourages you to exercise because it is fun
- Helps you forget your problems and feel happy
- Can help you lose or maintain your ideal weight
- Can be done at home for free
- Can be fun even if you have no training; just let the music move you
- Is an activity good for any age—even infants love to be held and danced around

So whether you dust off your dancing shoes or just dance barefoot in the grass, turn up the music and move your body! See if it makes you smile. There are plenty of online radio stations as well as Pandora radio at www.Pandora.com. You have many choices in style of music so listen to what works for a positive influence for you and your family. I get up early and tune in to www.KLOVE.com to start my day out right. I turn it up real loud and sometimes I dance while I am brushing my teeth or making the bed. That might not be your style but it tunes me in to the good stuff as a way to start my day.

PRACTICE A HEALTHY LIFESTYLE

If you feel strong and healthy and up for the challenges that are before you, then you are probably already engaged in some healthy lifestyle habits. However, if you feel tired and discouraged, anxious and overwhelmed, then you can help turn things around. Did you know that most degenerative disease are related to lifestyle habits that can be changed? Well, they are and this is really good news because it means that no matter what condition your health is now, there are simple things you can do to improve it. Give the following an honest try and you may gain many more years to watch your grandchildren and great-grandchildren grow up:

- <u>AVOID OVERINDULGING</u>, especially in alcohol, junk food, or snacking. If you are using food for comfort, replace that with journaling and reaching out to connect with supportive people
- <u>DRINK MORE WATER</u>. My childhood doctor used to have a sign in his waiting room that said, "I can't believe you pay me this much money to tell you to DRINK MORE WATER!"
- <u>EAT FRUITS AND VEGETABLES DAILY</u>. At least six servings a day. This one habit can add years to your life. Use dessert items sparingly and start teaching kids early to eat their fruits and vegetables. My kids use to love eating frozen blueberries while waiting for dinner.
- <u>BE ACTIVE WITH YOUR CHURCH</u>. Many studies show that families who are regular, active participants in a spiritual community show a significant decrease in health problems and a significant increase in living longer, healthier, happier lives. These results are true for both adults and children. If the

church or other place of worship you have been attending is not working for your new family system, visit others and try to find one that meets your needs.

- <u>GET REGULAR EXERCISE</u>. Kids benefit as much from physical exercise as adults do. We all need it, and it is especially important for kids with mood or behavior disorders, and for adults with stress, anxiety and depression. In your grand-parenting role you will need to stay as healthy as possible and keep your stamina up so that you can keep up with the kids. Exercising in the fresh air gives more oxygen to the brain and you are going to need all the brain power you can muster to thrive in your current situation. Kids with high energy and/or behavior problems should get at least an hour a day of fun exercise, outside if possible. (I do not recommend sending a child to run laps alone in the back yard for an hour, or any other exercise program that is isolating and punitively administered).

- <u>GET FRESH AIR AND SUNSHINE</u>! Get outside as much as possible and breathe deeply. Oxygenate your brain and your body. Get at least 20 minutes of sun every day if you can. There are many health benefits to air and sunlight. We are not bats you know! Couch potatoes die prematurely; you have a reason to live as long and well as you possibly can.

- <u>SLEEP AND REST</u>. The amount of sleep required for optimal health varies from person to person. Pay more attention to how you feel than to how many hours you are "supposed" to have and experiment to see what works best. No matter how much sleep you get, it is important that you have some time each week, preferable one day a week that you let go of all the burdens of life and just REST. The Sabbath, or weekly rest day, was made for this purpose and apparently we humans do a lot better when we regularly rest from the burdens of life. And you will feel much more rested at the end of the day if you get outside in nature and have some relaxing fun with people you love rather than passively sitting in front of the TV all day. Rest from the burdens of life, not from life itself. Once you get used to it, you won't remember how you ever lived without it.

BREATHING, MEDITATION AND PRAYER

Two more methods successfully employed in resolving anger and other negative emotions are meditation and breathing exercises. There are many good books on the market about these topics. There is scientific evidence for the effectiveness of meditation and breathing exercises, which are frequently used together, in improving mental, emotional, spiritual, and physical health. The same benefits apply when praying and also when singing joyful, happy songs. So whether you meditate, do breathing exercises, or pray, or sing, do something each day to calm and reassure yourself that no matter how things look right now, everything really is going to be okay. You will have the wisdom and confidence when you need them to make the best choices for yourself and your grandchildren. Ask for help when you need it and if you make mistakes (we all do), it's okay. Just get up again, dust yourself off, and keep going. Every day is another opportunity to refocus—a new start! "TODAY is the first day of the rest of your life"—as my first grade teacher used to say every morning (a phrase coined by Charles Dederich according to Wikipedia).

TEND YOUR MARRIAGE

Over a third of the grandparents who are raising grandchildren are married couples. Sometimes one of them is a step-grandparent and sometimes one spouse is more consumed with caring for the grandchildren and dealing with complicated family dynamics than the other. An important part of taking care of grandchildren is taking care of your marriage. When you take your grandchildren in, your marriage may be negatively impacted by many factors: grief; ongoing drama with an adult child; jealousy by a neglected spouse (male or female); financial stress; and fighting over how to discipline or set limits. One way or another, your marriage will be impacted by this.

Being a good role model is also about teaching your grandchildren what a healthy marriage looks like so that they will be able to form healthy relationships of their own. Here are some tips to keep your marriage healthy while raising your grandchildren:

- Raise them together—allow this project to be a joint venture. Focus on creating a *shared sense of purpose* around making a healthy, vibrant life for the kids and for the two of you. Share ideas, struggles and responsibilities. By being inclusive you can actually improve your marriage as you set out on this new venture.

- Ask your spouse for input before making decisions. If you think you have all the "right" answers, you will likely jeopardize your marriage. Always take the time to present the situation and ask for ideas and feedback from your spouse before making major decisions about your adult or grand child. Then be sure to share your ideas with your spouse and do your best to come to an agreement or compromise that honors both of you, before making announcements to your adult or grand children. Respect each other's perspective and hear each other out in areas where you disagree.

- Request your spouse's involvement in all family activities. It should not be that one grandparent is always heading off with the grandchild while leaving the other spouse out. If your grandchild is becoming a surrogate spouse, that will surely bring problems to everyone involved, including your marriage and the child. Of course, one spouse may be more involved in caring for the child, but this should never mean ignoring or excluding your spouse.

- Have a monthly date away from the kids, every month. During this date do not discuss the kids or any other family problems. Do something together that you both enjoy. If you can't think of anything, sit together and talk about what you enjoyed doing together when you first met. Do more of that or do new things that you've always wanted to try but haven't. If the kids have visitation with other relatives, plan your dates during the times that they are gone.

- Spend at least 10 minutes a day checking in with each other. This is what healthy partners do. They both share their joys and their struggles. They both listen and tune in to each other. Make it a point to know what is going on your spouse's world, both physical and emotional.

- If your marriage is struggling, seek professional counseling with an experienced family therapist or marriage counselor. Raising grandchildren might be stressful, but a failing marriage will just make it more stressful and might take one more parent out of the child's life. Of course, there are sometimes good reasons for separation or divorce. An example would be domestic violence. If that is going on, please seek professional help for yourself and your grandchildren.

- Make time for sex. When life is stressful and chaotic, there is nothing like a good long hug from your best friend. If you feel too tied in knots to be sexy, try just hugging and stroking each other's back and head until you both feel calm and relaxed. Take the time to comfort each other without words. Having sex from that point will be much easier. Share with each other your best memories of past times when you were having great sex and that will help to reignite the flame, if you are struggling in that area. According to author Joan Price, an orgasm has wonderful health benefits. At least one orgasm a week offers great health benefits with positive effects on mild depression, risk of heart disease, immune function, pain management, and tension release, to name just a few.

By tending your marriage, you have an automatic support system in place, which you will definitely need in order to give your grandchildren the best care possible. A good marriage is worth keeping, and a struggling marriage is worth tending.

GOOD FOR YOU = GOOD FOR THE KIDS

Take the time to do other things that you enjoy as well, such as read, pursue creative interests, garden, or knit if that's your thing. Don't fall prey to using alcohol or drugs, veg'ing out in front of the tube, or getting lost in cyber space as a default. If you find that the family is more irritable after certain activities or TV shows, stop providing them in your home. Increase the amount of time spent in positive, lively, connected pursuits, and less time in passive, negative, or isolating activities. If you have a habit of isolating, you must break out of that for the sake of your grandchildren. It is never too late to change and have a better life. I have known people in their late 70s who made drastic lifestyle changes and improved the quality of their lives by doing so.

Remember, what's good for you is ultimately good for the kids. If you are a whole and happy person, you will be a much better role model and support to your grandchildren.

Healing Activities

Every person has their own time and way of healing. Besides what was described above, there are many other activities and paths that lead to healing. Here is a quick guide with some specific actions that have proven to be very beneficial to many people who have been dealing with strong and/or negative emotions and some of them may be helpful for you too. It's a smorgasbord, so start by picking two or three that appeal to you to try out and don't feel you have to do them all.

Express intense negative emotions by:

- Journaling as described above
- Draw or paint a picture with no plans and no rules; use bold colors
- Make a collage to expresses how you feel, using old magazines
- Write a song or poem that tells your story or expresses your feelings

- Listen to songs that tap into the emotions or experiences you are having

To process anxiety or comfort yourself:

- Take a long bubble bath or a hot shower
- Take a walk or a run
- Get a massage or a pedicure
- Rub your hands/arms/feet/legs with lotion
- Listen to soothing music
- Snuggle up in a comfy chair and watch an old comedy

When you feel lonely and empty do one of these:

- Call a good friend or supportive family member
- Write a thank you note to someone that you have appreciated in the past. Do not be afraid to go back 10 or 20 years, or more. Send it, or better yet, hand deliver it
- Bake some cookies and take some to your neighbors
- Get online and join an online support group for whatever it is you are struggling with
- Go online and join some meet-up groups in your area. www. meetups.com

When you are very angry or extremely stressed out, try one of these activities:

- Exercise vigorously for at least an hour—walk, run, play tennis, ride a bike, throw a Frisbee or a football, dance, whatever you like to do (I get in a racquetball court alone and try to drive the ball through the far wall until the intensity passes)

- Write letters to the people you are angry with and then destroy the letters
- Bake bread and knead the dough vigorously or make Aggression Cookies (recipe in Chapter 10)
- Tear an old newspaper in strips, crumple them up, and throw them in a trash can across the room
- Do yard work, rake leaves, clean the house
- Talk to someone you trust. Tell them what you are angry about, what you want to do about it and get feedback before taking action

If you find you have ongoing issues with anger, anxiety, depression, prolonged grief, or severe conflict, find a good family therapist, counselor or social worker who can help you understand and work through your problems and family situations. Another good option is to join a small group dealing specifically with the issues you are struggling with, such as:

- 12-Step groups such as Al-Anon, Alateen or Alcoholics/ Narcotics Anonymous
- Grief recovery
- Grandparenting or kincare
- Co-dependency

The Return from Grief

Chances are pretty high that you and/or your grandchildren are dealing with issues of loss and grief of some kind. To help them get through it, you will need to help yourself get through it. Whether you are grieving the loss of an adult child who has died or been lost to drugs or a life of crime, you will need to grieve this loss in order to do the best job possible raising your grandchildren. There are many ways to grieve a terrible loss, but there are also stages of grieving that are most common for those of us who have lost someone we love. These stages do not occur in this order for everyone:

- Denial—The feeling that what has happened is not real and is not part of your life
- Anger—Feeling that what happened was not fair with a strong desire to blame someone
- Bargaining—Seeking some alternative to the inevitable loss, such as a promise to God in exchange for a desired remedy
- Depression—Feelings of sadness, fear and acceptance with regrets
- Acceptance—Making peace with what cannot be changed

No one can really say for sure which of these stages you will experience or how long you will take to go through any of them. Do try to recognize each stage and do something to help yourself if you feel that you have become stuck. Being stuck in denial can result in numbing behaviors while being stuck in anger can lead to bitterness and cynicism. Depression can become chronic if feelings are left unexpressed. There is also the grief of ambiguous loss. This is often the case when dreams are lost, for example if your beloved, adoring daughter turns to drugs and abandons her children to your care. Loss that has no clear beginning or end and no formal ritual can be an even harder grief to process. Here are some steps to take if you feel that you are suffering too long:

- Find understanding friends to talk to about the person/ dream you have lost. Make sure they are not the children you care for and that grandchildren are not listening in on your conversation.
- Journal as instructed previously in this chapter
- Take the time to process your feelings and do not try to pretend that it is okay. Some healthy ways to process are:

  o Collect photos of the person lost or make a collage of the dream lost and spend time crying or just feeling your sadness and pain

  o Find a symbolic object or photo that you can keep somewhere that you can see every day to stay in touch with your memories of the person lost

  o Do an art project that allows you to express your feelings

  o Play, sing, or listen to music that expresses what you are going through

  o Write a letter to the person lost and read it to them at the cemetery or read it to a picture of the person. Let them know how much they meant to you and tell them how you plan to live your life now that they are gone. You do not need to give this letter to a living person you may be grieving over, for example, a son or daughter who is incarcerated

- Get some exercise each day and eat as healthfully as you can. Taking care of yourself is a gift you can't afford not to give
- Practice gratitude for the good times you had with the person lost, for the motivation and inspiration you felt for a dream

before you lost it, or for the grandchildren in your life who may carry on the family traditions and values

- When grieving becomes overwhelming and exhausting, put it away for a day or a week. You can always come back and finish with it when you need to. When life gets hard, it's important to go on sleeping and eating and living as if it isn't. Structure can help

- Find some way to help someone else, such as your grandchildren, knowing they are grieving too

- Join a grief group or a support group of some kind

- Find another grandparent raising their grandchild that you can regularly connect with, or perhaps an online support group

- Be patient with yourself and your grandchildren. Grief takes time

- Cry—don't try to hold in the tears or the anger or any other emotion. Just find appropriate ways to express them. Appropriate means it doesn't hurt you or anyone else

Realize that some losses are very hard to work through and that the passage of time all on its own does not bring healing. In the first year that you have your grandchildren, your focus may be much more on surviving and recreating a life without the missing parents. If your adult children are not completely out of the picture, but come and go due to incarceration, drug addiction, mental illness, or some other tragedy, the loss may seem like it happens over and over again. Losing a child or a parent is not something that one can just "get over" due to the fact that love is stronger than death or disease. That longing ache may never completely disappear, but you and your grandchildren can indeed learn to live joyful, fulfilling, and meaningful lives in which you are all thriving in spite of it. As you continue creating the Healing

Circles, remember that you must first be inside the circle yourself before you can bring in the grandchildren. So, if it's been a while since you felt joy and exuberance, put on your dancing shoes or your roller skates and start the Hokey Pokey today! I'll see you in the rink. Turns out that to do the Hokey Pokey, and turn yourself around, really is what it's all about.

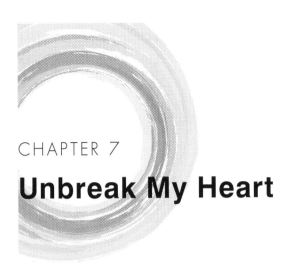

CHAPTER 7

Unbreak My Heart

*"The more healthy relationships a child has, the more
likely he will be to recover from trauma and thrive.
Relationships are the agent of change and the most
powerful therapy is human love."* ~by Bruce Perry

To understand the importance of this quote from Dr. Bruce Perry, you
must understand who he is. Dr. Perry is a neuropsychiatrist, and one of
the world's leading experts on children and trauma. For two decades,
he has done extensive research on, and worked with, many children
who have endured the worst kinds of trauma. In his book, *The Boy Who
Was Raised As A Dog,* he tells the story of a young boy named Justin
who's fifteen-year-old mother left him permanently in her mother's care
when he was just eight weeks old. His grandmother cared well for him
for the next nine months and then she became very ill and died. This
left him with his grandmother's live-in boyfriend, Arthur, who knew
nothing about taking care of babies.

Of course, due to these two significant losses in his first year of life,
Justin began to have some significant behavior problems, including

crying and tantruming frequently. While waiting for Child Protective Services to find a permanent home for the child, Arthur, who was a dog breeder, took to keeping him in a dog cage most of the time. He fed and clothed him and kept him clean, but not much more than that. For five years Justin lived in this cage before he was brought to the attention of Dr. Perry when he was admitted to the hospital for pneumonia.

Brain scans revealed a brain that was badly underdeveloped, particularly in the area of the cortical system, which you may remember from Chapter Two is responsible for logic, planning, and reasoning. At that time, many medical professionals were unaware that the cause of this underdevelopment was due to the severe neglect he had suffered and not a congenital defect. He had none of the skills normal for a six-year-old and the medical team was unable to treat him due to his extreme behaviors. Among other things, he could not stand, walk, or sit in a chair. He could not talk and he threw food and feces, shrieked, and pulled his IVs out. Because of the anxiety and fear he experienced in this new setting, and his complete lack of logic, planning, and reasoning skills, his Emergency Response Center had full control and all he could do in response was fight for survival. This is an extreme case, but it does show the direct cause and effect that neglect and trauma can have on a child.

Your grandchildren also have suffered an impact on their brain development, but likely to a lesser degree. I include this story because it reminds us of that link between trauma and brain development, and because all children are vulnerable to being misunderstood and mislabeled. They must have the help of consistent, caring adults in their lives to develop normally and to heal. You will be happy to know that after just two years of consistent care and training by his new foster family, little Justin was able to function normally enough to start school. Although children are vulnerable, and easily wounded or developmentally stunted, they readily respond to proper care.

Knowing what that proper care is does not come naturally to most people, not when you are dealing with children of trauma and loss. Whether your grandchildren are acting out, or they are overly compliant and perhaps withdrawn, you can learn to be that healing person in their lives. The fact that you care enough to read this book tells me that you are teachable and that you already have the most important ingredient in a healing relationship, courageous love. I say "courageous" because sometimes what you are doing might be hard or frightening. You may have to change some ways of parenting that have been working for generations in your family, and change takes purposeful effort. That courageous love and that purposeful effort are why I call you Super Parents!

WHAT DO KIDS NEED?

"I remember the traumatic moment when my world came crashing down. I was only four years old but I still remember it. I was watching out the window as my mom walked away and I was screaming but they wouldn't let me go after her. She never came back.

I keep wondering what do I do, or what have I done, that might cause a moment like that for my son. How can I avoid that? I have so much anger and guilt because

I simply can't care. I want to be stable and I want to be there for him, but I can't. I constantly have this feeling like I am never where I want or need to be."
~ A Drug Addicted Parent

Many children, traumatized by loss and/or abuse, begin to act out based on the experiences they have been through and the deep feelings of powerlessness and hopelessness that grow out of that. We already discussed in a previous chapter the many ways that trauma affects children. When they act up in school and they act up at home, they get less and less of this sense of love and welcome that they need. Instead they often get cross words, labels and medication, punishments, extra chores, lectures, scolding, time-outs, and other consequences meant to "teach them a lesson" and help them to behave better. Even the very best behavior modification programs are seeking to squelch or eliminate these "bad behaviors" that are only the symptoms of much deeper problems. The evidence is now in that behavior modification programs, although they may bring relief in the short run, do not bring the inner transformation and healing that children so badly need. What needs to happen, instead of controlling problem behaviors or managing negative emotions, is an internal healing and growth that eliminates these problems at their source.

But let's not forget the compliant, quiet children who are trying so hard to please. Their needs are just as profound and significant. In an art therapy session I had recently with a nine-year-old compliant child we were talking about anger. I asked her what kinds of things make her feel mad or angry. She said, "Well, mainly when my grandpa doesn't notice all the good things I do. He always tells me what needs to be done, but he does not celebrate with me when I do them. He doesn't notice my progress in doing good things and that makes me mad and sad." So don't think that just because you are not having problems with a child, that they are not suffering. They have the same needs as the children who are acting out. They just don't demand attention quite as loudly. If you are caring for an infant and it never cries, don't assume that's good. Normal, healthy babies cry when they are hungry, lonely, uncomfortable, tired, anxious, or scared. If a baby is not crying at all, it could indicate more serious issues and should be checked out by a health care professional. It is the same for children who are so completely compliant that they seem too good to be true. Normal children are energetic and curious and can sometimes tax an adult who has too much on their plate already.

All children of trauma, both those who act out and those who are compliant, need to develop the parts of their brain that will allow them to make responsible choices. They can only do that when they have the ability to regulate both the Decision Making and the Emergency Response Centers. A traumatized brain does not have the same choices that a well-developed brain has. As it turns out, much of what children needs is also what grandparents need to have the strength and joy to raise them. This is good because that means that all of you can obtain many of your needs together in joint family or community settings. Let's talk about what your special child needs in order to enter the Healing Circle that you are creating.

THE POWER OF JOY

Dr. Allan N. Schore is considered the world's leading expert in developmental neuropsychoanalysis (the study of the organ of the brain, the processes of the brain, how they are formed, and how that impacts the emotions and behaviors of a person). Some consider him the "Einstein" of psychiatry. He is on the clinical faculty of the Department of Psychiatry and Biobehavioral Sciences, at the University of California Los Angeles (UCLA) David Geffen School of Medicine, and at the UCLA Center for Culture, Brain, and Development. It is no wonder that he studies the brain because he is so brilliant and brainy that the many huge books and research articles he has published cannot be understood by most common people. Even if you could understand them, if you are raising your grandchildren I don't think you'll have time to get through them!

Fortunately, there are some people who have read through his huge, thick books and translated them into simple terms for the rest of us. One such person is Jim Wilder, Director of Shepherd's House in Pasadena, California. He has also written several books to help people understand and apply complex neuropsychological scientific theories in practical everyday ways under highly difficult circumstances. I own two of Dr. Schore's huge volumes which I have read parts of and I have attended a workshop that he gave a few years ago. I also own and have read several of Dr. Wilder's books and listened to over 20 hours of his DVD workshops. It is all fascinating information and I will try to condense the most important parts of their work into a few pages for you so that you will gain the benefit of thousands of hours of work put in collectively by the three of us . . . least of all by me.

The core of their message, as best as I can tell, is the same truth that Dr. Perry came to in all of his research on children of trauma, that the main healing ingredient, and the magic ingredient of normal, healthy development is love. Furthermore, that love is delivered through an exchange of joy between two people. The more consistent the experiences of joy in a person's life, the more whole, healthy, and happy they will be. Children who do not have someone giving them this joyful exchange of love in a consistent way will suffer in many ways. If it is not corrected at some time, and the sooner the better, they will function far below the potential they were born with. Love and joy is everything. **Please think of the Healing Circles as protective containers for the love and joy that your family will use to apply as healing salve to your grandchildren.**

They discovered by studying the brain using new imaging technology, the same things that Dr. Perry discovered in studying traumatized and neglected children and what healed them. Neuroscientists are looking through cameras that show activity as it is happening in the brain. But both Dr. Schore and his team, and Dr. Perry and his team, discovered that seriously traumatized, broken-hearted or wounded people only heal when they are in a community that shares deep bonds of love. The other kinds of bonds are trauma bonds, otherwise known as fear bonds.

Our brains only develop as a result of a response to some kind of stimulation. According to Dr. Caroline Leaf, another extremely brilliant neuroscientist, the brain grows pathways that look like trees when you photograph them. Negative interactions with others and negative thoughts actually grow ugly little shrunken, dead-looking branches with thorns on them. Positive, loving interactions and positive, grateful thoughts grow pathways that look like beautiful, healthy trees. Neglect and isolation do not grow many trees at all, which is why little Justin, the boy who spent several years in a dog cage had a very small brain. In fact his whole head was much smaller than normal for his age. As adults we can learn to choose what we want to think or who to let in, but as children, we take what we get and that causes our brains to wire up and develop in one way or another without our permission.

The amount of healthy trees we have in our brains equates to "joy strength" and the amount of joy strength that we have determines how much loss or trauma that we can handle and still function well.

Joy Bonding

There are bonding periods through infancy and childhood that allow us to bond and become more like those we bond with. Before a baby is born, he senses his "universe" through <u>emotion, taste, smell,</u> and <u>temperature.</u> All of these continue to be bonding factors throughout life. Think about it, don't you feel close to people who are joyful to be around, offer you some tasty food, burn a wonderful smelling candle and keep you warm in the winter or cool in the summer? Sounds pretty good to me! When my husband does these things for me I feel really happy and I feel loved. Think of joy bonding as activities you can do which will bring a child back into the Healing Circle any time that they fall out, are drawn out, or are kicked out.

By three months of age, a normal infant is able to see clearly and then will begin to look at faces, especially mother's face (or the primary caregiver's face). They will coo and smile and <u>seek eye contact</u> and respond to expressions of joy in other's faces. This just adds to the ways that they can be told they are loved. What they are looking for is someone whose facial expressions say "I am happy to be with you," which registers as "I love you and you are safe."

Around 12 months, babies begin to hear more clearly and then they add to the growing list of ways to receive love, a voice tone. They are listening for a tone that says "I am happy to be talking to you." Children need to know that they are the sparkle in their caregiver's eye, and that they not only receive joy, but they give it. This knowledge makes them feel loved and excited. Once a child gains language skills the words spoken to them also convey a message. Babies can understand words long before they can say them clearly back to you.

Babies will feel the emotions that are reflected in the facial expressions and the voice tone of the person who cares for them. It absolutely determines how the brain grows. Anger, depression, anxiety, or any other negative emotions reflected in a caregivers face begin early on to grow the stunted little thorny trees in the brain. Joy and love and attentiveness grow strong healthy trees in the little brain.

Babies are born without a formed Decision Making Center which ideally will become roughly one-third of the mature adult brain. There are two ways to have a reduced Decision Making Center—one is that it never develops in the first place (neglect), and two is if that part of the brain is not used once it is developed. Then the little healthy branches will die and eventually be trimmed away.

This important infant bonding time starts around three months and peaks at about the ninth month of age. There are other bonding peaks as well.

- At three to five years of age a child will naturally strive to develop a strong bond with a father figure.
- During growth spurt of ages seven to ten years of age

- Around fifteen years of age, teenagers experience the bonding euphoria that we call "puppy love"
- A mother during pregnancy with her first child
- A grandmother when her first grandchild is born

Whether or not a child (or any person) is in a peak bonding time, the Decision Making Center of the brain never loses its ability to grow as a result of experiences. This is a good thing because our ability to function well when bad things are happening is related to the development of this center of our brain. It is also the part of the brain responsible for pain control, emotional control and our immune system. A healthy, well-functioning Decision Making Center also has the power to shut down the Emergency Response Center, giving us the ability to choose how to respond when we are afraid, angry, hungry, or sexually driven. If our Decision Making Center is dwarfed, the Emergency Response Center will have full reign in a person's life. They really do not have the same choices as other people.

And remember, this is all based on the amount of joy bonding that a person has been able to experience. A child's identity also is developed by their experiences of joy bonding, or lack thereof. If a child is only noticed when there is a problem and they are in trouble, or the caregiver does not light up and give that message of "I am so happy to be with you" the child will have a very negative picture of self and the corresponding brain function. It's not just children that need to receive this message regularly from someone. We all need it. I need it. You need it. All of us have hearts crying out to be noticed and loved, esteemed worthy. Children who do not get this have impaired brain function. Don't expect them to make good choices all the time. They can't.

Seeking joy

Children are born seeking this joy. In fact, seeking this **joy exchange** is the only thing that motivates a child during their first year of life. They want and need desperately to be inside the Healing Circles, where love and joy reign. When infants and children need this joyful connection they will find some way to signal that to their caregiver. If they get the desired response, they can go on. This is why it is important to allow little interruptions from small children. Interrupting a thirty-minute conversation with another adult for a ten-second joy exchange with a small child is a very sound investment. This exchange requires that you somehow give the child the message that you see them and you care about them. They repeatedly need the message from you that you see something beautiful in them.

There are several ways that children's joy seeking missions get messed up by their caretakers:

- When a caregiver does not respond to requests for the joy exchange the rejection to the child is extremely painful. In fact it is so painful that after a certain number of failed attempts an infant or child will stop trying. This is known as **Avoidant Attachment** style. Eventually these children will also not respond to other's emotions or requests for a joy exchange because they come to believe that their needs will not be met anyway.
- When a caregiver gives a child joyful, loving attention based on the adult's needs rather than the child's needs, it creates other problems. When a caregiver ignores a child's requests, but then tries to attach later when the child is not seeking

an exchange the child does not experience this as soothing. Eventually this will cause **Ambivalent Attachment**, because the child believes there is no reliable source for getting their needs met. This child is at risk for becoming "parentified," believing that it is her job to tend to the emotional needs of the parents, while denying her own. This may occur in situations where the caregiver is in so much stress or grief of their own that they have no energy left to attend to the child. The previous chapter addresses the need of caregivers to find healthy ways to take care of themselves. As a grandparent raising grandchildren, you may be having your own struggles with what has happened with your adult children. Do your best to not let this cause you to be unavailable for your grandchildren.

- It is very frightening to children when caregivers yell and scream at them or someone else in front of them, or when caregivers are scared themselves. You cannot get comfort from someone who frightens you which puts these children in a real bind, and leads to a **Disorganized Attachment** style. If it is bad enough, it can lead to Post Traumatic Stress Disorder or Dissociative Identity disorders. These children find themselves drawn to fear and other frightening people. They may spend their lives feeling confused and hopeless in regards to getting their needs met.

In order to form a **Secure Attachment** the caregiver must offer consistent healthy joy exchanges when the child needs them. These healthy bonds will grow stronger as child and caregiver find safe ways to share both positive and negative emotions in ways that honor the needs of the child and do not overwhelm him. They contain a balance of freedom and connection. As the bonds become strong enough, they will continue to grow and be strengthened by stretching the limits slightly because the child will have learned by experience that their needs will be met. They will be able to withstand and grow through periods of closeness and moving apart and coming back to closeness. This ability to move further away before coming back to reconnect should grow and stretch as a child matures.

If your grandchild has an impaired attachment style, there are many things you can do to repair that and help them to have a strong joy bond. Being the consistent loving caregiver they need may not be easy in the beginning, but the longer you apply the healing principles laid out in this book, the easier it will become. And there is nothing better than to see joy in the eyes of your grandchildren as they light up when they see you. This beautiful joy exchange benefits both of you! It keeps you both in the Healing Circles, where you belong.

RETURN TO THE HEALING CIRCLES

All of us fall out of our **Healing Circles** at times. All of us suffer pain. It is part of the human condition and embracing life means embracing the difficult times as well as the good. One of the most important skills that we all need to learn, and that we need to teach to our children, is how to return to joy, to the center of the Healing Circles, after we have fallen out. Sometimes this ability to "return to joy", or to go from negative emotions back to positive emotions is called "emotional regulation". Exercise is a wonderful way to help increase the brain's ability to return to joy is it increases natural endorphin activity. Exercise is one of the first-line defenses against depression, dysregulation, or getting stuck in negative emotion. Exercise that you and your grandchildren enjoy doing is a very good tool for helping you learn to return to joy.

Children of trauma live in a heightened state of alarm due to their hypervigilant, over-active **Emergency Response Center**. This state of alarm often puts children (or adults) outside of the circles. There are actually pathways created in the brain from each of the negative emotion areas back to the place of love and joy in mature, healthy individuals. If you yourself do not have this ability to get back to joy from anger, sadness, fear, or other negative emotions, you will not be able to pass this gift on to your grandchildren. This means that you will need to go back to the chapter titled *Do the Hokey Pokey*, and do your own recovery work so that you can have this ability to return to joy yourself. And remember that a loving community is critical to you and your grandchildren while developing this skill. You cannot do it alone.

In a normal, healthy child, this pathway should be in place by 18 months of age. When children do not have this pathway back to their Healing Circles you will see behaviors indicating out-of-control emotions like temper tantrums or night-terrors. If children are punished or verbally berated when they have these problems, it only makes their problems worse as what they really need is a calm loving person to help them back to joy. That does not mean giving them the candy they are demanding in the grocery store line. We will get to the details of what it means in a minute. Adults who are "moody" are simply people who do not yet have a joy path back to the Healing Circles from some part of the brain. As adults we must be responsible for our own recovery, but children must depend on us to help them. Remember that joy exchanges are registered in the face and in the tone of voice.

That is how we communicate the important message that "I am happy to be with you!" Yelling at a child who is having a temper tantrum does not help them learn to return to the Healing Circles. **They will control their own temper when they have built up enough internal joy strength to endure the pain of disappointments or rejection.** Rather than working to control the behavior of the child, your new focus is to control your own response to them and to be sure that you are communicating love even in the difficult moments.

The Healing Circles filled with love and joy is where we will picture our natural setting. This is the place that we want everyone in the family to be at the end of every interaction and at the end of every day. Of course there are times for setting limits and delivering consequences, but at the end of that, you will want to be sure everyone is back in the Healing Circle as soon as possible. Perhaps the greatest of all fears is that of being found unworthy of love and the greatest pain, that of rejection. **None of us will be loved and adored by everyone, but each of us needs a place to go where we are always welcomed, a place where we are wanted and appreciated for who we are. That place, when we find it, is home.** When everything is going wrong in a day, to have a home like this to come back to makes everything else endurable. To have someone light up when they see you walk in the door, to be hugged and listened to, and to be told that everything will be okay, that is home to a child.

On the other hand, if the family home is a place where stress, chaos and criticism reign, that will not be the safe haven for a child to come home to. Even if a child comes and goes from your home due to unstable parenting or other circumstances, and the remainder of their environment continues to be chaotic, the time they spend with you in your home can make all the difference in the world. Sometimes it is the impact of one person in a child's life, even if for a limited time, that helps them to believe in themselves even when everything else is going wrong.

The Language of Love

About a decade ago and for close to three years, I spent some time every day in the pursuit of understanding what love really is and how to apply it in the everyday and the difficult places in my life. I studied and I prayed for understanding and I did my best to put into practice what I learned. With some understanding of love and with my human tendency toward failure, I limped along doing my best and getting some mixture of success and failure through my focused attempts. In the spring of 2008 I attended a one day training of The Nurtured Heart Approach® by Howard Glasser. That day I felt as though I had stumbled upon a new language that sounded vaguely familiar.

I was not at all fluent in either speaking or receiving it but it had a huge impact on me, on all of my relationships, and on the work I was doing as a therapist, a manager, and a trainer. I came to recognize this language as the language of love. It is not perfect, and neither are those of us who believe in it or follow it or use it in our daily lives. But it is good and it can help you make huge strides toward offering your grandchildren what they need in terms of emotional nutrition. (Please note: I will not be teaching this approach in this book because it is already so well done in several other books. See "Recommended Book List" at the end of the book for my recommendations.)

I believe that the magic of The Nurtured Heart Approach® is that it gives caregivers powerful ways to bring children back into the Healing Circles in any given situation. I will give an example from a foster group home for little boys that I worked with. There was one boy, Aaron, six-years-old, that everyone working in that group home agreed would be sent to prison as soon as he was old enough. When the staff came to the first week of Nurtured Heart training, they told me that he was beyond help of any kind. He was "too wicked . . . too far gone" to be reached by any of them. Being in that particular group home setting was as close to prison as a six year old can get. On week four of training, they had begun to change their minds and one of the staff who had been most resistant to the idea of using a nurturing approach in this group home shared the following story. All of the boys were going on an outing except for Aaron. He had an appointment with his social worker and had to stay home. He was very upset as the van was leaving and he was left behind. He ran into the house screaming, with this staff member, Eva, and the social worker following behind. He threw himself on the couch face down and was screaming and pounding on the couch.

Eva, determined to use the Nurtured Heart Approach, said to him, "Aaron, I know you are so angry and disappointed right now because you have to stay here and they all left without you to go and have some fun. I am really proud of you right now for using such self-control as you show how bad you are feeling." The social worker immediately challenged her on this statement. "How in the world can you say Aaron is using self-control right now? Look at him! He is throwing a temper tantrum!" "Well, replied Eva, "he is screaming and crying and hitting the couch. But he is not calling me names or hitting me or punching walls or breaking things. Right now he is being really respectful of me while he is expressing how bad he feels. And who wouldn't be upset to have to stay here when everyone else is going off to have fun? I am really proud of him for using self-control, being respectful and expressing his feelings without hurting anybody." Of course Aaron heard the whole conversation and at this point sat up, and with tears still running down his face he looked up at Eva and started to smile a bit from the corner of his mouth. She put her arm around his shoulder and pulled him close to comfort him. Within moments he had calmed himself down and was completely cooperative with Eva and a very befuddled social worker.

What Eva did right there, was offer understanding and empathy to Aaron. She also told him in very clear terms what was great about him. Even in the midst of a "tantrum" he was showing self-control, respect, and expressing his emotions without hurting anyone. By highlighting that aspect of Aaron, Eva reached out caring hands and an open heart and pulled little Aaron tenderly back into the Healing Circles. I teach this approach because it is simple enough for anyone to understand and it is powerfully effective. I highly recommend learning the Nurtured Heart Approach® if your grandchildren have behavior or mood problems. Actually, I recommend the approach for everyone to use all the time, because I believe it spells out the language of love that we are all so hungry for. It is the language that belongs in the Healing Circle and I try to keep it in mine. Of course, I fall out sometimes too, but I am in a real hurry to get back in because I prefer joy to pain. What I hate most is when I discover that I have pushed someone else out of the healing circle, but I am afraid I am guilty of that sometimes too. When I do, I want to get them back in (if they belong in my circle at all). More on that later . . .

I can write another book on the experiences I had using and failing to use the approach in all areas of my life. I have done my best also to use it and live it and teach it to anyone I work with. In one clinic setting where the entire team was trained and using the approach, we experienced incredible effectiveness and satisfaction in our working environment. One day I was sitting in my office alone, working on a project. A young man that had been working on the team for over a year came in and asked to speak to me for a minute. I invited him in and he told me the following story:

"I don't know if you knew that I used to be a drug user. Of all the drugs I used, my favorite was Ecstasy. It gave me a feeling that I was lovable, and that everyone was my best friend and they loved me. It made me feel accepted and like I belonged. I never felt that good at any other time in my life until we started using the Nurtured Heart Approach® here. Now for me, coming to work is better than being on Ecstasy because I really do feel loved and accepted and in a much deeper way this time. And now I know how to share that experience with others. I just wanted to let you know that and to thank you for the difference you've made in my life. I only had one other person, my third grade teacher, who made me feel valued like this."

As you can imagine, I had tears running down my face by the time he was done and I have never forgotten that conversation. No, I had no idea he had ever used drugs. I considered him one of the most valuable employees on the team. He was early to every assignment. He took initiative to get things ready to go out to the field without being asked. He showed leadership skills in getting his team together. He had great ideas that he contributed to every discussion that we had around our big meeting table. He noticed what others needed and went for it before they had a chance to ask. If there was something hard or inconvenient that needed to be done, I always knew I could count on him to be there. He was tall and good-looking and smart. He had a huge heart and connected well with the kids out in the field. It was hard for me to imagine that he had ever felt unworthy of love, recognition or respect. But many of us, even as adults, carry the pain of abuse or unmet needs from childhood around in our hearts every day.

As humans we are first and foremost social creatures, requiring respectful loving relationships in order to thrive. Children cannot get better in isolation just as grandparents cannot be healthy in isolation. Children will learn to be trusting and to receive and give love through relationships. In the words of Dr. Perry, "Healing and recovery are impossible—even with the best medications and therapy in the world—without lasting caring connections to others." Where you find or create that caring community is through all of your social interactions, at school, church, daycare, extra-curricular activities, family, friends, and neighbors. Each family can look at where the richest social environments are that they can tap into. Being close and connected can make all the difference in the world for both children and grandparents. Do what you can to foster your healthiest relationships, and learn to ask for help when you need it.

Healthy Peer Relationships

Caregivers are the child's first playmates but at some point friends become an important part of the socially rich environment that children need. Peer relationships are important for the development of social and emotional intelligence skills. Children with siblings who are relatively close in age have a built in peer system. When children have free time to play together, uninterrupted by hovering or overprotective adults, they learn and develop skills that they cannot learn by themselves, such as:

- Problem solving
- Teamwork and cooperation
- Leadership and planning
- Language and conversation skills
- Physical skills and cognitive concepts
- Negotiation and conflict resolution
- Increased attention span and memory
- Social roles
- Sharing and empathy
- Creative skills
- Muscle control
- Cause and effect principles

More than that, children begin to create their own personal nurturing community, a skill they will need throughout life. Children can be healing agents in each other's lives as well.

Children can be terribly mean at times, and when they are it can bring a training opportunity. Children, when trained and encouraged by caring adults, can begin practicing empathy in their peer relationships. It is normal to become more anxious with the unknown, and when children do not understand the behavior quirks of a "problem child" or they react to a heritage or race that is different from their own, explanations of the other child's life experience, condition, or culture can help to foster acceptance. Many times children with similar wounds will help each other feel understood and offer a sense of belonging.

Play Time

Many studies and reports indicate that as free play activities are dwindling for children, a complimentary increase in anxiety, depression, and narcissism is also occurring. Children need free play in order to become confident and competent adults. Free play is play that children engage in, on their own initiative. It is not organized, planned or directed by adults. It does not include the use of electronic devices. This kind of play benefits kids by allowing them to discover what it is that they really enjoy and helps them to become more self-directed and independent. Children who have plenty of time in free play learn to do and accomplish things for their own sense of satisfaction and accomplishment, not to please others. This leads to greater self-motivation and self-control, more natural curiosity and better problem solving skills. When children are allowed to make their own rules and make their own decisions they get better at it. They also feel they have more control over their own lives and their own emotions as they mature into adulthood.

In addition, children who engage in free play with other children develop social skills including conflict resolution and cooperation, organization and leadership, team work and fairness, sharing and compassion, and the ability to cope with stress and fear. While all of these things are important, the feelings of joy and happiness that come from free play are the most important, aiding in healthy brain development. The ability to play and experience joy, and to return to joy after disappointments enhances the development and strength of the Decision-Making Center of the brain. Free play would include such non-directed activities as:

- Playing with blocks, dolls, tinker toys, cardboard boxes, and other toys with no specific function
- Playing outside with other children
- Playing with children of different ages
- Free, imaginative play directed by children
- Lack of adult organization, interference and direction

While safety is always the concern of the grandparents or other caregivers, children should not be hovered over continuously. They need space to grow and you can keep an eye on them from a safe distance that honors their needs for autonomy and safety both. When they need connection, they will come to you.

Music & Dance

Just as music and dance can be healthy for grandparents, it can help to restore the rhythms of the brain and body. A rhythm and dance class will do wonders for children who have experienced neglect and that have developmental delays. If you are not able to spend the time and money on special classes, you can play music together and dance at home. Small children and infants love to be held and "danced" to good music. Soothing music will calm an anxious child, and joyful music will lift the spirits of a sad child. Remember that children listen to and learn from lyrics in songs, so be sure that what they are listening to contains appropriate, life-building lessons. There are many styles of music and whatever style they respond well too is good music for them. Do not be stuck with any certain type of music or believe that there is only one "good" kind of music for kids. Pandora online radio has some fun stations for children and many stations that you will love as well. Most communities have a variety of family friendly radio stations. It will benefit you and your family to listen to music every day, whether in the car or around the house. Music can be a central part of every family's life and will benefit everyone.

Massage

In some cultures such as India and Africa, infant massage is standard practice, and many studies reveal that humans are never too old or too young to benefit from regular massage. For children who are stressed, traumatized, grieving, or who have asthma, ADHD, or other behavior disorders, a 10-15 minute massage at bedtime is a wonderful way to help them calm down, fall asleep and continue to benefit the entire following day. My son fondly remembers his grandpa stroking his hair, which he would do at night or in church to help him keep calm and quiet. They called it "picking ticks and fleas" out of his hair. Sometimes he would climb up in grandpa's lap and say, "Grandpa, will you pick the ticks and fleas out of my hair?" What he was really asking for was love and comfort and a way to calm down. My sister remembers Dad rubbing her head when she was little, a tradition that she used to help her boys unwind at the end of every day.

Get the child's permission to massage and never force touch on a child. They naturally seek touch when they feel safe and connected. If you do not yet have this kind of relationship with the child, or for children who have suffered neglect and have not had the physical affection they needed, it may be hard for them to get used to your touch at first. If you have such a grandchild who resists massage you can help them get started by having them rub lotion into their own arms, hands, legs and feet at night as part of the bedtime routine. If they work up to getting more comfortable with touch, regular massage from you or a therapist will help to replace the physical affection they missed. People of all ages who do not get regular affectionate touch from someone safe can develop "skin hunger" and this adds significantly to stress and a compromised immune system. Kids will be happier and healthier with regular massage which translates to a happier, healthier grandparent too!

Safe Hugs

Hugs are also a wonderful way to offer the affectionate loving touch that all people need. In our very unsafe world, where many children are physically abused or sexually molested, some adults have avoided any physical contact in order to assure safety to children. But when we become so afraid of touching kids for fear of being accused of sexual abuse, we increase the likelihood that they will become victims due to emotional detachment or skin hunger, which will lead them to gravitate toward highly affectionate people, some of whom may be pedophiles. Any touch to a child with sexual intentions, obvious or hidden, is sexual abuse. Any touch from a person who is sexually aroused is inappropriate. The best way to safe guard your grandchildren is not to overprotect and isolate them, but to help them become part of a vibrant community. Take the initiative to meet your neighbors and invite people over who have kids the ages of your grandchildren. Do not let children play in rooms with doors closed or allow adults you don't know well to be alone unobserved with them. Reach out to extended family if that is available to you.

Children need healthy touch, and daily safe hugs are a must. So what is a safe hug? When you are an abuse survivor and horrible things have happened to you by abusive people, hugging may be very frightening. Children who have been sexually abused may not want your hug, or may want an inappropriate hug from you. It is important to know what a safe hug is. Just because you are safe, does not mean your hugs feel safe to your grandchildren. A hug is a SAFE HUG when:

- The child wants the hug—You might ask, "Do you want/need a hug right now?" if you are not sure.
- The hug meets the child's needs, not the adult's needs—NEVER say: "Grandma needs a hug. Please?" or in any other way coerce or guilt a child into hugging you. For an abused child this keeps the link between intimacy and power alive.
- There is no genital contact of any kind
- Adult and child are clothed
- Neither person is sexually aroused
- It's not too long—A safe hug lasts only as long as the child wants it to. If a child is pulling away, let them go
- It's not too short—Pulling away before a child is ready may be felt as rejection. Some kids might need lots of hugging and daily rituals that include hugging help them know they will get more
- You are not disinterested or emotionally pre-occupied—Get into a caring frame of mind while hugging. Remind yourself how much you love this child and tap into your affection and love. A hug is as much about the heart-to-heart connection as anything else.
- It's not too tight—If the child stops breathing or starts moaning in pain loosen up! Make sure when hugging an infant that their face is free so they can breathe easily

In addition to hugging, eye contact, a hand on the shoulder, a pat on the back, sitting close on the couch, or lap sitting up to a certain age are all healthy and appropriate means of offering affection. Co-sleeping is often helpful to children who are experiencing a lot of fear at night. In general, same rules apply to co-sleeping as hugging. Most countries around the world have regularly engaged co-sleeping with infants and small children. Babies and children who have someone to sleep with experience fewer sleep disorders. Infants might especially benefit from co-sleeping, which aids the attachment and bonding process, but be sure to look into the pros and cons yourself if you are considering co-sleeping and provide appropriate safety measures. Regular, safe physical touch is critical to bonding, to emotional healing, to healthy brain development. It is also critical for a child to receive safe physical affection in order to develop trust.

THE RETURN TO JOY

In summary, at the end of every interaction and at the end of every day, children need their caregiver to usher them into the Healing Circles by finding a way to see what is beautiful in them. By reflecting this truth to them you can continually bring them back to a place of love and joy where healing is possible. Practice seeing beauty in your grandchild and practice building a rich language of love, by verbally sharing the beauty that you see in them. I am not talking about physical beauty here. I am talking about values and character strength, and any efforts made to obey, cooperate and be a part of your family and community.

At any given moment, any child can be found to be exhibiting some positive behaviors or at least making efforts to do so. If you have trouble recognizing the values and character strengths that they are beginning to develop, you will need extra help with that. The best place I know to start is by learning the Nurtured Heart Approach® and the most accessible way for anyone to do that is to purchase the book, *Transforming the Difficult Child Workbook* by Glasser, Bravo, and Bowdidge. This book is wonderful in its simple explanations and activities that will help you identify and magnify the beauty of each child. With this new approach, a time out is simply an opportunity for you as the grandparent to take the time to figure out how to turn things around to get all of you back into the Healing Circles, back to joy. You will be amazed how simple this turns out to be. Here's an idea! Stop reading right now and order the book online. By the time you finish this book, it may be in your mailbox. You can order it through www. amazon.com or call your local bookstore and ask them to get one in for you. They are available at many Barnes and Noble and other bookstores already.

This very powerful act of helping a child return to a place of love and joy before going to bed turns out to be very important to the healing of the brain. Children who are still on high alert when they go to bed have cortisol and adrenaline pumping through their systems and this keeps their little brains from being able to rewire themselves in the ways that ultimately lead to healthy development of the brain. Bringing them back into the Healing Circles before sleep will increase the healing and rewiring of their brains and their ability to make consistently healthy choices. The quality of sleep is at least as important as the quantity of sleep.

LEARNING TO DANCE

It is imperative that you learn how to bring your grandchildren back into the Healing Circle of love and joy at the end of every day. At the end of every interactio, would be even better. You may need to take a break to get yourself back in first. That's okay. You are learning too. When you make a mistake, forgive yourself. Own up, 'fess up, dust yourself off and do it better the next time.

This return to the Healing Circles after any kind of emotional upset is a critical developmental process. When people do not have a path back to joy from any place of pain in their lives, they can easily get stuck in fear, depression, anger or other negative emotions that make long term relationships very difficult for them. This inability to return to joy can even lead to personality disorders and mental illness. The path back to joy is one of the most important paths to help your grandchildren develop in their brains and it may take some time for you to do it. It will also take patience, understanding, empathy, love, kindness, and absolute resolve to get some children there. You just need to know that this labor of love is a lifeline of hope to your grandchild. It can make all the difference in the world to their future. And you too will sleep better at night, knowing that you have just practiced excellent neuroplastician skills!

This whole process of maneuvering from the Healing Circles to a behavior problem and a consequence; and then back into the Healing Circles; should become a natural dance that you do. If you have ever taken a dance class then you have probably had to learn to either follow or lead. My husband and I recently took a lesson in Swing dancing. We both have done this dance in the past, but never together. At first it was a struggle for both of us and our dance instructor told us to try doing it with our eyes closed so that we could feel each other better. That really helped. If you are having trouble leading this dance of love with your grandchild, close your eyes and try overlooking their problem behavior. Just tune in and feel them with your heart. Use your heart, not your head or your ego, to step into their world and see things from their perspective. Ask them more questions about their experiences, feelings, and thoughts when you see them struggling. Make it a habit to be available for them at key talk times, generally early morning or just before bed, depending on the child. Give them the benefit of the doubt whenever you can. Forgive, love, and forgive again. Remember their Decision-Making Center is under construction and needs further development. At the same time, they may often be overwhelmed by their Emergency Response Center and feel as though they are trying to operate a semi-truck with motorcycle brakes, when they can't even see over the steering wheel.

CHAPTER 8

Is This Normal?

"You see a child play, and it is so close to seeing an artist paint, for in play a child says things without uttering a word. You can see how he solves his problems. You can also see what's wrong. Young children, especially, have enormous creativity, and whatever is in them rises to the surface in free play." ~Erik Erikson

This chapter honors the brilliant work of Erik Erikson in the area of life stage development, while acknowledging the impact that trauma and neglect can have. As he alludes in the quote above, a lot can be seen while watching a child play, as long as no one is directing the play. Sadly, many adults feel compelled to micromanage a child's play, as if there were a "right way" or a "wrong way" to stack blocks, to build a fort, or to cook a pretend dinner. Play is a child's work and free play is a "university" of creativity, initiative, and self-confidence.

I love doing play therapy with children, because children are so transparent about what is going on inside of them when they are allowed to lose themselves to play. When children are traumatized, it shows up in the play therapy room when they are given the freedom to use their own initiative and creativity to do their work, which is simply play. They play out what they know. Children only know what they have seen, heard, or experienced. It is always alarming to me when a child comes into the play room and does not know what to do, or lacks the interest in life to engage playfully in a room full of toys and props carefully chosen for expressive play. We can "read" a child's story by watching them play, and equally important, we can also read something of a child's story by their lack of play.

We have already seen how trauma and neglect affect brain development, but that's not where the damage stops. Trauma, neglect, and multiple failed placements profoundly impact the social and emotional development of a child as well. The fact that your grandchild was born eight years ago does not mean that they have accomplished the normal developmental tasks of a typical eight-year-old. Having the expectation that they do, when they don't, causes frustration for the grandparent and a deep sense of failure and rejection for the child. Neglect can severely delay all kinds of development in a child, because through neglect the child lacks the resources and experiences that would help him to develop in many ways.

On the other hand, many children have had to mature quickly in order to survive. They may appear to be developmentally advanced in many ways, but keep in mind that these children have missed out on much of their childhood due to these same circumstances. The best thing to do for them is to back up and only ask them to do those tasks which are age appropriate. They will need to back up and just be children. Avoid overcompensating and letting them off the hook because you feel sorry for their past. All children need free time and all children need chores and age appropriate responsibilities. Be sure to include both in their lives.

When neglected and abused children come to live in their grandparent's home, they often have not had experiences that lead to "normal development" according to Erikson's widely accepted life stage development cycle. Many times they have also not been taught the tasks that most children their age already know. Often there are serious hygiene issues, a complete lack of proper and healthy eating habits, and no history of chores, routines, or other structures that would teach a child how to do life. This chapter is for grandparents who want to parent purposefully and may be doing so from a disadvantaged point. It will cover what to expect in the different developmental stages, offer guidance for dealing with the unexpected, list learning tasks, chores and responsibilities that may be "stage" appropriate rather than "age" appropriate, while acknowledging the differences between the chronological and developmental ages of kids.

DEVELOPMENTAL STAGES

As you read through this section of the book, recall your own experiences of childhood and also your parenting of your own children. Which stages did you accomplish and where might you also need to learn and grow in order to best tend to your grandchild, and possibly your adult child as well? Examine yourself as you consider your grandchildren and seek ways for all of you to learn these life lessons and grow together. The human brain continues to grow and develop throughout life. As we mature, our ability to think and process ideas and experiences changes too. Sometimes traumatized children find ways to cope with life that allow them to sail beautifully through one stage of life, and then these very same survival skills blindside them suddenly in a later stage of development when they do not bring the desired effect. Often the coping and survival skills that work in one stage do not work in another. Sometimes children remember things in one stage of development that they did not remember before or because they begin to think differently. Then suddenly, the "smooth waters" erupt into "tidal waves" of trouble, either for them or for those around them, like you.

Due to our past experiences, many of us have become stuck in some stage of development that does not line up with our chronological age. Because our brains are continuously being rewired by experiences and relationships there are many things you can do to help your grandchildren make up for lost time. Each stage requires that the skills of previous stages be accomplished before moving on. Do not skip ahead to the chronological age of your grandchild as you go through this chapter because chances are they have not yet reached that developmental stage. Each stage is important and builds on the last one. On the other hand, some children appear overly mature for their age because they have had to take care of themselves in order to survive. They also need help in establishing a firm developmental foundation. Some children have not had the opportunity to simply be children and those who are overly mature or extremely responsible may also need help to go back and experience the stages they missed.

The ability to trust is foundational to all adult relationships and most traumatized children have significant trust issues because their relationships and experiences did not build a strong psychological, emotional, and social foundation. When it comes to developing skills of trust, it is much easier to "do it right the first time" then to go back and do the repair work. However, many of you did not have that opportunity, and in fact, most of us start recognizing that something needs to be fixed after it is apparent that it is broken.

In 2008 when I first learned the Nurtured Heart Approach® my two kids were already grown and launched. I had to do a lot of repair work after-the-fact and am still working on that today. Life is a journey, and going through it with a "get it right the first time" attitude will only set everyone up for failure and remorse. It is important to develop a good strong repair program, a willingness to keep trying, and a heart to forgive many times, both yourself and others. It will take a lot of patience and understanding to repair all the cracks in your grandchild's foundational ability to trust, but the journey is well worth it.

A FOUNDATION OF TRUST

In his book, *Whale Done: The Power of Positive Relationships*, Kenneth Blanchard and his co-authors reveal the secrets that whale trainers use to teach the amazing acrobatic stunts to killer whales so large they could easily swallow the trainers whole. There may be days when you feel as overwhelmed about raising your grandchildren as you would if you thought you had to train a 10,000 pound killer whale to wave a fin or leap from the water on command. There may be times that you feel frightened by your grandchild's behavior, your own emotions, and your inability to control either. If so, you might be interested in applying the same principles to raising your grandchildren that Shamu's trainers use at SeaWorld in Orlando, Florida. The very first thing that the trainers learned from the whales was that they could not teach the whales anything without first gaining their trust. You can't put a whale in time-out, take their electronics away, spank them, or isolate them and expect that at the end of the day they will follow your command and entertain crowds! In Blanchard's book, one of the whale trainers commented, "Shamu wasn't about to do anything for me or any other trainer until he trusted us . . . . Whenever we get a new whale, we don't attempt to do any training for some time. All we do is make sure they're not hungry; then we jump in the water and play with them, until we convince them . . . that we mean them no harm." In the end, it was the whales that taught the trainers the power of having patience and building trust. Both are required in training killer whales, and both are required in successfully raising children of trauma.

The other two big lessons that the trainers learned were to train by noticing and rewarding the positives; not just the "doing well" but also the "doing better." So any movement in the direction of improvement is an opportunity to notice and reward with lots of enthusiasm. If you are looking for perfection, for model adult behavior, in a traumatized child, you are setting the child up for failure. But if you notice and enthusiastically celebrate the efforts made and the movement towards mature behavior, that is encouraging to a child and they will flourish and grow. Focusing on positive accomplishments significantly reduces the negative behaviors that are often the focus of parenting. By redirecting the problem behaviors and giving the child a chance for a "redo" when things are going wrong, you give them hope and build trust and maturity. This is why I recommend the Nurtured Heart Approach®. It teaches a simple and effective method of parenting that builds relationship and brings inner transformation, not just momentary compliance. When you are parenting a traumatized child, patience is more than just a virtue. It is a necessary ingredient for success. And it turns out, trust is where it all starts.

Infancy (Birth-18 months) Trust vs. Mistrust

When a caregiver offers consistent affection and care, an infant will develop **trust** and the capacity to build and maintain trusting relationships with others. A lack of consistent and reliable affection and care will lead to **mistrust**. Developing trust is the foundation of loving relationships and is critical to developing many adult skills. An adult who successfully accomplished trust will have a sense of hope and the drive to accomplish worthy goals. Children learn to be trusting and to be consistently caring of others through their experience with trustworthy parents or other caregivers. If your adult children or your older grandchildren have missed out on building trust due to traumatic, chaotic, abusive or negligent care in the past, here are some trust-enhancing actions you can take now, regardless of their age:

- **Be patient**—It will not happen overnight. Building trust with anyone who has a history of neglect or betrayal takes a while.
- **Show respect**—Criticism, sarcasm, ridicule, teasing all serve to humiliate others and break down trust. Playing favorites or showing disgust also give the message that the child is not loved.
- **Have clear rules**—Be the adult, not the friend of the child. They should know that you are in charge and in control of yourself at all times. Clear, unchanging rules allow kids to know what is expected. Don't be a moving target.

- **Daily hugs and affection**—Children require physical touch and affection in order to build trust. This must be safe touch as covered in a previous chapter. Hugs, a pat on the back, rocking, lap sitting, massage, and wrestling, any touch that is safe and loving and combined with a positive relationship is not only good for the kids, but good for grandma and grandpa too!

- **Tell the truth**—When changes are happening, tell your grandchildren the truth from the beginning. Be sure to keep your conversations age appropriate and don't give all the messy details when that is not necessary—it may overwhelm them. Answer all questions in simple ways and if kids want more information, they will ask for it. Hiding the truth breaks down trust, creates feelings of shame and guilt, and causes kids to blame themselves for the problems.

- **Always keep your promises**—Kids who have had a lot of disappointments through broken promises have a very hard time trusting. Keep your word. Don't say it if you don't mean it or can't deliver it. Promising something and then not delivering actually teaches kids to be manipulative and to be untrustworthy themselves. If you say you'll do it, it is a promise. Let your word be a promise.

- **Provide consistent consequences**—When kids know what to expect and it is not dependent on mood or circumstance they feel more freedom to explore their environment. Inconsistent consequences create anxiety and rebellion, and break down trust. A word of caution: consequences should match the broken rule and not be inflexible. They should be reasonable and take into account the child's emotional state and ability to understand cause and effect. Overly harsh and punitive consequences can be discouraging and further traumatizing to children that have been abused. Physical discipline of any kind should not be used on children who have been physically or sexually abused.

- **Keep a regular structure**—Mealtimes and bedtimes should be the same every day, as much as possible. Having a bedtime routine is very helpful to kids. If they have visitation with a parent, it should be at the same time every week. When kids know what to expect, it helps them to recover from trauma more quickly. If a routine must be broken, be sure to offer an explanation and let them know what will happen and when.

- **Tune in and listen**—Be aware of the moods and emotions of your grandchildren. Take the time to check in with them when they seem stressed or upset. Let them know you care and always be ready to listen rather than advise. Just listening to their dreams, fears, ideas, or worries can work wonders for the child. Learn to ask questions that encourage kids to think through their own solutions to their problems.

- **Be honest and genuine**—As you respond to your grandchildren, be kind and be honest about your own feelings. If you have fear, sadness, or anger over what is going on, be honest about that but don't dump on them either and don't allow yourself to seek emotional support from them. You must have your own friends and support group where you have an opportunity to vent and get feedback, comfort, or encouragement. Do not vent or talk about sensitive or hurtful topics in front of the children, EVER, until you are ready to do so in a way that is respectful to the kids and to their parents.

- **Believe in them**—Rather than expecting the worst from troubled kids, expect the best. Be a source of emotional support as they explore their world and their own emotions.

For infants, feeding time is an important time to offer affection by holding a child lovingly, and giving them undivided attention, with lots of eye contact and attentiveness. This is not the time to watch your favorite soap opera or send text messages. The baby needs face-to-face contact during feedings, even if a bottle is being used. Humans are wired to connect and a lack of connection is frightening to babies.

Infancy is the time in which the brain is most like a sponge, soaking up about half of what the person will ever learn in their entire lifetime by the age of two years. Learning new skills during this time period is particularly important as there are windows of opportunity that will eventually close. The two greatest dangers to development during this period are depriving them of a rich variety of experiences or of overwhelming them by creating expectations beyond their capacity to achieve. For this reason, it is important to know what infants and toddlers need, and what is normal during each age or stage.

In America it is quite common for parents to begin early to drive their children toward independence, for example, by moving them into their own crib and nursery right away. Parents are sometimes cautioned not to "spoil" their babies by holding them too much or by jumping the instant they begin to cry. In many other cultures around the world, however, parents are more likely to have infants strapped to their bodies most of the day, and to co-sleep at night. In Japan, for example, children generally sleep with their mother's through early childhood, and continue to sleep with a family member until adolescence. In cultures where children sleep with their parents, sleeping problems in children are very rare. Recent research also shows that heart rhythm and breathing/sleeping cycles are regulated in infants by the person who is near them. When they are left alone for long periods of time it can be harmful to the development of natural body rhythms, and can lead to sleep disorders and other regulatory problems.

Early Childhood (18 months to 3 years) Autonomy vs. Shame and doubt

The developmental task for this stage is to develop <u>autonomy</u>—or a sense of independence and confidence of control over one's own physical abilities. Failure to accomplish autonomy leads to <u>shame and doubt</u>. Adults who have accomplished autonomy will have the will power to make wise decisions and carry them out. If not, they will exhibit dependency on others and/or rebellious attitudes towards authority figures. Also during this stage, most children are able to master toilet training. Traumatized children often experience a setback or delay in this area.

If your grandchildren have not had the opportunity to develop autonomy there are some things you can do to help at any age. Autonomy is having the ability to confidently make choices and act on them. If children are not allowed to fail, they will also not be able to succeed. These actions on your part will help them:

- **Don't do for your grandchild what they can do for themselves.** If you jump in at the first sign that they are having a challenge, they will not be able to learn and practice, and will develop fear of trying new things, or of failure. WAIT until they ask for help. If a child wants to dress themselves, let them do that, even if the colors don't match. If a child wants to try doing something on their own and won't hurt themselves or someone else, STOP yourself from jumping in and let them try it. I still remember how stunned I was as a teenager the day my mother announced to my sisters and me that she would no longer be doing our laundry. She had noticed that we were throwing everything in the laundry to avoid hanging it or folding it. With four kids, she had had enough. Once we had to take responsibility for our own clothes, we were much more careful about what we threw in the laundry. Of course you want to instruct your child in how to do chores and tasks, but then let them learn and let them come up with their own methods, which may be different from yours. As long as it works, who cares? Do not RESCUE your child, EMPOWER them instead.

- **Do not be a wet blanket!** If a child, or anyone, has a dream, let them hope and plan and pursue. If your granddaughter has a dream to compete in a beauty pageant, let her. If your grandson wants to try out for the high school football team even though he has never played, let him. If you let them and it does not work out, you won't be to blame and they will have learned some important life lessons along the way. If you don't let them, they may feel resentment toward you for their failed football or modeling career.

- **Do not fight their battles.** Be a shoulder for them to cry on. Be a cheerleader. Be someone who always believes in them. But do not try to take care of all of their problems. Solving their own problems will help them develop the independence and confidence in their own abilities. Of course if they are being abused, or are in danger, you need to step in. But, if you make a big deal every time they complain about something and rush off to "slay the dragon" for them, they will likely not want to tell you about other problems. If you show up at school the next morning and start scolding the teacher for being unfair, your child will probably suffer more as a result and will not want to be open with you about their struggles in the future. If a child or teen asks for reasonable help or appears to be experiencing overwhelming frustration, by all means, do what you can to help them solve their problems, but operate as a mediator, not as a rescuer.

- **Respect their "No!"** Do not treat it as rebellion or non-compliance. Children in early childhood begin to first explore their independence and personal power through use of the word "No!" They have just discovered that they are not "Mommy", they are separate individuals. The way they practice being separate is by asserting the power to say "no." Having the ability to say "No" is a skill that will serve them well throughout their lives. If they do not learn how to say "No" then they may become dependent people-pleasers who are also unable to say "No" to their peers when being pressured to do something wrong. Respect their "No" and use reason to help them understand they "whys" of life. Remember their brains are little sponges at this age.

- **Encourage exploration and experimentation.** Toddlers love to try new things with as many senses as possible. They will touch it, taste it, bang it, smell it, throw it. They want to know how things work. They experiment by throwing the same toy on the floor 1,000 times (it seems like) just for the joy they get when <u>you</u> pick it up. Turns out it is not always the kids that have short attention spans, it is often the adults who get tired of the toddler games. Hang in there, they are learning to explore and the more they experience your applause and joy, the more autonomy they will develop. This can be even more frustrating if you have an older child who is still in this stage. Be patient, this too shall pass. Allow kids of all ages to fail and to figure out how to solve their own problems as much as is possible and safe. Believe in their abilities to figure things out rather than jumping in to rescue and help.

- **Offer safe choices.** For a two year old, a safe choice might be choosing which book to read, which shirt to wear, or which fruit they want for a snack. For older kids, encourage choices that reflect their age and maturity. Allow kids to choose within the guidelines that you establish. I used to let my kids choose any breakfast cereal they wanted when they went grocery shopping with me. It just had to have 9 or less grams of sugar. Be creative and offer as many safe choices as possible.

Preschool (3-5 years) Initiative vs. Guilt

Think of this time as the age of imagination and free play. Through free exploration of their environment, preschoolers learn to take initiative and begin to attempt to gain power over the environment around them. If they are able to do this, they develop the ability to face challenges, take responsibility, learn new skills, and have a sense of purpose. If not, they develop guilt. Often intense or strong willed children exert too much power and are met with strong disapproval from the adults in their lives. This leads to feelings of guilt and frustration. Adults who have accomplished the task of initiative will have a clear purpose in life and will have the courage to take the steps necessary to accomplish that purpose. If not, they are more likely to allow others to make their decisions for them, to be overly competitive, and at the same time, to have a need to always be in control. This need to have others make the decisions while needing to be in control puts people in a terrible bind that is detrimental to all relationships.

During this stage, it is very hard for children to grasp the reasons behind their parent's divorces, drug or alcohol abuse, incarcerations, abandonments, etc. They tend to blame themselves and become insecure as they come to believe that they can be fully abandoned by all caregivers. This anxiety often gives way to behavior problems that increase the chances that the caregivers may in fact do so. Children who are hard to manage are often moved from daycare to daycare as parents try to find someone who can manage their out of control behavior. Other children take the opposite stance and become more mature and take on the burdens of parenting either their younger siblings or the parents who have become incapable of proper parenting themselves. Although these responsible children may be easier to live with and may not garner the type of negative attention of the children who are acting out, they are generally suffering just as much (or more) and generally harbor resentments or other harmful beliefs that will eventually come to the surface and negatively impact all of their relationships.

Here are some things you can do to help a grandchild of any age develop initiative in spite of setbacks they may be experiencing:

- **Free play.** More and more I see playtime being structured for kids. Video games, board games, and team sports are examples of structured play. If there are rules, it is generally structured. It is very good for kids to create their own play using simple or rudimentary items. My fondest memories as a child are of playing outside with neighbor kids. We lived surrounded by orchards. The trees were anything we wanted them to be. Of course create safety and always know where and with whom your children are playing.

- **Encourage goal setting.** Help kids set small goals they can easily accomplish. Even very young children can set a goal and achieve it. When I was working with a 10 year old girl who had not accomplished initiative I took her bike riding as part of her therapy. I noticed that she loved to ride her bike so I took her riding at the beach. I told her that when she met the goal of riding 5 miles in one outing that I would then take her to the park with dirt trails and show her how to trail ride the following week. It took her a few weeks and I reminded her of her goal each week. When she accomplished that goal we celebrated by stopping at Del Taco on our way to see the park where she would ride the following week. Smaller goals might be learning to tie shoes, read a small book, write their name, etc.

- **Do Community Service.** Make this a family event and do community service of some kind on a regular basis. Kids who help others develop more empathy and confidence, and the best benefit is the good feeling they will get when they do so. Doing community service does not have to happen outside of the home. We all do "community service" when we do something that benefits others. Even doing small kind acts, or helping someone with a chore that is not theirs, provides a feeling of accomplishment and well-being. Teach children to do random acts of kindness by your example. It is especially good for children of trauma to realize that there are others who are suffering more than they are in some way. By doing community service and helping some of these people, children can become more grateful for what they do have and develop greater empathy and the satisfaction of sometimes being a giver. The Bible says "it is more blessed to give than to receive" and modern science backs that up. We really do get more joy out of giving and serving others than we do out of receiving.

- **Reward with words not things.** According to research, positive attention is far more valuable in terms of developing internal motivation than tangible rewards. If you are short on knowing how to encourage with words, please make learning the *Nurtured Heart Approach®* a top priority. Develop a rich language of love and encouragement. When children experience success in accomplishing the details of everyday life, and when they learn that when they mess up it is not a big deal, they will be more motivated to try new things. This becomes fertile soil for the growth of initiative, which will last a lifetime.

- **Be playful and comforting.** Any caregiver that comes at a child with a demanding and annoyed attitude contributes to shutting down their development of initiative. Guilt is at the other side of initiative, discourages children from trying new things. Courage is having the ability to do something challenging even though you well know your limitations and your past failures. For example, what you are doing now in raising your grandchildren takes initiative and courage. If you are continuously annoyed with your grandchild or their parents, this contributes to the development of shame and guilt rather than initiative.

- **Finger paint.** It is much better for children at this age to have the freedom to create their own drawings, scribblings, or paintings, than to be given a coloring book and expected to color in the lines. They develop more confidence when you give them unstructured art projects in which it does not matter how they do it. Fewer rules are better, during this exploratory age. Finger painting is one idea. Play dough is another very good example of free play material. Tinker toys, Legos, the great outdoors. I am sure you can come up with many other ideas. How about mud pies? Or the plastic containers in your kitchen? If it won't break or hurt them, let them play with it. Give them opportunities to explore and try different textures, tastes, and activities.

- **You can't love too much.** Remember that when children are clingy, whiny, aggressive, or "attention seeking" it is not because they have 'too much' or feel 'too good.' It is generally a sign of unmet needs. Children want to please the adults in their lives if they believe they possibly can. Kids are taught empathy, kindness and generosity by how others treat them. They learn it from you when they see you manage your own emotions and while they watch you live out the qualities you demonstrate. You don't teach a three-year-old not to kick a dog by beating him or kicking him to show him how it feels. You teach by being patient, loving, and gentle with the child, even when he misbehaves, even when he has to serve reasonable consequences.

School Age (6-11 years) Industry vs. Inferiority

During elementary school years, the main tasks of children are to develop social skills and to devote themselves to academics. If children are successful in navigating this challenging territory they develop competency and <u>industry</u>, but if not, they develop deep feelings of <u>inferiority</u> instead. Competent is the word that best describes those who have accomplished this task. If children do not accomplish this, they will continue to suffer from feelings of inferiority through adulthood, and will struggle much harder to accomplish their goals. People lacking industry find it much easier to focus on task oriented activities and they may develop perfectionistic attitudes, or obsessive compulsive tendencies.

Generally, girls are ready to enter this stage earlier than boys are. While your granddaughter m., , be "chomping at the bit" by age 5 to go to school, your grandson is more likely to have an adverse reaction to it. If you do have a boy experiencing great difficulty with entering school, consider holding him out until age seven or eight if that is a possibility. If you are home or there is a daycare situation that will allow him to continue with another year or two of free play and exploratory time, he may benefit greatly from this and have a more successful experience by entering school at the right time for him. He will have a much greater chance of success in school if he enters when he is ready.

This is also a time when things can begin to go terribly wrong for children. Academic failure, harsh teachers, rejection or bullying by peers, and over bearing or punitive parenting can completely derail a child. Add to that a history of trauma or loss, plus grandparents who are feeling overwhelmed, and things can get very complicated. At this stage, if kids have accomplished the previous stage of **initiative**, they tend to become much more focused on rules and the need for them to be followed. That often is enough to keep them in line during elementary school, but by middle or high school, they may begin to act out more and more, either by withdrawing, giving up, hurting themselves, or by becoming angry, rebellious, and hurtful to those around them.

Remember that trust, autonomy, and initiative must be developed first. Some things you as a grandparent can do to help build industry in your grandchildren are:

- **Let them be kids.** Provide opportunities for them to get involved in activities they express interest in and at the same time help them to develop broad interests by continuing to expose them to a variety of experiences. But most of all, let them just be kids. This is not the time to push them into being a child prodigy of some kind. Even if you recognize the talent and greatness that is there, do not turn their special talents into a curse by over-focusing on one area. Kids at this stage need encouraging caregivers, caring teachers, and accepting peers. They need to have some place in their life where they experience themselves as successful.

- **Offer sports opportunities.** Every child needs to have the opportunity to participate in playing with other kids. Children in this stage make up their own organized team games and rules which allows them to experiment with winning and losing with little personal risk. There are also plenty of opportunities in most communities for adult led organized sports. Regardless of whether sports are organized by adults or by children, many valuable life lessons can be gained. If your child is participating in adult organized sports, the following recommendations will help this to be a valuable experience rather than a damaging one:

o Allow each child to choose their own type of sport and do not push them to participate in something they do not enjoy. If they find they do not enjoy a sport or activity that they thought they would, let them try something different.

o For kids under age 9, it is more important to focus on skill building (dancing, swimming, kicking, throwing, running, etc.) and simple games in which all kids have equal opportunity to participate.

o In any sport, let kids play for fun and at their own pace. Becoming an expert should not be the focus, and pressure to perform should not come from parents or coaches.

o Do not allow practice time to take over time to spend with family, friends, or homework. A couple of practice times per week for 30-60 minutes each time is good.

o Do not focus on winning vs. losing. Focus on effort, teamwork, cooperation, empathy, and skill building. Avoid criticism and lecturing like the plague as they snuff out desire to participate or create anxiety, leading to less chance of success and enjoyment.

o Focus on their success and compliance, giving lots of appreciation for that. Focusing on instances of non-compliance will only escalate problems and undesirable behaviors.

o Do not use this as an opportunity to fulfill your own lost dreams. Let them have their own. Watch to see what they seem most interested in.

- **Offer non-sport group activities.** There are many other groups or organizations that are wonderful places to help kids develop the skill of industry. You can check in your community for 4-H Clubs, Girl Scouts or Boy Scouts, YMCA, Community Parks & Recreation activities, gymnastics, dance, drama club, or music lessons that involve groups, such as band or choir. Help your grandchildren discover their special strengths and interests. Study them to see what they enjoy and what they are naturally good at. Everyone has something they do well. Provide as much opportunity as possible for them be around other people and to be successful at something. This helps their identity development and improves self-confidence.

Make sure your grandchildren are exposed to many different activities and events, such as art, music, dance, sports, history, etc. Look for community events that are within your budget. Many events, especially around the holidays, are free to attend. Take them hiking and gold panning and ice skating and fishing and to watch other people doing a wide variety of activities. The more rich experiences a child has, the more their brains become wired for success and creativity. If they express interest in riding bikes or gardening or painting, find a way to get them started with it. Many activities are hard when you first start so keep that in mind and encourage them to continue practicing until it becomes easier. Kids that are truly passionate about a particular activity should be allowed to continue even if they do not appear to have the aptitude for it, until they make their own decision to try something different. Remember that Billy Joel was told by his choir teacher that he did not have a good voice and would never be a singer. Many other successful people, as children, were surrounded by adults who did not believe they could possibly succeed in their area of passion.

Children who are widely liked by their peers are less likely to develop feelings of inferiority. Social skills can be taught and there are specific skills that help kids to be more popular or accepted among their peers. The idea behind "Social Skills" is to be able to behave in ways that maintain healthy relationships with other people. Helping your grandchildren learn these skills will decrease the chances of them withdrawing or rebelling during these pivotal years. In general, kids are more popular with their peers if they have: good verbal skills; are relaxed; know how to have fun; are inclusive when playing rather than isolating; are empathetic and even tempered; can lead out in free play; and express joy frequently. While popularity is not the goal here, being accepted by healthy peers is a very important preventive measure against becoming either the bully or the bullied. Remember that children learn by watching and by experiencing you, so whether you decide to do some of these with or around your grandchildren, it will help you all become better socializers:

- **Read to your grandchildren every day.** Read age appropriate books/stories of successful people or of people who overcame great odds to contribute something wonderful to the world. Read adventure stories. If you can't afford a vacation to the Greek Isles, read a book about a family that lives there. Find out what your grandchildren's dreams are and read to or with them about that. Remember to check your local library. Weekly trips to the library can be very enriching experiences. Also, being knowledgeable on many topics helps kids to be more conversational.

- **Have lively conversations at the dinner table.** Turn off all electronic devices at least once a day and have a family meal. Show interest and appreciation for the children. Make sure that they are both SEEN and HEARD. Adherence to the old adage of "Children should be seen and not heard" is not good for kids. Ask questions that invite stories and bring up topics that the kids are interested in. Tune in to their emotions. If they seem to be withdrawing, let them know that you noticed it and ask if you can help. Children that are spoken to freely at home have an easier time socializing with strangers and non-family members.

- **Lead an active family life.** The more your grandchild does, the more they have to talk about and the more shared experiences they have with others. An active, fun, family life, infused with good humor can be a tremendous boost to a child's self-confidence. Including their friends on these outings is an excellent way to help them build friendships. Be sure that humor NEVER comes at the expense of anyone. Teasing and humiliating for a laugh can be very damaging.

- **Accept the flaws and focus on the positives.** Every one of us are imperfect. Focusing on a child's problems or flaws deflates their sense of self confidence. Focus instead on everything that is good about them. If you can't see the good, maybe you need new lenses to look through.

- **Give lots of smiles and eye contact.** Kids who receive lots of smiles and eye contact develop the ability to connect more easily with others. This is why "unplugged" time is so critical for families to practice. No one gets that kind of personal affirmation through electronic media. A gentle but reassuring hand on the shoulder and a smile can turn someone's day around. When in public, engage with others. You can model the behavior you want to see in your grandchildren.

- **Focus on others.** Often the withdrawn or the rebellious are completely focused on their own needs and feelings in the moment. Spend some time each day watching the people around you just to try to experience life from their view. Teach your grandchildren to see things from the perspective of others, not to excuse objectionable behavior but so they don't take it so personally. Model this by seeking to understand your grandchild and by looking at the world through their eyes.

- **Be interested in others.** Rather than bringing up controversial subjects and trying to impress others by being an expert, become an expert on caring about other people. What others remember the most about you is how they felt about themselves when they were with you. People feel cared about when others show an interest in them and remember from one visit to the next little things they said or did.

- **Mind your manners!** If your grandkids have not been trained to use good manners, do not criticize or blame them. Show them by example and patiently explain what you are doing and why. Celebrate the slightest movements in the right direction. Sharing and asking permission rather than fighting and grabbing, greeting others rather than ignoring them, introductions to new people, asking for help rather than complaining, apologizing when you know you're wrong, etc. You can add manners books to your library list. You can teach these skills on purpose and make a fun family activity out of it.

- **Be caring and helpful.** It is not the huge acts of philanthropy that matter the most in relationships. It is the small caring acts in moments others may not notice that show empathy and kindness. Pick something up when someone drops it, open a door, listen to people when they talk, care when people are sad or upset, and rejoice with them when they have something to celebrate. It is important to do this without being a people pleaser or allowing others to manipulate or use you for selfish reasons. It is also important to give with no expectation of a payback. Being *genuine* in your caring is the most important aspect. If you are "caring" for your own gain, or with an agenda for some certain outcome, that is considered manipulative. Being a caring and helpful person to your grandchildren, and to others in front of your grandchildren, is the best way to teach this skill.

- **Help kids label and understand emotions.** By being understanding and caring of your grandchildren, you teach them empathy. The better they accept and understand their own emotions, the more accepting they will be with other's emotions. Empathy is a social skill that is learned through the experience of having others care deeply for you.
- **Teach the steps of connecting.**

  o Smile at people you don't know. If they don't smile back just keep on going, no problem.

  o Smile and greet people you don't know. A simple "Hi" is enough. If they don't smile or say hello back, just keep moving, no problem.

  o Smile, greet people and make a pleasant comment. Comments can be about the weather, something they are doing, or even the standard "How's it going?" or "Are you new here?"

  o Notice people that seem as uncomfortable and alone as you and reach out to them. You know how they feel and you just might make a new friend!

Adolescence (12-18 years) Identity vs. Role Confusion

By exploring independence, teenagers learn to develop their own personal identity, a secure sense of who he or she is in terms of a career path, political ideas, and moral and sexual issues This identity will be in some ways unique and in some ways similar to others in their family. If they accomplish this task and commit to a well-formed identity, they will have self-confidence and enjoy much greater independence and self-control. If they do not, they will instead experience insecurity, role confusion, and an "identity crisis". Adults who have not been able to form a true sense of identity will likely be enmeshed with their families and will be childish in social situations.

Has anyone ever told you, "Just be yourself. People will like you more." It leaves you standing there thinking, "Well, who else would I be if not me? What are they talking about? Am I not okay being the me that I think I am right now? Do I need to be some other me that I don't know yet?" If you have ever met a teenager and had the urge to say those words, stop yourself. They are not helpful. What teenagers really need to do is try lots of different things until they find what really fits them. If they are not allowed to experiment, fail, change their minds, quit a project or class mid-stream, get different friends, change their hair color, and a whole list of other things that seem very odd to the adults in their lives, they might just get stuck in a place that never really feels like home to them.

Young people who have yet to establish their true identity or their "place in the world" must have the opportunity to explore different styles, views, career goals, family roles, and moral, sexual, or political ideas, until they find those that feel right enough for them to make a commitment to it. This should not be someone else's dream for their life, but their own dream. If life circumstances do not allow this exploration, for example, if a teenager begins using drugs and alcohol to numb their emotional pain, that numbing process stops the exploration phase and leaves them stuck in emotional immaturity and a lifetime habit of following the path of least resistance, rather than following their dreams or achieving their true calling. If a girl becomes pregnant during her teen years, the birth of a baby may stop her ability to continue exploring as she goes into survival mode. Or if she has an abortion she is more likely to seek numbing behaviors due to the emotional trauma. If a person makes a commitment to a career or a lifestyle without doing this exploration then they may always have the feeling that they are missing out on something but not quite sure what. It is finally making a commitment to an identity that leads to greater health, happiness and life satisfaction. At this point in your life, being a grandparent has become a big part of your identity. Your commitment to being the best grandparent you can possibly be will be a benefit to your life in many ways. One grandmother who is raising her granddaughter because of her daughter's meth addiction, stated the following:

> "I have sacrificed. I have lost the 50s where I finally should get to live for me. Instead I play the role of a young mother. The other grandparents in her life play the grandparent roles, whereas I set everything aside to play mom and grandmother roles, but I feel no resentment about that. I do not feel that I am missing out on spas or bunko or anything. This is so much more important a role to play. Before my granddaughter

came into my life I enjoyed a full and social life. It is different now, but in a good way.

"I have hopes and dreams for my recovering daughter, that she dig herself out of her hole as quickly and painlessly as possible. It will take her more than a decade to turn it around. Most people by age thirty have family and home. She is a felon for life, just got her driver's license back, owes a lot of money, has a GED but little college, so it will be hard. I hope for my granddaughter that everything she has gone through she will take and turn into positives in life and be able to have a full life. I hope she is compassionate and makes a mark on the world. I hope she finds a good husband and has kids and that she does not play the victim role, but rises above it all. That's why I try so hard to keep her life stable. For me, I have no time for hopes and dreams other than to stay healthy and watch my kids and grandkids grow up . . . and get rid of my wrinkles."
~A grandmother

There is a pretty good chance that this grandmother will realize the hopes and dreams for her granddaughter. Research shows that even those who suffer losses in childhood can do well. Their resilience can help them to "rise above it all" and you as a grandparent can contribute greatly to Post Traumatic Growth and resilience by giving them a warm, well-organized family life and by offering them a support system and by modeling positive coping skills. To help your teens establish an identity that they can make a commitment to, here are some steps you can take:

- **Encourage exploration** of different aspects of life, such as educational pursuits, career possibilities, family roles, romantic interests, and major hobbies.

- **Arrange for teens to job shadow** any career they believe they might be interested in. Do not get discouraged if they change their minds a dozen times or more. The exploring is important as they put on different hats and wear them around for a while. One day they will put on a hat that feels right and then commit to it!

- **Give them the freedom to try** different clothing styles, hair colors, peer groups, hobbies and clubs, college degrees, etc. Do not be alarmed when they change their mind several times. This is normal and they will be better off if they explore some before committing.

- **Allow them to fail.** Create safety within reason, but do not step in before necessary and cut them off from learning the life lessons that will be much harder to learn once they have a mortgage and three children to take care of.

- **Encourage and support travel** to other countries or other areas in our country where they can experience a wide variety of lifestyles and ways of thinking, valuing and expressing themselves. Perhaps you can get involved with a church that has an active youth group that does mission trips. These can be life changing events for teenagers as they see people with much greater needs who have wonderful attitudes towards the adversity in their lives. They can also see themselves as someone who can help others and gain confidence and meaning by that.

- **Recognize your teens need to fit in** and belong to a group at school. Do not criticize their desire for the status symbols that go along with "belonging" in that group. Encourage healthy expressions of **belonging** and recognize the need behind the apparent materialism and role playing.

- **Watch for and celebrate any movements toward adult behavior.** Do not be alarmed by your teen's move toward activities that are tabooed pleasures which they may engage in to prove their independence from family restrictions. Do not change the rules or consequences, but do not moralize or judge your teen. Simply deal out the consequences without all the hype, judgment, and drama.

- **Provide opportunities for healthy, exciting adventures**—as many as possible. Most teenagers are curious and love to do daring or unusual things. It is better if those daring activities are associated with learning a new skill or achieving an accomplishment, such as running a marathon, painting a huge mural, doing a summer adventure or political camp, etc. Tap into their natural interests and abilities.

- **Do not react emotionally to their rebellious rejection** of family, social or spiritual values. They generally have very idealistic views which they will have to try out long enough to discover which of them are practical and hold up over the long haul. Arguing and criticizing will only create a tug-of-war that causes them to be even more determined to be different from you. Accept their ideas. You can always respond with, "Hmmmmm . . . Could be" or "That's an interesting idea. How did you come up with that?" Do not use sarcasm. Be genuine and be kind.

- **Do not react emotionally to their identification** with a celebrity role model who does not reflect your family values. This is a normal way to safely explore a different identity and generally does not mean that they plan to take on their values or lifestyle. It is their way of living vicariously while they are exploring.

- **Be as understanding and kind** as you possibly can while your grand-teenagers get through the trauma of the physical and sexual changes that are occurring without their permission in their own bodies. They may also be dealing with the rejection by their peers if they are developing sooner or later than the main crowd.
- **Accept their religious or spiritual questioning** as a genuine spiritual quest, not as skepticism and doubt. Unless they investigate the spiritual or religious views of their parents and others, they cannot genuinely commit to any.

CHORES AND RESPONSIBILITIES

The two main reasons that children of all ages need to have chores and responsibilities is: number one, that childhood is a training ground for adulthood; and number two, that children who have chores and responsibilities have greater confidence and self-esteem. We all need to be needed and when kids have chores they not only feel they are an important part of the family, but also learn that they can do things themselves, which is empowering. Let them know that you need their help to keep the household running smoothly, however, do not think that a huge number of chores will give them even more confidence. There are limits.

I am sure you have experienced very young children who want to help with everything. No bigger than a tiny mite, barely walking, and little Maree wants to help sweep the kitchen floor! Let her! Celebrate that "accomplishment" and remember that the true accomplishment is the enthusiasm for doing chores. What you celebrate grows, so acknowledging the effort and the desire to help that was behind the action is where you want to focus. Do not worry that your chore of sweeping the floor just took three times longer and was not done perfectly; you just contributed to the healthy development of a helpful and competent child, and eventually a responsible, contributing adult member of society.

Many people ask, "What is normal?" in different areas of raising a family. What follows is a list of common chores and responsibilities that will be important for your kids to know before they leave home. They will be listed in age appropriate categories, but please remember that if kids come to you not having accomplished what is normal for their age group, it is not their fault. Do not blame them or become impatient with them while teaching them to do chores and take responsibility. Simply start by celebrating where they are and don't expect overnight change. Just add a couple of new things when they have mastered the old ones. The more you offer positive feedback and celebrate their accomplishments the more confident and independent they will want to be. Criticism has the opposite effect, and encourages rebellion as they come to see themselves as "a failure" rather than as capable and accepted as they are.

No matter how old kids get, they still need free time to play every day. Make sure that your grandchildren are neither overburdened with homework, chores and extracurricular activities, nor bored enough to get into trouble. Having kids help with chores helps you to take care of yourself. However, I know one grandmother that stayed in her room in front of the TV most of the time and made the kids do all the work and chores of the house. For her they were slaves and I am sad to say that she neglected her role of caregiver. She justified this behavior through her bitterness over what her daughter had done to "screw up her own life and my life too." Since you are reading this book, I cannot imagine that this could be what you are doing. You are obviously putting effort into being the very best grandparent you can be and that inspires me to know that there is an army out there, over two million strong, of grandparents who have stepped up to the plate to give this generation a chance at a safe and normal life. I only wish there were more like you.

CHORES AND RESPONSIBILITIES—Kids will become engrossed in just about any activity as long as the goals are doable but a bit challenging and they are getting frequent, positive and clear feedback. Try making a list of all the chores that need to be done, broken up into doable tasks and let the children come and choose their next assignment and then check it off when it is done. You might even copy the appropriate list below and let your grandchild know that you are training them to become an independent adult someday. Kids want to grow up and they will feel a sense of accomplish as they see themselves getting more and more ready to be adult. If they need training for something they choose to do, join them until they have mastered it well enough. Kids love learning new things and they feel grown up when they work with you. Or you can have older siblings teach younger kids. Don't forget the frequent, positive, and clear feedback—for both the trainer and the trainee! Schedule a two hour time period each week where everyone in the family will pitch in and get all the weekly chores done. Crank up the music and have fun with it! Who said chores has to be dull?

Ages 2 and 3

Usually up until age 3 toddlers will be helping an adult or older sibling when they do chores. Remember they learn a lot by watching, which they have already been doing for a couple of years.

- ❑ Brush teeth and wash face as part of getting ready for bed routine
- ❑ Wash hands before meals and after using toilet
- ❑ Make their own bed (keep bedding simple)
- ❑ Put their toys away (can be easy with a toy box which does not have to be fancy)
- ❑ Put their laundry in the hamper and help pull it out of the dryer
- ❑ Help dust with dust mitts or sox on their hands
- ❑ Wash pet dishes or other non-breakables (kids love to have their hands in water)
- ❑ Help feed the pets
- ❑ Put books back or stack them

Ages 4 and 5

They may continue to need help but let them ask for it and then only do what they really can't do

- • All of the above with reduced supervision, plus the following with supervision as needed

- ❑ Get dressed (may need guidance for seasonal and occasion choices)
- ❑ Help choose their clothes when shopping
- ❑ Put their own things away
- ❑ Set and clear the table
- ❑ Help select and put away groceries
- ❑ Help prepare meal or bake goodies
- ❑ Empty a small trash can
- ❑ Get the mail
- ❑ Help with simple yard tasks
- ❑ Complete simple laundry tasks
- ❑ Help clean floors

Ages 6 to 8

At this age kids are becoming less excited about helping but more excited about becoming independent. Foster this growing sense of independence which leads to confidence by giving them lots of positive feedback on the skills and value traits they are using to accomplish their chores. Continue to offer help only as requested so that the child has the opportunity to gain confidence through mastery of a chore.

- All of the above with reduced supervision, plus the following with supervision as requested

  - ❑ Bathe unsupervised and comb their own hair
  - ❑ Choose appropriate outfits most of the time
  - ❑ Fold and put away their own laundry
  - ❑ Pour their own drinks

- ❒ Mop and vacuum (they may need help with this—don't push them to exhaustion)
- ❒ Write simple thank you notes
- ❒ Feed, water and exercise pets
- ❒ Put clean, dry dishes away
- ❒ Learn to answer the phone using proper manners

Ages 9 to 12

The two things that will help out the most with this age group are using the Nurtured Heart Approach® credit system and having a regular schedule that they have helped to create during a family meeting. Consistency and routine are key and remember you have three years to teach them all of this so don't expect them to have this down the month after their ninth birthday!

- All of the above with reduced supervision, plus the following with supervision as requested

  - ❒ Take care of their own personal hygiene
  - ❒ Clean their own room
  - ❒ Bring notes and homework assignments home from school
  - ❒ Take completed homework back to school
  - ❒ Take care of their own things, indoors and outdoors
  - ❒ Iron clothes
  - ❒ Use an alarm clock to get themselves up
  - ❒ Load the dishwasher or wash dishes
  - ❒ Help prepare family meals
  - ❒ Fix a simple meal or pack their school lunch
  - ❒ Scrub the bathroom sink and tub

- ❐ Help with yard work (should not be left to mow without supervision)
- ❐ Wash the car
- ❐ Use the washer and dryer (but should not be saddled with the entire family's laundry)
- ❐ Take trash cans to the curb and put away when empty

Ages 13 to 18

Children become teenagers on their 13th birthday, but they do not develop maturity overnight. While they may be as big and as strong and as smart as you (or bigger, stronger, and smarter), this does not mean they are as capable of handling the responsibilities of a home and family. Be aware of the emotional, physical and spiritual changes that are occurring for them as they become more involved with their peer group and with school and extracurricular activities. Try to keep life balanced for them so they do not become exhausted and overwhelmed even though they may know "how" to do everything.

- ❐ Set their own alarm clock and learn to manage their own time and schedules within the framework of school and family obligations
- ❐ Change and wash their own towels and bed sheets on a weekly basis
- ❐ Begin to do their own laundry
- ❐ Help with deep cleaning projects of their own and family spaces
- ❐ Be responsible for their own electronics devices and maintaining them

- ☐ Plan small parties and get-togethers
- ☐ Create and send invitations and thank you notes in a timely manner
- ☐ Write letters, send emails, manage social media safely and responsibly
- ☐ Change light bulbs and check smoke alarms
- ☐ Learn basic auto care (fill with gas, change oil, and other maintenance tasks) and take care of the car that they drive, including keeping it clean inside and out
- ☐ Vacuum whole house and change vacuum cleaner bags
- ☐ Clean the entire kitchen including refrigerator, appliances, counters, sink and floors
- ☐ Clean the bathroom including toilets
- ☐ Clean windows and mirrors
- ☐ Take First Aid and CPR
- ☐ Learn to babysit or to care for younger siblings or dependent elders
- ☐ Mow the lawn
- ☐ Plan and prepare family meals
- ☐ Make a grocery list
- ☐ Go grocery shopping on their own
- ☐ Be responsible for earning and spending their own money
- ☐ Learn to manage checking and savings accounts
- ☐ Purchase their own clothes
- ☐ Purchase stamps and mail letters and packages at the Post Office
- ☐ Get a library card and know how to find resources
- ☐ Be responsible to return books, DVDs, and other borrowed or rented items
- ☐ Notice when others need help and pitch in without being asked

One word of caution here: Remember that these are your grandchildren, not your servants or slaves. Everything should be done in balance. Teaching kids to do chores and allowing them to help out and be a needed part of your family will give them a gift that will help them for the rest of their lives. When they have a home of their own, they will be confident in their ability to run their own household. But children should have as much time for free play without being directed by adults as they have in homework time or chore time. If a child is coming home from school and doing homework for 5 hours and organized sports for 2 or 3 hours after school every day, that is not recognizing that children of all ages NEED to play. It is a big part of developing independence, confidence, imagination, creativity, mastery and zest for life. Play is the work of childhood so make sure that amongst all the chores and responsibilities they have time to play.

CHAPTER 9

Plugged In

"Excessive media consumption contributes to a reduction in happiness for today's children. Replacing connectedness to self, friends and the natural world with the pseudo-connectedness of the online world doesn't work. Nature offers opportunities to decompress, reduce stress and improve relationships, helping kids feel lighter and happier."

~by the National Wildlife Federation

NO LICENSE TO DRIVE

It's not just grandparents that struggle with raising children and teens. All parents are experiencing more challenges in raising their families today than in previous generations of American history. There are many more temptations and opportunities for getting off course than ever before. The Internet and the unlimited number of electronic devices which provide easy access to others and anything they want to put out there has grown exponentially in the last ten years. It has become an information superhighway. Do your grandchildren have a license to drive it? Do you? Staying balanced is a real challenge for all of us and it is hard to know if you have crossed the line from responsible and appropriate Internet use to Internet Addiction Disorder, recently recognized by the American Psychological Association as an official diagnosis.

When I was a teenager I talked on the phone a lot. It was not unusual for me to get anywhere from five or even ten phone calls from friends a day, sometimes more. I was connected. But we had one phone in our house. It was mounted to the wall in the kitchen and we had a party line. This meant that every conversation that I had on the phone, EVERY conversation, someone else was most likely listening in. One day I was drinking iced lemonade waiting for the other people on our party line to get off so I could call a friend. For some reason I thought I could hear them but they could not hear me so I was chewing on ice. Then one of the ladies on the phone said, "It sounds like someone is chewing on ice. Can you hear that?" I immediately hung up the phone, but knowing that others could hear everything you said in those days, and that your parents might know them, meant we were all a lot more careful. Today, there is often a sense of total privacy for kids connecting with anyone and anything in cyberspace, and there are few reasons left for them to be careful. Kids are usually more computer savvy than the adults and are able to hide things and hack their way around software that grandparents use to try to keep them safe. It is a scary world.

If a broken family is not enough to deal with, the information superhighway has kids scared, anxious, overstimulated and overwhelmed. To deal with their fears and the isolation that comes with too much time "plugged in" and too little time in face-to-face relationship with others, kids find ways to escape. If a child is trying to escape from fear and pain, they easily fall prey to temptations to use drugs and alcohol and to engage in risky sexual activities. Kids also escape by spending hours playing video games or living in the virtual world available on the Internet. Part of why this is appealing to kids is that it is something they can control, it is predictable and they are guaranteed an experience of success. When parents try to take control by confiscating the items, or isolating the child by grounding them, they take away their ability to survive if they do not deal with the root issues of pain, fear, grief, or loneliness that drive the need the kids have to escape from reality. This increases the fear and feelings of lack of control, most often exhibited as anger, which can throw the family into a black hole of conflict and out-of-control emotions.

By planning ahead on what times will be used for certain activities, such as computer and gaming time, you can help to minimize the amount of conflict over these activities. It may be hard at times, especially when you are tired or feeling distracted by other stressors, but try to keep to the schedule as much as possible. Of course there will need to be some room for flexibility, but this should not be a common, daily occurrence. Do not be so flexible that you lose structure, but do not be so rigid that you become unreasonable.

CONNECTION ADDICTION

One of the biggest areas of stress in families, and one of the areas for the greatest conflict between kids and their care-givers, is surrounding electronics such as cell phones, Internet, and video games. Many grandparents are not really up to speed with the latest and greatest in the electronics arena so it can be very confusing. I have received so many calls about teens that have gone ballistic over having electronic devices taken away as a discipline technique. Some have torn up the house and had to be removed by police. Some have resorted to yelling and swearing at their parents and punching holes in walls. Others have begun cutting themselves and attempting suicide when they have become so distraught over losing their ability to stay "plugged in." Indeed, the virtual world has become such a huge part of their identity that the virtual world feels more real to them than the real world does.

It's not just the kids who are pulled away from meaningful connections with those around them. We are all drawn to whatever is moving and emitting the most energy around us, and when that is on a screen, we are drawn to it like moths to light. I have the latest copy of *Newsweek* magazine (July 16, 2012) in front of me as I write. The featured article of this issue is "iCRAZY—Panic. Depression. Psychosis. How CONNECTION ADDICTION is Rewiring Our Brains." In this article, MIT psychologist Sherry Turkle is quoted as saying after interviewing hundreds of young people, that children are finding their parents "unavailable in profound ways, present and yet not there at all." When mothers are continuously texting or checking Facebook, even while breastfeeding, children get the feeling that they are alone, disconnected. I have had children in therapy complain of mothers who "love their friends more than me." How do the children know? Because some parents or grandparents are all too often tuned in to their electronics and all too often tuned out to their kids.

I see many families out together, but everyone, including small children, has a hand-held electronic device they are interacting with rather than interacting with each other. They are together, but disconnected. Often I hear kids cry out, "Look at me, watch me!" And nobody looks, or maybe just for a moment, but it is not what the child really needs. They need the focused attention of the adults in their lives. They need to see joy, not disinterest or irritation reflected there.

Dr. Turkle also states that people are reporting that "their phones and laptops are the 'place for hope' in their lives, the 'place where sweetness comes from.'" High school and college kids are creating alternate identities online when they should be forming their identity in real life. The social media profile becomes who they are to the outside world and when reality does not reflect this virtual profile it creates unnecessary depression and anxiety. Kids judge their own worth and value based on how many "likes" or comments they get to pictures they post. They also compare themselves to the images that others build in the virtual world. Disconnected and plugged in has become America's latest addiction. Even the shapes of people bodies are changing as they sit for hours, hunched over their laptop or cell phone.

Earlier today, to take a break from my computer and writing, I went out for a walk. While I was out, I saw two young boys, about five and seven years old. They each held a plastic, toy cell phone and were totally focused on clicking the little buttons like they were texting. I guess that now when kids play "house" they play that they are plugged in. When my kids were little, they would sit for hours, even days as we drove cross country in the car. There was a box of toys between them and they were well behaved. I know children today who will not take the fifteen minute trip to town if they don't have a DVD plugged into the backseat player or a hand-held electronic device in their hands. The temptation parents have to hand a kid an electronic device as a means of keeping them quiet and entertained so the parent can have their own online time, or chore time, or driving time—uninterrupted, is wiring the children's brains in a whole new way. Electronic addictions create the same brain anomalies that drug and alcohol addictions create.

Professionals are beginning to see people with symptoms of Dissociative Identity Disorder (previously known as Multiple Personality Disorder) as a result of their multiple avatars (a graphic personality belonging to an Internet user). And that's not the only mental illness or emotional disorder related to high Internet usage. In short, people need real, face to face interactions with real, breathing people who care about them. We all need that. Anything that takes us farther away from connecting meaningfully with the people around us is taking us further and further from health—emotional, social, spiritual, and physical health.

A recent study in China shows that with Internet addiction, shrinkage occurs in the part of the brain where speech, emotion, memory, and sensory processing occurs. The more time online, the more the shrinkage or atrophy. How much time on the Internet is considered "Internet addiction"? Thirty-eight hours-a-week is the standard used, making most of us "Internet addicts". The line between an addict and a regular person in the course of their work week has become very unclear. Many studies have linked a heavy use of texting and Internet connecting with increased depression, stress, and suicidal thoughts. Most people report being exhausted with Internet activities. Do you ever do like I do and dream of going to stay at a rustic cabin on a remote lake with NO ELECTRONICS for a month? Could be you have Internet exhaustion too.

CONNECTION BENEFITS

Don't get me wrong; I am not saying that all electronics and social media programs are not bad. Kids also gain some cognitive and social skills from time spent on electronics. Personally, I use Facebook as many people do to keep up with what is happening with my family and friends. I saw my granddaughter take her first steps and say her first words on Facebook. I missed both events in my daughter's life because I was at work at the time they occurred and no one took videos. Those moments are lost to me forever. The babysitter or my parents told me about most of her major accomplishments. Today, many people are able to connect with friends and have meaningful connections because of Facebook and other online social gatherings. Texting has become very common and allows families and friends to stay much more connected by having short conversations throughout the day. Some video games help kids to learn useful skills and gain aptitudes that will be helpful to them in their careers later on. Today almost every job has some type of computer, electronic device, or Internet skill requirement.

The Internet also allows people who would be otherwise isolated to stay in daily contact and feel connected. Many people post their daily successes and struggles and are able to have a large community of caring people respond to them. For them it is life saving and therapeutic. For all the problems it might cause, the Internet has some pretty strong benefits. Have you ever been under a lot of stress or feeling blue over something and then watched a few funny YouTube videos? During college when we were studying like crazy during exam week we occasionally got together for study and laugh evenings together. We would study for a while and then show each other our favorite YouTube videos and laugh until we cried. Then we could study some more and it helped us get through it. Laughter is still one of the best medicines for depression, stress and even cancer!

In our increasingly plugged in world, technical skills are a must. On the other hand, the Internet is the place where many kids lose their innocence by accidentally running into porn sites. The average age that kids stumble onto pornography online for the first time is nine years old. They do not have the emotional maturity at that age to handle this information. This experience can taint their views of sex and love for life if it is not handled well, or if it develops into an addiction. Many times parents do not find out for months or years. Pornography addictions in younger children, including girls, are becoming more common, and responsible care-givers should be knowledgeable on how to protect kids against it. There are some basic rules that can help you offer some amount of safety, although no system is completely fool proof. Many kids are much more computer savvy than their care-givers will ever be and there are many teens who admit to getting up in the middle of the night when everyone else is sleeping to sneak onto Internet sites where they are not allowed. It can be quite shocking to grandparents to learn that some of these activities have been going on.

ELECTRONIC LIMITS

If you are feeling overwhelmed by all this electronic information, you might be grateful for some simple and general rules that will help you to be balanced and responsible as you seek to protect your grandchildren without having to lock them up completely:

- Keep computer in a common room of the house where the whole family can see it and there is no privacy. It should not face a wall so that only the person on the computer can see the screen. If everyone has a laptop they can all be gathered up at curfew time and locked away until morning
- Do not allow kids of any age to lock themselves away in their rooms with the door shut on their laptop or a television set that provides the possibility of inappropriate selections
- Time online for any reason other than homework should be considered a privilege and should be earned through a credit system and limited to times and places that you permit. (PLEASE use a credit system that never takes points away)
- Children under age seven should not spend more than one hour per day total time on all electronic devices (TV, computer, cell phone, video games)
- Make sure you have login and password information for all cell phones and computers, including online pages. Stay involved with their Internet activities and make it part of your schedule to check in on them periodically. Kids that are isolated and emotionally disturbed are much more likely to become victims of online abuse or addictions. If you are concerned for their safety consider monitoring software that lets you know what sites they go to and any other activity on the Internet that you

might need to know to keep them safe. This is a controversial issue so research it well before you decide to take such drastic measures. Starting something like this when they are young will make it easier on both of you and will help them form better Internet boundaries, knowing that you are involved

- Be sure they know not to post personal information online that would allow others to track them down. Address, phone number, school, date of birth, and other identifying information should not be made available for the public. For example, help them with the security settings on their social media applications. This will force you to keep current on your computer skills, but doing these things *with* your grandchildren and not *to* them will help a lot.

- Talk to them openly about the value of their reputation and the image they create out there. It may close doors for them that they will regret down the road. Even completely decent and good people sometimes forget their manners at the keyboard because there is no immediate feedback for how people will take things. Remind them at least occasionally, that sometimes *everyone* can see things they write or pictures they post online. They will never be able to truly take something back that they put out there once others have seen it.

- The most current reports show that today's kids are spending on average 7.5 hours per day on electronics of some kind. This is compared to the four to seven minutes spent in unstructured play outside. The effects of all this? Behavior problems, low grades, an increase in mood problems and risky behaviors, decreased emotional bonding with parents, weight gain, and/or sleep problems. Instead of trying to keep track of how much time your child is spending, try establishing electronic-free zones, such as in the car, at the dinner table, during homework unless required, as possible examples. Bedtime should absolutely be an electronic-free zone. Take the electronics and lock them up until morning if necessary. These rules should apply to grandparents and parents as well. Electronic free zones should apply to EVERYONE in the house. Remember, they learn more by watching you than by hearing your lectures.

- Encourage your grandchildren to spend time with their friends and to include as much face-to-face time as possible in their friendships. This way the social media aspect will only enhance, rather than replace relationships.

- To judge if your children or family should be watching certain shows, moves, or playing certain games, ask the question, "Would I allow the kids to do this in real life?" If the answer is "No" then they should avoid watching it or engaging in it in virtual life. The more your real and virtual lives line up, the healthier and happier you and your grandchildren will be.

- Check out "Movie Night" at www.PluggedIn.com to find great movies with family activity and discussion guides to go along with them. Find out BEFORE you go to the movies if it matches your values or not. That way you can avoid the stress and embarrassment of walking out in the middle of a movie. You might not mind, but believe me, your grandchildren will!

- Avoid the extremes of permissiveness and legalism. An "anything goes" style of grandparenting may expose your grandchildren to inappropriate and damaging information, while an attitude of "No way! It's all bad!" can cause rebellion and an inability to make good decisions for themselves. You can strike a balance by asking questions, researching, and thoughtfully deciding what is appropriate, for whom and when. Do the research together so they feel included. A cell phone may be an important security device and a laptop may be necessary for school, or they can be stumbling blocks to security and success in school. Make sure you know which it is for your grandchild and act with proper and informed authority. Be sure that you and the kids are ready for the responsibilities that come along with each new electronic device.

- Be a good role model. Unplug yourself and get outdoors with the kids frequently. Spend time each day in physical activities, preferably out in nature. This is even more important for kids with ADHD. If you are a couch potato, chances are your grandchildren will be too.

In short, electronic media on its own is not bad. As a grandparent and as an authority figure in your grandchild's life, be sure that electronics do not rule your household. Do everything you can to make sure they are used for good and not to harm your family. Start by controlling your own use and being available for face-to-face relationship. Keep life outside of electronics rich and rewarding for your grandchildren and this will go farther in helping them curtail use than all the behavior modification techniques known to man.

Other Cautions

- ❖ Be aware of all the features of any cell phone given to a child or teen. Most of today's phones come with Internet access from which pornography or other inappropriate information can be viewed or downloaded. Know what you are putting into your grandchildren's hands and remain vigilant at your post and involved in their lives.

❖ Many kids text a lot. By "a lot" I mean literally thousands of texts per month. Be sure that you know what your cell phone company charges for texting and if you do not have an "unlimited texting" package make sure that both you and your grandchildren are keeping under your limit. Some parents have been surprised with really huge phone bills due to texting.

❖ For decades, auto accidents have been one of the leading causes of death among teenagers. Now, texting or talking on the cell phone while driving is making this an even greater danger. Make sure that your teenagers know that this is never acceptable, and don't do it yourself. Remember, "do as I say and not as I do" does not work with kids!

❖ It is a good idea to be "friends" with your grandchildren on Facebook or any other social media platform that they use so that you can monitor their use. Stress to them that it is inappropriate for them to put any photos of themselves or their friends in bathing suits, pajamas, or indecent or sexy outfits. Teach them to focus their pictures on *activities* rather than *poses*. That is one of the rules I have with the kids I work with. I only take pictures of kids *doing things*. I do not take pictures of them posing. It sends the wrong message to them and to their viewers. Also remind them frequently that even if they delete things they have posted in the past, their comments have already been read and cannot really be "taken back"—ever!

❖ It is important to ask people for their permission to post their photo online, especially somewhere like YouTube where it is available to the general public. Some people have been subject to lawsuits as a result of posting pictures without proper permission. Especially avoid posting pictures of strangers anywhere that they will be available for the public. Help your grandchildren set all of their photo album privacy settings so that only their 'friends' can see them. You should do the same if you are posting pictures of your grandchildren. This keeps the general public from gaining access to them.

❖ Be aware that it is an all-too-common practice for kids to use their phones to take pictures or videos of themselves which they send to friends. Sometimes, more often that we would like to think, kids are sending pictures of their own genitals and such. Even if they are sending it themselves, it still constitutes child pornography, which is considered a felony. Make sure your children know this even if you think they would never do something like that.

❖ Along those lines, any crude or sexual behavior posted online is a very bad idea. Many kids today are trying to outdo each other with their outrageous acts online. Even young girls that we would ordinarily never suspect are being influenced into some of these activities by peer pressure or by the lure of getting boys to like them. Kids should be educated and reminded occasionally that it is much harder to fix a damaged reputation that to keep it clean to begin with.

❖ Have your grandchildren delete any inappropriate pictures or comments that others post on their page. When they know that you are keeping an eye out, they will be more responsible and more respectful and it is a great way to train and protect them. I hate to admit it, but I have also seen parents and grandparents posting pictures of their babies or small children in the nude, or nearly nude, online. Make sure that you are not doing anything you would not want them to do to you. It might not be a problem for most people, but it only takes one who views it and responds inappropriately. It is not worth the risk or the message it sends.

❖ Have clear rules and appropriate, consistent consequences for broken rules, regarding all electronics in your home. Teach, expect, and require responsible behavior and if you are lucky, someday your grandchildren will thank you for it. If they don't, you can satisfy yourself with the knowledge that you did the best job you could to protect them and raise them up for responsible adulthood.

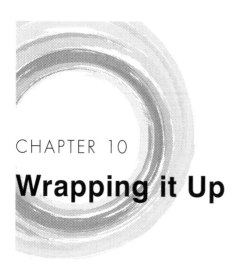

CHAPTER 10

Wrapping it Up

I packed as much information and as many tools as I possibly could into this book while trying not to make it overwhelming or too large and heavy to carry around. I hope that by this point you have a much greater understanding of why your grandchildren behave the way they do. I also hope this may have shed some light on your own life and on your understanding of your adult child. Unresolved childhood trauma is the root cause of so many problems in our world, but the hopeful news in all this is that, as Ron & Nancy Rockey like to say, "It's fixable! If you are teachable, you are fixable." The fact that you are reading this chapter means that you have read the entire book and that tells me that you are teachable. By learning and taking steps forward you have the power to change destiny for your grandchild and your entire family line. That is very hopeful news. Yes, you can and you do make a difference for your grandchildren. When you make a difference to one child, you make a difference for an entire community. By impacting a community, you change the world. Don't underestimate your value just because you get little or no thanks.

The follow-up book to this one has already been started and is going to be a collection of thank you letters written to grandparents from the grandchildren that they helped to raise. Often, grandparents are faithfully planting seeds even though sometimes both grandchildren and adult children can be ungrateful and resentful. Sometimes grandparents do not get to stay around long enough to watch those seeds grow into producing fruit trees. Most of the letters in the book will be from adults who are writing letters to grandparents who are no longer living. I think sharing them with you will encourage you to press on when it seems as if you can't. I include one letter here to give you a taste of how much it means to grandchildren to have a grandparent, or two, to love them.

Dearest Grandma and Grandpa,

You knew most of how terrible my childhood was. Thank you so much for fighting to take me in and raise me—especially on the days I was the most unlovable and rude. Thank you for understanding when I had to leave the light on all night and for not pushing me to talk about things I didn't want to tell anyone. I was not overly happy when you insisted that I exceed in spelling, grammar and English, but today I thank you for having high expectations and goals for me. There were a lot of trials and rough times to go through (sorry about that), but you hung in there with me and gave me the best chance at life that I could ever have. You never knew how many times I thought of suicide or dying, but somehow you always knew when I was down and you were right there for me, to lift me up. Thank you so much for giving me the gift of learning of Jesus, and for setting an example of what people are like when they know Him and follow Him, and share that love with others.

I think of the times you made me sing silly songs with you, of drives and picnics we went on, of grandpa puttering in the garden and showing off his prize flowers that meant so much to him. I think of grandma in her cute apron serving Thanksgiving dinner to all the friends and relatives in the enclosed patio, and her favorite saying: "You can never learn too much or have too many friends." She had SO many friends.

Now I laugh when I think of the time my cousin and I were going to sneak out to ride with some guys and we found Grandpa leaning in his chair against the door. He said, "Good evening ladies, can I help you?" We were so mad then, but now I'm really glad he did that to protect us. Your love and guidance has made me the person I am today, and is the reason that I have excelled in so many things. I wish I could have realized back then all the sacrifices you made for me, but I did understand that your love for me was real and unlimited.

Thank you with all my heart for everything. You were the most special grandparents on this earth. I think of you both every single day, and I wish I could hug you right now.

All my love forever, Trenee'

I hope that after reading this book, you have a much better idea of what you can do to make the most positive difference for your grandchild. If you know anyone who would like to contribute a thank you letter to the book, please send it to ThankYou@CourageousLove.org

I want to end the book with a simple summary to remind you of all that we covered. Go ahead and bend the corner of this page so that when things get difficult and you feel lost you can read the letter above and the book summary below. You may need to remind yourself often of your value in the life of a child who would be lost without you.

CREATE HEALING CIRCLES

What I hope *Courageous Love* has offered you is the hero status you deserve and the encouragement to continue to fight for the lives of the grandchildren you love. Because they have experienced such complicated family dynamics, heart breaking loss, abuse and neglect, it has broken their hearts and affected their brain development. Understanding the devastating impact of trauma on brain development and function makes it easier to be more patient and purposeful with your grandchildren. In addition to understanding, you also now have the tools you need to help your grandchildren experience Post Traumatic Growth rather than Post Traumatic Stress Disorder. Creating the Healing Circles for your family will give you greater confidence and courage. Think often of the Healing Circles and move quickly to get yourself and your grandchild continuously back into them:

Circle One: Safety, basic needs, and structure

Circle Two: Family gatherings that create identity and foster
                a sense of belonging
Circle Three: Clear rules, authority agreements and non-toxic
                relationships

Then remember that these Healing Circles are simply containers for the healing ingredients of *joy* and *love*, a powerful combination for delivering hope to children of trauma and to you!

Take care of yourself, un-break the hearts of your grandchildren, and re-write their brains for success. These are three of the key responsibilities of grandparents raising grandchildren in a high tech, high stress, unpredictable world. I hope this book has given you the confidence and tools you need to run this parenting marathon as well as the desire to read more books and to gain more knowledge, understanding and tools for living life on purpose.

FILL WITH JOY AND LOVE

Here are a few activities that you can do with your family to bring a little more joy into your home. Remember, laughter is one of the very best medicines and you can hardly laugh too much. The next few pages contain a few fun family activities to get you started. Notice what brings the most joy into your family and then come up with some on your own activities. The goal is to bring movement, love and laughter into your family. So get moving and let the healing begin!

FUN WITH CIRCLES #1: HULA HOOP

All this talk about circles is making me think of Hula Hoops. I learned to Hula Hoop as a child and on my 31st birthday I won a Hula Hoop contest at Bee Bops in Portland, Oregon. It is so important to have fun and get your grandchildren moving and here is a great family activity that will have you all laughing in no time:

> **Go to a local toy store and get Hula Hoops for everyone in your home. If they are too lightweight to get a good swing going, wrap them with duct tape. Get one for yourself too so that you can show them how to get inside the circle. Crank up the tunes and Hula Hoop to the music you danced to when you were in your teens. It will create joy and laughter and it is good, clean fun that never goes out of style.**

If you are short on room, you can all take turns with one or two Hula Hoops. This activity will serve as a metaphor or model for what you will be doing in life. You will create circles and fill them with love and joy. You will get into the circle yourself and then you will draw your grandchildren in. There you can have lots of good clean fun and laughter and their broken hearts can heal.

FUN WITH CIRCLES #2: BAKE SOME COOKIES AND EXPRESS YOURSELVES!

Get the whole family involved in this activity. You can mix up the dough and then divide it up evenly among yourselves. Even small toddlers can sit up on the counter or stand on a chair and help to measure and pour ingredients into a bowl if supervised.

Aggression Cookies

This recipe is great for adults and children who want to express some pent up emotions in a totally fun and healthy way!

This recipe makes about 3 ½ dozen cookies. Preheat oven to 350°

Ingredients:

- ❏ 2 Cups rolled oats
- ❏ 1 Cup all-purpose flour
- ❏ 1 Cup brown sugar—packed
- ❏ 1 Cup butter
- ❏ 1 tsp. baking soda

Directions

1. Measure all ingredients into a bowl
2. Here's the aggression part. Put your hands right into the bowl and punch, mash, knead, and squeeze until there are no lumps remaining. The more you do this the better you feel and the better the cookies taste!

3. Form small balls about an inch across. Place on ungreased cookie sheet. Flatten each ball of dough into a circle with the bottom of a glass which you cover in butter once and then dip in granulated sugar each time you press a cookie.

4. Bake at 350 degrees F (180 degrees C) for 10 to 12 minutes. Place on cookie rack and cool.

5. Pour a glass of milk and eat cookies. When you are full, take a plate of cookies to share with at least one neighbor. If you ate all the cookies, then exercise for thirty minutes while playing loud music.

FUN WITH CIRCLES #3: DO THE *HOKEY POKEY*

If you have access to a skating rink, take all the kids and go. When you get there, strap some skates on yourself too. If you can't get to a skate rink, don't worry. You don't have to be on wheels to do this fun song and no doubt you remember it well no matter how long it's been since you last sang it. If you are at home get the family together; neighbor kids too if you can. Stand in a big circle, do the *Hokey Pokey* and turn yourselves around. That's what it's all about!

You put your right hand in, you put your right hand out,

You put your right hand in, and you shake it all about,

You do the hokey pokey and you turn yourself around.

That's what it's all about.

1. Left hand
2. Right foot
3. Left foot
4. Head
5. Shoulder
6. Back side
7. Whole self

You can ad lib and use any body part that you want.

FUN WITH CIRCLES #4: THE SURPRISE PACKAGE

According to Janice Cohn, PhD, in her book *Raising Compassionate, Courageous Children in a Violent World*, studies show that helping other people reduces the risk of depression and anxiety disorders, and also increases social and academic skills. Here is a family activity that will be fun and helpful at the same time!

Children love mystery and surprises! Here is an activity that will give your grandchildren the opportunity to learn first-hand that there is a lot more satisfaction in being sneaky for positive, rather than negative, activities. Get the family together and have everyone sit in a circle on the floor. Talk about who you know that is going through a rough time and needs some encouragement. Decide on the person that you would most like to help. Then make up a surprise package for them and deliver it, without letting them know who did it. If it is a neighbor, you can have the kids drop it on the front porch, ring the bell and run off before someone opens the door. Find some anonymous way to deliver it and try to make sure they never find out.

FUN WITH CIRCLES #5: WATCH FUNNY VIDEO CLIPS

Families who share their online activities with each other stay more connected than those that isolate and retreat each to their own corner of the house to plug in. Get everyone in a circle around the computer with the best video capabilities. Go to www.YouTube.com and try these activities:

- Put "funniest video ever" in the search bar. Have each person choose one funny video for the family to watch together. One of my favorite videos ever was the "Baby Panda Sneeze." I don't know why it made me laugh so hard but I must have watched it 100 times. I shared it with anyone that would take the minute to share a laugh with me. (Make sure it is good, clean comedy and let everyone know ahead of time that if it is offensive it will be turned off immediately. Avoid bad language, nudity or sexual content, violence or injury related, and anything that makes fun of others.)

FUN WITH CIRCLES #6: VALIDATE ME

There are many ways to validate each other as a family. One of my favorite short movies is entitled "Validation" by Kurt Kuenne. It is just over 15 minutes long. Here is a great way to use it to improve how your family relates to one another.

- Use this link: http://www.youtube.com/watch?v=Cbk980jV7Ao or simply put "You Tube Validation" in the search bar and watch the black and white video of the parking lot attendant. The video is titled "Validation."
- Then sit in a circle and tell each other what you appreciate about each other. Go around the circle and take turns validating each other. Make sure everyone gets validated at least 2 or 3 times and that no one is left out. If a child refuses to participate just validate them anyway and ignore the fact that they are ignoring you. Eventually they will want to be part of this activity.

Make a habit of sharing as a family the positive things that you find online and make sure that you find a way to talk and share and laugh together. It is in these moments that bonding occurs—laughter, eye contact, stories, sharing—they matter a great deal to kids and it will make your life richer as well.

FUN WITH CIRCLES #7: ROAD TRIP STORY HOUR

Road trips are another way that families often spend time together. Unfortunately, since the electronic age has entered automobiles, families can be in this very small area and still be isolated. If each kid has their own hand held electronic device or DVD player then it may be quiet in the car, but there will be no relationship happening. Use this time well and your road trips can be wonderful bonding times. Be careful to use this opportunity to build others up and not to use this to criticize or make fun of others. Some children are very sensitive about being "laughed at." Be careful to laugh "with" them, not "at" them.

- Take turns telling "the funniest thing that has ever happened to me" and make sure everyone has a chance to be included if they want to be.
- Children love to hear stories about when they were little, when their parents were little, and when grandparents were little.
- Tell about how the world was when you were growing up and then compare and talk about the differences between "then and now"
- Sing songs and see how many different states license plates you can find.

You probably have many other road trip games that you can remember and teach your grandchildren.

FUN WITH CIRCLES #8: POLLYANNA AND THE GLAD GAME

Find a comfortable place in your home to make a "reading circle". Get a set of the *Pollyanna* books, which are perfect to read with your grandchildren. You can purchase a set of the *Pollyanna* books, written by Eleanor H. Porter at www.Amazon.com for next to nothing or find them at a used bookstore in your community. My grandmother gave me my first set back in about 1969. It is the story of a young girl who has lost both of her parents, but makes life better for herself and others by playing the *Glad Game*. Read just one chapter a night (if you can stop at one) and have your grandchildren sit on your lap or close to you on the couch. If you have a resistant child who does not want to sit with you, allow him to play quietly by your feet with Legos, latch-hook, Tinker Toys or some other activity that will allow him to listen while you read but won't require him to sit completely still. Kids can listen and play quietly at the same time. After you read the chapter with the Glad Game in the book, stop and talk about how you can play the Glad Game in your home on a regular basis. Then do it! Even boys will enjoy this book, especially when Jimmy Bean shows up!

FUN WITH CIRCLES #9: CLASSIC READING CIRCLES

There are many classic books that are great for the reading circle. Many of them are available in movie form as well. I am sure this is not an exhaustive list, but it will get you started:

- *The Little House Collection,* by Laura Ingles Wilder
- *The Secret Garden,* by Frances Hodgson Burnett
- *Heidi,* by Johanna Spyri
- *Sound of Music*, by Maria von Trapp
- *Anne of Green Gables*, by L.M. Montgomery
- *Are you my Mother?,* By P.D. Eastman
- *Where the Wild Things Are*, by Maurice Sendak
- *Amelia Bedelia*, by Peggy Parish
- *Little Women*, by Louisa May Alcott
- *Where the Lilies Bloom,* by Vera Cleaver
- *Daddy-Long-Legs,* by Jean Webster
- *The Homecoming series*, by Cynthia Voigt
- *Sarah Plain and Tall* series, by Patricia MacLachlan
- *Mandy*, by Julie Andrews Edwards
- *The American Girl* Series, by Meg Cabot
- *Hatchet*, by Gary Paulsen
- *A Separate Peace*, by John Knowles
- *The Adventures of Tom Sawyer,* by Mark Twain
- *The Adventures of Huckleberry Finn,* by Mark Twain
- *The Little Prince*, by Antoine de Saint-Exupery
- *Little Lord Fauntleroy*, by Frances Hodgson Burnett
- *The American Boy's Handy Book,* by Daniel C. Beard
- *A Boy at War* series, by Harry Mazer
- *The First Edition of the Boy Scout Handbook*

- *The Red Badge of Courage,* by Stephen Crane
- *The Chronicles of Narnia*, by C.S. Lewis
- *Canoeing with the Cree*, by Eric Sevareid
- *Lord of the Flies*, by William Golding
- *Treasure Island*, by Robert Louis Stevenson
- *James and the Giant Peach*, by Roald Dahl
- *Holes*, by Louis Sachar
- *The Indispensable Calvin and Hobbes: A Calvin and Hobbes Treasury*, by Bill Watterson
- *Harris and Me*, by Gary Paulsen

I am sure that you remember the books that you loved as a child as well. Share those with your grandchildren and allow them to choose some they are interested in from the library. Choose reading material carefully and remember, garbage in—garbage out! In the next section you will read a list of books that are recommended for you if you want more information on any of the topics in this book. I hope that this is one of many books that you read to make your life and your grandchild's life better. Thank you for reading *Courageous Love*! Laura

RECOMMENDED READING

RECOMMENDED BOOK LIST

Reading all of these books is not necessary. However, if you find you are really interested in any of the topics covered in this book, or you need more help in any specific area, here is where you can find more information so that you can dive in and really study and understand it.

A Child Called It, by Dave Pelzer

A Man Named Dave, by Dave Pelzer

*ADHD Without Drugs: A Guide to the Natural Care of Children with ADHD, b*y Sanford Newmark, MD

Authentic Happiness, by Martin E. P. Seligman

Belonging: Overcoming Rejection and Discovering the Freedom of Acceptance, by Ron & Nancy Rockey

Better Than I Ever Expected: Straight Talk about Sex After Sixty, by Joan Price

Beyond Consequences, Logic, and Control: A Love-Based Approach to Helping Attachment-Challenged

Children with Severe Behaviors, by Heather T. Forbes and B. Bryan Post

Dare to Love: The Art of Merging Science and Love into Parenting Children with Difficult Behaviors, by Heather T. Forbes

DIVORCE POISON: How to Protect Your Family from Bad-mouth and Brainwashing, by Richard A. Warshak

Flourish, by Martin E.P. Seligman

Forgive & Love Again: Healing Wounded Relationships, by John Nieder & Thomas M. Thompson

From Fear to Love, by Bryan Post

Grandparents as Parents, Second Edition: A Survival Guide for Raising a Second Family, by Silvie de Toledo LCSW & Deborah Edler Brown

Healing the Shame that Binds You, by John Bradshaw

Healing Your Emotional Self: A Powerful Program to Help You Raise Your Self-Esteem, Quiet Your Inner

Critic, and Overcome Your Shame, by Beverly Engel

Naked at Our Age: Talking Out Loud about Senior Sex, by Joan Price

Necessary Endings: The employees, businesses and relationships that all of us have to give up in order to move forward, by Henry Cloud

Notching Up Workbook, by Lisa Bravo with Howard Glasser, and co-authors

Notching Up, by Howard Glasser, and co-authors

Pollyanna Grows Up, by Eleanor Porter

Pollyanna, by Eleanor Porter

Reclaim Your Family from Addiction: How couples and families recover love and meaning, by Craig Nakken

SAFE PEOPLE: How To Find Relationships That Are Good For You And Avoid Those That Aren't, by Dr. Henry Cloud and Dr. John Townsend

Setting Boundaries with Your Adult Children: Six Steps to Hope and Healing for Struggling Parents, by Allison Bottke

Sometimes It's Grandmas and Grandpas Not Mommies and Daddies, by Gayle Byrne

The 7 Habits of Highly Effective Families, by Stephen R. Covey

The Betrayal Bond: Breaking Free of Exploitive Relationships, by Patrick J. Carnes, Ph.D.

The Great Behavior Breakdown, by Bryan Post

The Language of Letting Go: Daily Meditations for Codependents, by Melody Beattie

The Lies We Believe, by Chris Thurman

The No-Cry Sleep Solution: Gentle Ways to Help Your Baby Sleep Through the Night, by Elizabeth Pantley

The No-Cry Sleep Solution for Toddlers and Preschoolers: Gentle Ways to Stop Bedtime Battles and Improve Your Child's Sleep, by Elizabeth Pantley

The Sneaky Chef: Simple Strategies for Hiding Healthy Foods in Kids Favorite Meals, by Missy Chase Lapine

The Sneaky Chef to the Rescue: 101 All-New Recipes and "Sneaky" Tricks for Creating Healthy Meals Kids Will Love, by Missy Chase Lapine

The Speedy, Sneaky Chef: Quick, Healthy Fixes for Your Favorite Packaged Foods, by Missy Chase Lapine

Transforming the Difficult Child Workbook, by Howard Glasser and co-authors

Transforming the Difficult Child, by Howard Glasser and co-authors

When a Child You Love is Grieving, by Harold Ivan Smith

When Dad Hurts Mom: Helping Your Children Heal the Wounds of Witnessing Abuse, by Lundy Bancroft

Why Does He Do That? by Lundy Bancroft

Writing to Heal: A Guided Journal for Recovering from Trauma and Emotional Upheaval, by James W. Pennebaker

RECOMMENDED ONLINE RESOURCES

I hope you will stay in touch with me by going to the Courageous Love Facebook page at www.facebook.com/courageouslove. You will see updates, encouragement, and links to other helpful resources by clicking "Like" on the face-page.

AARP has a wealth of information for grandparents raising grandchildren. I have found their website to be the most helpful in practical, every day ways and they have links to resources in every state. Get started by going to this link, or you can simply search online for "AARP grandfamilies" and it will take you there.

> http://www.aarp.org/relationships/friends-family/info-08-2011/grandfamilies-guide-getting-started.html

Other great web sites dealing directly with family or children and trauma issues:

www.attachmenttraumanetwork.com

> A great website for more information on attachment issues as they relate to trauma in children. Their mission is to promote family healing

www.beyondconsequences.com

> Beyond Consequences Institute, Heather T. Forbes, LCSW—Resources and online training

www.childrenandnature.org

Encouragement and resources for getting your family outside

www.childrenssuccessfoundation.com

The Nurtured Heart Approach®—Resources and online training

www.focusonthefamily.com

A wealth of information to help families thrive—from a Christian perspective.

One caution here: When you are dealing with a traumatized child, spanking (which they recommend in some cases) is more likely to be a trauma triggering event than an effective discipline method. I recommend not spanking any traumatized child, but if you insist on spanking any child, please follow the seven steps they outline

www.grandparents.com

This website has great articles for grandparents on the topics of: Grandkids; Family & Relationships; Food & Leisure; Health & Wellbeing; Money & Work www.grandparentsasparents.org

GAP offers resources, services, and programs to help grandparents and other relatives who are raising at-risk relative children.

www.griefspeaks.com

Excellent source of information on grief and healing

www.pluggedin.com

Offers family friendly advice on selecting appropriate movies, videos, music, TV, and games

www.postinstitute.com

"A love based family-centered approach for helping children with challenging behaviors" Resources and a home study training program based on the work of Dr. Bryan Post

www.raisingyourgrandchildren.com

An online support group and resource founded and run by Karen Best Wright, a grandmother who raised her granddaughters for six years

www.theartofmanliness.com

A great resource for raising boys, especially if you are a grandmother raising a boy alone

http://tlcinstitute.org/PTRCtrauma.html

Lots of information and resources for parents who have children suffering from grief and trauma. Includes many activities to help children heal and feel safe

REFERENCE SOURCES

What follows are lists of books, journal articles and web sites that I read in my search for the best information possible in writing this book. These may or may not show up on the recommended reading list because many of them are frankly burdensome or not well suited for the lay reader. While studying for my Master's degree in Marital and Family Therapy, I was required to read as many as 20 or more books per quarter. In addition I am sure I sat through more than 400 lectures by brilliant professors and other experts. Some of the information that I read then remains embedded in my brain and naturally flows out as I write without my being conscious of where I learned it. That education will cost me the $140,000 I currently have in student loan debt plus any additional interest that accrues in the next thirty years while I am paying it off. I wrote this book so that you do not have to go through such extreme measures for information that I think should be readily and affordably available to everyone. I hope that my investment in time and money pays off for you and your family and that this book, COURAGEOUS LOVE, whets your appetite for more learning. I did not include footnotes because personally I find all the numbers and notes distracting. With easy access to so much information through search engines, you will be able to find anything you really want to pursue on your own personal journey. Nonetheless, I have provided as complete a reference list as I possibly could.

BOOKS REFERENCED

A Child Called It, by Dave Pelzer

A Gift to Myself: A Personal Workbook and Guide to Healing the Child Within, by Charles L. Whitfield MD

ADHD Without Drugs: A Guide to the Natural Care of Children with ADHD, by Sanford Newmark, MD

AFFECT REGULATION and the Repair of the Self, by Allan N. Schore

Authentic Happiness, by Martin E. P. Seligman

Belonging: Overcoming Rejection and Discovering the Freedom of Acceptance, by Ron & Nancy Rockey

Bold Love, by Dan B. Allender & Tremper Longman III

Born to Run, by Christopher McDougall

DIVORCE POISON: How to Protect Your Family from Bad-mouth and Brainwashing, by Richard A. Warshak

Family Evaluation: The role of the family as an emotional unit that governs individual behavior and development, by Murray Bowen and Michael E. Kerr

Flourish, by Martin E.P. Seligman

Forgive & Love Again: Healing Wounded Relationships, by John Nieder & Thomas M. Thompson

Ghosts from the Nursery: Tracing the Roots of Violence, by Robin Karr-Morse and Meredith S. Wiley

Healing the Child Within: Discovery and Recovery for Adult Children of Dysfunctional Families, by Charles L. Whitfield MD

Heart Connection: Science Reveals the Secrets of True Intimacy, by Nancy & Ron Rockey, PhD

Joy Bonds, by E. James Wilder (DVD)

Necessary Endings: The employees, businesses and relationships that all of us have to give up in order to move forward, by Henry Cloud

Pollyanna, by Eleanor Porter

Pre-Parenting: Nurturing Your Child from Conception, by Thomas R. Verny and Pamela Weintraub

Raising Compassionate, Courageous Children in a Violent World, by Janice Cohn, PhD

Stumbling on Happiness, by Daniel Gilbert

The 7 Habits of Highly Effective Families, by Stephen R. Covey

The Boy Who Was Raised as a Dog: And Other Stories from a Child Psychiatrist's Notebook, by Bruce Perry and Maia Szalavitz

The Developing Mind: How Relationships and the Brain Interact to Shape Who We Are, by Daniel J. Siegel

The Healing Power of Play: Working with Abused Children, by Eliana Gil

The Hour that Matters Most: The Surprising Power of the Family Meal, by Les & Leslie Parrott with Stephanie Allen and Tina Kuna

The Language of Letting Go: Daily Meditations for Codependents, by Melody Beattie

The Lies We Believe, by Chris Thurman

The Secret Life of the Unborn Child: How You Can Prepare Your Baby for a Happy, Healthy Life, by Thomas Verny and John Kelly

The Tiniest Humans, by Jerome Lejeune and Albert William Liley

Too Scared to Cry: How Trauma Affects Children . . . and Ultimately Us All, by Lenore Terr, MD

Transforming the Difficult Child, by Howard Glasser and co-authors

Trauma and Addiction: Ending the Cycle of Pain Through Emotional Literacy, by Tian Dayton, Ph.D.

Trauma and Recovery, by Judith Herman

Vital Involvement in Old Age, by Erik Erikson, Joan Erikson, Helen Kivnick

Whale Done: The Power of Positive Relationships, by Kenneth Blanchard, et.al.

When a Child You Love is Grieving, by Harold Ivan Smith

When Dad Hurts Mom: Helping Your Children Heal the Wounds of Witnessing Abuse, by Lundy Bancroft

Who Switched Off My Brain: Controlling Toxic Thoughts and Emotions, by Dr. Caroline Leaf

Why Does He Do That? by Lundy Bancroft

Writing to Heal: A Guided Journal for Recovering from Trauma and Emotional Upheaval, by James W. Pennebaker

JOURNAL ARTICLES REFERENCED

Bandura, A., Ross, D., and Ross, S.A. (1961). Transmission of Aggression Through Imitation of Aggressive Models. *Journal of Abnormal and Social Psychology*, 63, 575-582.

Beazley, J.M. (1980). Assessment of life in utero. *Nursing Times*, 76 (19). 825-828.

Berrick, J.D. (1998). When children cannot remain home: Foster family care and kinship care. *Protecting Children from Abuse and Neglect, 8(1),* 72-87.

Bowling, A. and Grundy, E. (1998). The Association between Social Networks and Mortality in Later Life. *Reviews in Clinical Gerontology* 8, 353-361.

Brooks, D., & Barth, R. P. (1998). Characteristics and outcomes of drug-exposed and non drug-exposed children in kinship and non-relative foster care. *Children and Youth Services Review, 20*, 475-501.

Chipman, R., Wells, S. W., & Johnson, M. A. (2002). The meaning of quality in kinship foster care: Caregiver, child, and worker prospective. *Families in Society, 85(5/6)*, 508-521.

Dubowitz, H., Feigelman, S., Harrington, D. & Starr, R. H. (1994). Children in kinship care: How do they fare? *Children and Youth Services Review, 16*, 85-106.

Ehrle, J., & Geen, R. (2002). Kin and non-kin foster care: Findings from a national survey. *Children and Youth Services Review, 24(1)*, 15-35.

Gebel, T. J. (1996). Kinship care and nonrelative family foster care: A comparison of caregiver attributes and attitudes. *Child Welfare, 75*, 5-18.

Geen, R. & Berrick, J.D. (2002). Kinship Care: An evolving service delivery option. *Ci.. ..ren and Youth Review, 24,* 1-14.

Glanville, J., Sikkink, D., and Hernandez, E. (2008). Religious Involvement and Educational Outcomes: The Role of Social Capital and Extracurricular Participation. *The Sociological Quarterly*, 49: 105-137

Gunstad, J., Paul, R.H., Spitznagel, M.B., Cohen, R.A., Williams, L.M., Kohn, M., Gordon, E. (2005). Exposure to early life trauma is associated with adult obesity. *Psychiatry Research*. 142 (1), 31-37.

Keyes, C. L. M. & Waterman, M. B. (2003). Dimensions of well-being and mental health in adulthood. In Bornstein, M. H., Keyes, C. L. M., and Moore, K. A., *Well-being: Positive development across the life course*. Mahwah, NJ: Lawrence Erlbaum Associates.

Kiecolt-Glaser, J. K., McGuire, L., Robles, T. F., and Glaser, R. (2002). Emotions, morbidity, and mortality: New perspectives from psychoneuroimmunology. *Annual Review of Psychology*, 53, 83-107.

Kross, E., Berman, M.G., Mischel, W., Smith, E.E., and Wager, T.D., (2011). Social rejection shares somatosensory representations with physical pain, *Proceedings of the National Academy of Sciences of the United States of America,* 108, No. 15, 6270-6275.

Lin, F., Zhou, Y., Du, Y., Qin, L., Zhao, Z., et al. (2012). Abnormal White Matter Integrity in Adolescents with Internet Addiction Disorder: A Tract-Based Spatial Statistics Study. *PLoS ONE* 7(1): e30253. doi:10.1371/journal.pone.0030253

Lorkovich, T. W., Piccola, T., Groza, V., Brindo, M. E., & Marks, J. (2004). Kinship care and permanence: Guiding principles for policy and practice. *Families in Society, 85(2)*, 159-164.

Oman, D., Thoresen, C.E. and McMahon, K. (1999). Volunteerism and Mortality Among the Community Dwelling Elderly. *Journal of Health Psychology* 4. No. 3, 301-316.

Pearce, L.D., Denton, M.L. (2009) Religiosity in the Lives of Youth. *International Handbook on Youth and Young Adulthood*, Routledge Press.

Pennebaker, J.W., Kiecolt-Glaser, J., & Glaser, R. (1988). Disclosure of traumas and immune function: Health implications for psychotherapy. *Journal of Consulting and Clinical Psychology,* 56, 239-245.

Pennebaker, J.W. (1997). Writing about emotional experiences as a therapeutic process. *Psychological Science*, 8, 162-166.

Perry, B, and Marcellus, J (1997). The impact of abuse and neglect on the developing brain. *Colleagues for Children.* 7, 1-4.

Perry, B.D., Colwell, K. and Schick, S. (2002). Child Neglect. *Encyclopedia of Crime and Punishment*, Vol 1, 192-196.

Pinson-Millburn, N. M., Fabian, E. S., Schlossberg, N. K., and Pyle, M. (2011). Grandparents Raising Grandchildren. *Journal of Counseling & Development*, 74, Issue 6, 548-554.

Sawyer, R. J. & Dubowitz, H. (1994). School performance of children in kinship care. *Child Abuse and Neglect, 18*, 587-597.

Scannapieco, M., Heger, R. L., & Alpine, C. (1997). Kinship care and foster care: A comparison of characteristics and outcomes. *Families in Society, 78(5)*, 480-489.

Seppala, E.M. (2012). Connect To Thrive: Social Connection Improves Health, Well-Being & Longevity. *Feeling It*, August 26, 2012.

Snell, P. (2009). What Difference Does Youth Group Make?: A Longitudinal Analysis of Religious Youth Group Participation and Religious Life Outcomes. *Journal for the Scientific Study of Religion*, 48(3): 572-587.

Solomon, J., & Marx, J. (1995). "To grandmother's house we go": Health and school adjustment of children raised solely by grandparents. *The Gerontologist, 35,* 386-394.

Valman, H.B. & Pearson, J.F. (1980). What the fetus feels. *British Medical Journal. Jan 26, 1980, 233-234.*

Wilson, D., & Horner, W. (2005). Chronic Child Neglect: Needed Developments in Theory and Practice. The Journal of Contemporary Social Services. 86, No. 4, 471-481.

Winnicott, D.W. (1967). Mirror-role of the mother and family in child development. *The predicament of the family: a psycho-analytical symposium,* P.26-33.

WEB SITES REFERENCED

http://en.wikipedia.org/wiki/Courage

http://nlrc.aoa.gov/Legal_Issues/Family_Law/Grandchildren.aspx

http://psychcentral.com/blog/archives/2011/03/21/the-surprising-history-of-the-lobotomy/

http://ssw.che.umn.edu/CASCW/CWN/05.html

http://www.acrf.org/Self-StudyCourses/neglectcourse/n2brain.htm

http://www.artofmanliness.com/2009/11/15/50-best-books-for-boys-and-young-men/3/

http://www.helpguide.org/mental/self_injury.htm

http://www.hsph.harvard.edu/nutritionsource/pyramid/

http://www.massagetherapy.com/articles/index.php/article_id/470/Children-and-Massage

http://www.npr.org/2005/11/16/5014080/my-lobotomy-howard-dullys-journey

http://www.psychologytoday.com/blog/feeling-it

http://www.psychsight.com/ar-shame.html

http://www.theatlantic.com/health/archive/2011/10/all-work-and-no-play-why-your-kids-are-more-anxious-depressed/246422/

http://www.ucdmc.ucdavis.edu/CANCER/pedresource/pedres_docs/ChildrenLearnThruPlay.pdf

http://www.utexas.edu/features/archive/2005/writing.html

https://www.childwelfare.gov/preventing/supporting/resources/grandparents.cfm

www.aap.org/traumaguide

www.aarp.org/relationships/friends-family/grandfacts-sheets/

www.barna.org

www.childrenandnature.org

www.childrenssuccessfoundation.com

www.childtraumaacademy.com

www.difficultchild.com

www.grandparents.com/gp/groups/group/Grandparents-Caring-for-
Grandkids/index.html

www.griefspeaks.com

www.penzu.com

www.youthandreligion.org

Dates of reference: February 2012 through August 2013